The American Society for Public Administration (ASPA)

The American Society for Public Administration (ASPA) is a nationwide nonprofit educational and professional membership organization dedicated to excellence in public management and the promotion of public service. The Society seeks to achieve these objectives through

- The advancement of the science, art, and processes of public administration,
- The development and exchange of public administration literature and information, and
- Advocacy on behalf of public service and high ethical standards in government.

With more than seventeen thousand members and subscribers, ASPA represents a broad array of professional interests and disciplines from all levels of government, the nonprofit and private sectors, and the academic community, both in the United States and abroad.

ASPA has provided national leadership in the areas of public administration and management since its inception in 1939. The Society and its members have been involved and influential in virtually every significant development in the theories and practice of public administration for half a century.

Through its networks of 126 local chapters, 19 national special-focus sections, individual and agency members, and organizational supporters, ASPA promotes recognition of public service achievements, develops a substantive dialogue on relevant issues, and enhances the professional development of its membership. To further its mission, ASPA

- Communicates the importance and value of public service,
- Promotes high ethical standards in public administration,
- Speaks out in support of public service and seeks to improve the public's perception of government and seeks to restore confidence in public servants,
- Develops positions on significant public management and public interest issues,
- Publishes a prestigious journal—*Public Administration Review*—and issues-oriented newspaper—*PA TIMES*—and other special books and publications, and
- Recognizes excellence in public service through annual awards for special accomplishments in the literature or practice of public administration.

For additional information or membership materials, contact:

American Society for Public Administration
1120 G Street, NW
Suite 500
Washington, DC 20005
(202) 393-7878
Fax: (202) 628-4952

ETHICAL
FRONTIERS
IN PUBLIC
MANAGEMENT

James S. Bowman, Editor

ETHICAL
FRONTIERS
IN PUBLIC
MANAGEMENT

Seeking New Strategies
for Resolving
Ethical Dilemmas

Jossey-Bass Publishers
San Francisco • Oxford • 1991

ETHICAL FRONTIERS IN PUBLIC MANAGEMENT
Seeking New Strategies for Resolving Ethical Dilemmas
by James S. Bowman, Editor

Copyright © 1991 by: Jossey-Bass Inc., Publishers
350 Sansome Street
San Francisco, California 94104

&

Jossey-Bass Limited
Headington Hill Hall
Oxford OX3 0BW

Library of Congress Cataloging-in-Publication Data

Ethical frontiers in public management : seeking new strategies for
resolving ethical dilemmas / James S. Bowman, editor.
    p.   cm.—(The Jossey-Bass public administration series)
    Includes bibliographical references and index.
    ISBN 1-55542-345-0
    1. Public administration—Moral and ethical aspects.   2. Civil
service ethics—United States.   I. Bowman, James S., 1945-   .
II. Series.
JF1525.E8E84   1990
172′.2—dc20
                                                                90-23575
                                                                CIP

Manufactured in the United States of America

The paper in this book meets the guidelines for
permanence and durability of the Committee on
Production Guidelines for Book Longevity of the
Council on Library Resources.

JACKET DESIGN BY WILLI BAUM

FIRST EDITION

Code 9148

The Jossey-Bass
Public Administration Series

Contents

**Part Three: Developing New Strategies for Promoting
Organizational and Individual Ethics**

Preface

The decisions public servants make about policy and administration have a significant effect on American life. Such decisions are statements about what ought to be done; that is, they are ethical judgments. But what is the basis of these judgments? Are they clearly grounded in an understanding of the moral milieu of public administration, in an appreciation of the theoretical and professional underpinnings of the field, and in an awareness of the latest developments in the discipline?

With direct responsibility for making government work, career administrators confront many difficult issues—problems that demand resolution. As a result of these problems, citizen and professional interest in civil service ethics has increased dramatically in recent times. This book presents current research that defines the moral environment found in public management, examines how and why thinking about government ethics needs to be revitalized, and offers theoretical strategies to bring that renewal to fruition.

Throughout, the book provides perspectives on the social, political, and cultural context in which public service is embedded. By analyzing specific approaches and ethical strategies found in these perspectives, the book contributes to understanding the ethos of government management in a democracy. By emphasizing educational and ethical standards, it fosters the growth and development of the virtuous practice of administration.

Written by experienced scholars, *Ethical Frontiers in Public Management* is intended for all serious students of the subject. Academicians as well as practitioners from a variety of fields will benefit from the knowledge base provided here. Likewise, both pre-service and in-service students in graduate programs need to explore scholarly thinking on ethics in public service professions. Finally, reflective managers in the nonprofit and business sectors who interact with government will profit from the kinds of analyses found in these pages. Sponsored by the American Society for Public Ad-

ministration (ASPA), the book is a teaching tool that represents the
state of the art in management ethics and suggests how members of
the society can assist each other in best serving its constituents and
students.

Although journal articles and several books have been published concerning selected dimensions of government ethics, until
now no one reference has offered a selection of the latest research
in the field. Earlier publications have included casebooks, philosophical treatises, policy volumes, and textbooks that defined the
role of the public official and urged more inquiry into the subject.
However, a single source that presents current work on the nature
of the discipline has long been needed. This collection of original
studies on ethics in public administration seeks to meet the need.

To launch the 1990s, ASPA held an "Ethics in Government"
national conference in the waning days of the 1980s. Collected here
are a number of substantially revised papers from that meeting as
well as additional research studies. The result is a book in which
each chapter, although written from a particular vantage point,
provides fresh insights into a common phenomenon: honorable
management of the public's business.

Overview of the Contents

Part One contains three chapters that analyze the moral milieu of
government administration. In Chapter One, Darrell L. Pugh focuses on the development and limitations of ethics as they have
evolved in American public service. He examines alternative ethical
frameworks, as well as the codes of conduct derived from them, and
explains why there is an obligation to move beyond these ideas to
new frontiers. In Chapter Two, based on forty-two interviews, Harold F. Gortner documents this need by reporting that managers are
vitally interested in ethics but find little professional support or
guidance. In Chapter Three, Bruce Jennings suggests why this is
the case. The form and style of ethical thinking in government are
well adapted—indeed, too well adapted—to bureaucratic life; they
promote "ethical reasoning and inhibit ethical judgment." These
chapters examine contemporary ethical practices from historical,

empirical, and theoretical levels in different but complementary ways. Each also includes useful material pertinent to later chapters.

Part Two consists of four chapters that focus on the key implication of Part One: the need to search for new ethical territories in the field. Each author weighs the necessity for a deeper understanding of the elements of public administration ethics than is often found. In Chapter Four, Kathryn G. Denhardt excavates the moral foundations of public administration and maintains that the profession has a clear leadership role in creating change. In Chapter Five, Curtis Ventriss examines a compelling "embarrassing moral dualism" that the field must address before genuine progress can be made: the conflict between high moral standards (or what he labels *civic virtue*) and the ethos of the marketplace (referred to as *civic commercialism*). In Chapter Six, Brent Wall helps us to understand this dilemma by documenting the incomplete, if not misguided, character of the academic literature on public administration ethics. Finally, in Chapter Seven, Jeffrey S. Luke maintains that the rapid development of "global interdependencies and interorganizational webs" mandates a shift of focus from behavioral ethics to policy ethics in public service. Each of the authors argues for a new philosophy or ethos to assist in developing an effective approach to government morality. In so doing, they also briefly review the environment of government ethics considered in Part One and suggest ideas for change, discussed more in Part Three.

Part Three offers six chapters that detail strategies for exploring ethical frontiers in the years ahead: three at the institutional level and three at the individual level of analysis. In Chapter Eight, Mary E. Guy argues that "high reliability management" can be employed in agencies to effectively bridge individual and collective values. In Chapter Nine, beginning with a provocative critique of administrative customs, Gerald T. Gabris then suggests another method for dealing with the dilemma between personal and institutional ethics: the use of organizational development techniques. Judith A. Truelson, in Chapter Ten, examines the signal significance of specific institutional controls in federal governance. Chapter Eleven, the first of the final three selections, by Debra W. Stewart and Norman A. Sprinthall, presents data on the stages of individual moral development that point the way to effective change. In Chapter Twelve, Gerald M. Pops, after examining other important values, contends that the concept of justice constitutes a normative theory in executive decision making. In Chapter Thirteen, Douglas F. Morgan and Henry D. Kass provide a theory-directed, empirical capstone essay. Based on in-depth discussions with high-level public officials, it is evident that the concept of constitutional principles of stewardship can enrich many of the foregoing chapters and provide a meaningful interpretation of the managerial function.

Certainly no single compendium of current research in an interdisciplinary field such as administrative ethics can or should be complete. Yet a timely exploratory study of integrity in public service can be found in these chapters. The role of ethics in the administration of American democracy is a crucial subject for inquiry. As a presentation of recent scholarly advances in this pursuit, this volume seeks to foster greater ethical reflection and action in the future.

Acknowledgments

Many people have contributed to *Ethical Frontiers in Public Management*. First, of course, gratitude is extended to the contributors who educated me with their thoughtful papers. They worked to produce a book that includes a multitude of viewpoints and theoretical orientations representative of contemporary thinking. Their readiness to revise and resubmit attests to their respect for a complex subject and their skill in mastering it. This task was facilitated by the thorough, insightful, and prompt reviews of draft chapters by over twenty referees, including the late Michael Bayles (Florida State University), Peter Bergerson (Southeast Missouri State University), John Burke (University of Vermont), Donald Calista (Marist College), Ralph Chandler (Western Michigan University), Myron Glazer (Smith College), April Hejka-Ekins (California State University), Kenneth Kernaghan (Brock University), Elaine Johansen (University of Connecticut), Dalton Lee (San Diego State University), Carol Lewis (University of Connecticut), Michael McDanield (Florida State University), John Palguta (U.S. Merit Systems Protection Board), Thomas Pavlak (Fairleigh-Dickinson University), Jeremy Plant (Pennsylvania State University), W. L. Richter (Kansas State University), Frank Sherwood (Florida State University), David Speak (Georgia Southern University), James Svara (North Carolina State University), E. C. Wakham (U.S. Office of Personnel Management), and Robert Zinke (Eastern Washington University), as well as several anonymous contributors and readers. Many thanks are also owed to my family, who always wonder when Dad will be done with "work."

Tallahassee, Florida   *James S. Bowman*
February 1991

Contributors

James S. Bowman is professor of public administration at Florida State University. He holds B.S. (1967) and M.A. (1968) degrees in political science from the University of Wisconsin at Madison and a Ph.D. degree (1973) in political science from the University of Nebraska at Lincoln. Bowman is a former fellow of the National Association of Schools of Public Affairs and Administration Faculty, as well as a Kellogg Foundation fellow. He serves on the editorial board of three periodicals. He is editor (with the late Frederick A. Elliston) of *Ethics, Government and Public Policy* (1988).

Gerald T. Gabris is associate professor of political science in the Division of Public Administration at Northern Illinois University. He received his B.A. (1971), M.A. (1973), and Ph.D. (1977) degree, all in political science, from the University of Missouri at Columbia. He is on the editorial boards of *Review of Public Personnel Administration* and *Public Productivity and Management Review*.

Kathryn G. Denhardt is an assistant professor in the Graduate School of Public Affairs at the University of Colorado at Denver. She received her B.S. degree (1976) in political science from Kansas State University and her M.A. (1978) and Ph.D. (1984) degrees in political science from the University of Kansas. Her research and professional activities have focused primarily on public administration ethics. She is the author of *The Ethics of Public Service: Resolving Moral Dilemmas in Public Organizations* (1988), as well as articles that have appeared in such journals as *Public Administration Review* and *Administration and Society*. Denhardt is on the editorial board of the *Public Administration Review* and has served on the Professional Ethics Committee of the American Society for Public Administration since 1985.

Harold F. Gortner is associate professor of government and politics at George Mason University. He received his B.A. degree (1963) in political science at Earlham College. His M.P.A. (1966) and M.A. (1969) and Ph.D. (1971) degrees in political science are from Indiana University. He has published books and articles in the areas of public administration, organization theory, and public administration ethics.

Mary E. Guy is associate professor of political science and public affairs at the University of Alabama at Birmingham. She received a B.A. degree (1969) in psychology from Jacksonville University, a master's of rehabilitation counseling degree (1970) from the University of Florida, an M.A. degree (1976) in psychology from the University of South Carolina, and a Ph.D. degree (1981) in political science from the University of South Carolina. She has written numerous chapters and journal articles and is author of three books on managerial issues, including *Professionals in Organizations: Debunking a Myth* (1985), *From Organizational Decline to Organizational Renewal: The Phoenix Syndrome* (1989), and *Ethical Decision Making in Everyday Work Situations* (1990).

Bruce Jennings is executive director of the Hastings Center in Briarcliff Manor, New York. He received his B.A. degree (1971) in political science from Yale University (1971) and his M.A. degree (1973) in political science from Princeton University. His publications include *Ethics, the Social Sciences and Policy Analysis* (1983), *Representation and Responsibility: Exploring Legislative Ethics* (1985), and numerous articles on ethical issues in public policy, medicine, and the professions.

Henry D. Kass is currently professor of public administration at Lewis and Clark College in Portland, Oregon, and a senior associate with JMA Associates, Boston, a management consulting firm. He received his Ph.D. degree (1969) in government and public administration from American University. He is a past chairman of the Standards and Ethics Committee of the American Society for Public Administration. Kass coedited an issue of the *International Journal of Public Administration* dealing with public administration ethics and is coeditor (with B. Catron) of a recent volume, *Images and Identities in Public Administration*.

Jeffrey S. Luke is assistant to the vice president for research and is also associate professor of planning, public policy and management at the University of Oregon. He received his B.A. degree (1972) in urban studies and his M.P.A. (1974) and Ph.D. (1982) degrees in public administration from the University of Southern California. He is the coauthor (with J. Kerrigan) of *Management Training Strategies in Third World Countries* (1987) and (with C. Ventriss, B. J. Reed, and C. Reed) of *Managing Economic Development: State and Local Leadership Strategies* (1988).

Douglas F. Morgan is professor of public administration and director of the master's program in public administration at Lewis and Clark College in Portland, Oregon. He received his B.A. degree (1965) from Claremont McKenna College and his M.A. (1967) and Ph.D. (1971) degrees in political science from the University of Chicago. His articles on administrative ethics have appeared in various journals and books, including *Administration and Society, Problemi di Administrazione pubblica, Administrative Discretion and Public Policy Implementation,* and *Images and Identities in Public Administration.*

Gerald M. Pops is professor of public administration at West Virginia University. He received his B.A. degree (1957) in pre-medicine from the University of California, Los Angeles; his J.D. degree (1961) from the University of California, Berkeley; and his Ph.D. degree (1974) in public administration from the Maxwell School of Citizenship and Public Affairs at Syracuse University. He has taught and published widely in the fields of administrative law, justice, ethics, public sector labor relations, and conflict management. His books include *Emergence of the Public Sector Arbitrator* (1976); (with M. O. Stephenson, Jr.) *Conflict Resolution in the Policy Process* (1987); and (with T. J. Pavlak) *Administrative Justice* (forthcoming).

Darrell L. Pugh is professor of public administration and urban studies in the School of Public Administration and Urban Studies at San Diego State University, where he is also associate dean of the College of Professional Studies and Fine Arts. He received his B.A.

(1976) and M.P.A. (1977) degrees from San Diego State University and his Ph.D. degree (1983) in public administration from the University of Southern California. His research interests include the history of American public administration and the professional development of the public service. He has published articles in *Public Administration Review, International Journal of Public Administration, American Review of Public Administration, The Bureaucrat*, and *Journal of Contemporary Legal Issues*. He is also author of the book *Looking Back—Moving Forward: A Half-Century Celebration of Public Administration and ASPA*.

Norman A. Sprinthall is a professor and former head of the counselor education graduate department at North Carolina State University. He received his B.A. degree (1954) in international relations from Brown University. He also holds an M.A. degree (1960) in political science from Brown University and a Ph.D. degree (1963) in counseling psychology from Harvard University. Awards and honors include Phi Beta Kappa, fellow status in the American Psychological Association, and membership in the Academy of Outstanding Teachers. He is author of numerous articles and has coauthored two textbooks, *Educational Psychology: A Development Approach* (5th ed.) and *Adolescent Psychology: A Developmental View* (2nd ed.).

Debra W. Stewart is a professor of political science and public administration at North Carolina State University. She received her B.A. degree (1965) in philosophy and political science from Marquette University, her M.A. degree (1967) in government from the University of Maryland, and her Ph.D. degree (1975) in political science from the University of North Carolina at Chapel Hill. Stewart is the author and coauthor of three books and numerous articles. Her scholarly works have addressed administrative theory, equal employment opportunity policy, and women and politics.

Judith A. Truelson is associate professor of librarianship at the University of Southern California, where she is also director of the Crocker Business and Accounting Libraries and adjunct associate professor in the School of Public Administration. She received her

B.A. degree (1964) in history and her M.L.S. degree (1965) from the University of California at Los Angeles. She received M.P.A. (1981) and Ph.D. (1986) degrees in public administration from the University of Southern California. Her publications on whistle-blowing have appeared in *Combatting Corruption, Encouraging Ethics: A Sourcebook for Public Service Ethics* (1990), *Policy Studies Review* (1989), *Australian Journal of Public Administration* (with G. E. Caiden, 1988), *Corruption and Reform* (1987), and *The Bureaucrat* (1985).

Curtis Ventriss is associate professor of public administration at the University of Vermont. He received his B.A. and B.S. degrees (1973) in political science and environmental science from California State University at San Jose and his M.P.A. (1976) and Ph.D. (1980) degrees in public administration from the University of Southern California. He is coauthor of two books: (with H. Muller) *Public Health in a Retrenchment Era* (1985) and (with J. Luke, B. J. Reed, and C. M. Reed) *Managing Economic Development* (1980).

Brent Wall is an assistant to the county administrator for Leon County (Tallahassee), Florida. He received a B.A. degree (1964) in political science from Ursinus College, an M.A. degree (1969) in philosophy from Lehigh University, and an M.P.A. degree (1990) from Florida State University. He is presently finishing the degree requirements for a Ph.D. degree in public administration at Florida State University. He has over twenty years' experience in local, state, and national posts in the areas of planning, policy development, budgeting, and management.

ETHICAL
FRONTIERS
IN PUBLIC
MANAGEMENT

INTRODUCTION

Ethical Theory and Practice

in Public Management

James S. Bowman

The seemingly different interests and concerns of scholars and managers have long been recognized as an important problem in public administration. Unlike with similar conflicts in more established fields such as medicine, law, and engineering, the resulting lack of understanding has retarded professionalism in public administration.

If this fact is true for the field as a whole, it is especially the case for the study and practice of ethics in government. Whereas professionals of older occupations are steeped in the moral obligations of their practice, there is little ethical training for public service. Not only is the subfield in an embryonic state, but also executives are not mandated to complete an accredited management program. Yet ethics can be, and is, empowering in administrative life. Sharing a common boundary across which many ideas are exchanged, the challenge for academicians and managers is to nurture and ensure a mature symbiosis in the profession. This may be achieved by improving communications between the world of the scholar and that of the practitioner through resources such as this volume.

The transfer of knowledge for the kind of transformational leadership needed for genuine ethical reform is not a simple task. As Mark Twain once said, "To be good and virtuous is a noble thing, but to teach others to be good and virtuous is nobler still— and much, much easier." In searching for moral bearings it would, accordingly, be inappropriate to delineate implications from the contributions herein for those reading this book. Such an effort could deny the richness found in those studies as well as distort

1

what only a reflective reader can do: determine the personal significance of the chapters for him- or herself.

Yet as this book shows, ethics is action, the way we practice our values, a guidance system to be used in making decisions. Ethics is work—the labor of the individual and organizations trying to live up to closely held beliefs. The responsibility for ethics is seldom effortless for at least two reasons. First, ethics exists in the gap between the "is" and the "ought." To be reminded of this breach, where reach exceeds grasp, creates discomfort—and managers already have plenty of that. Second, we cannot, as Aristotle warned long ago, demand greater clarity than a subject will allow. Public officials have many difficult decisions to make, and ethical ones are tougher than most. In recognition of these realities, then, we endorse the adage that "nothing is more useful than a good theory." In that spirit, some of the ramifications of the chapters for the practice of management are highlighted below.

Darrell L. Pugh, in the lead chapter, examines the origins of ethical frameworks in the profession and the status of codes of conduct in professional education. Approaches that have determined what is regarded as proper behavior in public institutions and how they have shaped ethical standards are reviewed. Finally, the uncertainty and frustration created by these principles are analyzed. The implications of this state of affairs for educating managers and ultimately the practice of the profession are pondered.

In the next chapter, Harold F. Gortner assists managers in sorting out the multiple influences that impact daily organizational decisions. The factors affecting which issues are defined as ethical concerns and how they are analyzed are examined using five major categories. The taxonomy, validated through field research, serves to better clarify the moral complexities often encountered in bureaucracy.

Such complexities, Bruce Jennings argues in Chapter Three, may have the effect of relying on superficial legalisms or promoting spurious ethical reasoning at the expense of genuine moral judgment. Ironically, the same kind of bureaucratic logic that creates moral dilemmas is applied to ethical issues with the result that fundamental problems are disguised. This chapter reveals why administrators must engage in a more profound analysis than that frequently manifested in organizational reform efforts. Such a frame of reference provides a valuable perspective for assessing the quality of everyday decision making.

The concerns in Part One, reflected by professionalism, society, and scholarship, are explored in greater detail in Part Two. Professionals and their associations, Kathryn G. Denhardt contends, can play an important role as change agents. Articulating, studying, and internalizing the elements of a moral basis of public administration are an essential part of being a true civil servant. A strong foundation provides an anchor for resisting unreasonable demands that may emerge with shifting political currents. It serves as an essential guide to action as well as a defense of the legitimacy of bureaucracy in democracy.

Curtis Ventriss then provides a useful context for Denhardt's analysis by arguing that a renewed philosophy—based on public interdependency, learning, and language—is required to frame pertinent questions that bear on the decision-making process. Taken together, these elements promote an understanding of what public institutions aim to achieve and the civic culture necessary to reach these goals.

Brent Wall follows with a plea, based on an insightful review and critique of the extant ethics literature, for a new ethics for democratic public administration. A genuinely democratic approach—directly or indirectly rejected by most scholars—suggests that officials must be sensitive to and criticize the values that govern policy-making, recommendations congenial to Jennings, Gabris, Ventriss, and others. Advocating and designing institutions that facilitate such value assessments, says Wall, will diminish the unjustified control that some stakeholders have over the formulation and implementation of public policy.

Jeffrey S. Luke's chapter argues that today's globally interconnected world requires executives to consider policy ethics—the ethics of the outcomes and consequences of decisions—in addition to the more conventional arena of behavioral ethics. Policy ethics is guided by an ethics of foresight and responsibility: to ensure the continued existence of the human species and an adequate quality of life. Luke offers two guidelines, stewardship and intergenerational ethics, to assist executives in pursuing policy choices. Several

criteria—irreversibility, aggregate magnitude, and sustainability—
emerge as crucial decision-making factors.

The contributors in Part Three explore organizational and
individual techniques to be used to enhance research and practice
in the years ahead. By emphasizing the importance of personal responsibility, coupled with a focused set of collective values, Mary
E. Guy's "high reliability management" offers a framework for advancing integrity in public agencies. It blends the strengths inherent in the need for a strong sense of personal accountability with
the equally critical requirement for institutions to create its "beacon" values. Guy explains how managers can instill ethical sensitivity and promote public trust by combining both ethical means
and ends on the job.

Bureaucracies, Gerald T. Gabris claims in Chapter Nine, legitimize Machiavellian values—strategies that protect or enhance
one's hierarchical position. Indeed, conventional management
practices actually encourage such behavior. Subjected to Machiavellian value systems, managers face significant obstacles to ethical
action and organizational change. An organizational development
approach that fundamentally shifts established value patterns is
essential, according to Gabris.

Judith A. Truelson crystalizes these ideas in the following
chapter. An examination of ethics reform in the federal government
reveals the importance of structural innovation to nurturing individual honor and organizational conscience. Public managers,
therefore, need to be receptive to ethics training that goes beyond
mere legal compliance and conflict-of-interest statutes, be prepared
to engage in ethical dialogue with subordinates, and be able to set
an admirable example of how to deal with moral conflicts. Likewise, employees must be ready to discuss ethical issues with peers
and superiors, defend professional codes, and develop strategies for
exemplary behavior.

Debra W. Stewart and Norman A. Sprinthall, in Chapter
Ten, also agree with the significance of training to enhance ethics
in public service. They present data about and discuss the implications of the stage of moral cognition found among a sample of
managers. Stewart and Sprinthall suggest, and no doubt Gabris and
other contributors would concur, that bureaucracies narrow ethical

awareness. If a good government is one in which administrators reflect on ethical dilemmas using higher levels of analysis than apparently is typical, then both academicians and practitioners have an important challenge. The National Association of Schools of Public Affairs and Administration and the American Society for Public Administration can certainly influence academic and training curricula. The discussion and replication of Stewart and Sprinthall's research, followed by an identification of appropriate courses of action, would be vital initial steps in curricular design.

Gerald M. Pops maintains, in Chapter Twelve, that *justice* provides a conceptual framework that is at once familiar, understandable, and practical. Thoughtful managers called on to make decisions with moral dimensions should be able to apply the material in this chapter. Indeed, since administrative justice has not been an area of intensive research, it is perhaps more developed in the minds of practitioners than in the minds of those who study public administration.

Finally, Douglas F. Morgan and Henry D. Kass's concept of constitutional stewardship provides a way to interpret much of the material in previous chapters as it (1) documents the dominant ethical claims that compete for the loyalty of career administrators, (2) connects these claims to the larger American administrative tradition within which career administrators practice, and (3) orders conflicting claims by showing how each grows out of constitutional efforts to prevent majority tyranny, usurpation of authority, and incompetent administration. Morgan and Kass argue that administrators have an obligation to prevent democracy from falling prey to these dangers, and their research provides a legitimating framework for structuring the exercise of discretionary authority. Their findings aid in resolving the crisis of legitimacy that the profession has experienced for many years.

These chapters do not offer simplistic how-to suggestions and pragmatic advice. However, they do provide alternative ways to think about the ethical problems in government agencies and can thereby help identify, refine, and promote positive values and honorable policies. The real role of the executive, as Chester Barnard pointed out more than fifty years ago, is to create and manage the values of an organization. Today that role is called "transformational leadership," that quality of interaction between followers and leaders that guides both to a higher plane of morality. The result should be activities that satisfy the need for an enduring sense of purpose and community that honors democracy.

It is evident that this task—aided by the effective transfer of knowledge in the public administration community—cannot merely be reduced to another management "program" but instead must be an ongoing daily practice. This process must begin with an appreciation of the fundamentals and premises of ethical action in American public service. To treat management and ethics apart, to paraphrase Rousseau, is to not understand either. If this book contributes to bridging the gap between scholars and practitioners, then an important goal will have been achieved. In light of the ethical issues facing us today, the need to foster genuine change has never been greater.

PART ONE

Understanding the Context

of Ethical Issues in Government

1 The Origins of Ethical Frameworks in Public Administration

Darrell L. Pugh

An appropriate beginning to any exploration, whether ethics or otherwise, is a requisite understanding of one's point of departure. To begin their search, explorers must have a fix on their current bearing, knowledge of how they arrived at that particular point, and an awareness of why that point is no longer satisfactory but requires them to push ahead. The purpose of this chapter is to assist in this requisite understanding by focusing on the origins of public sector ethics in the United States and how they have come to limit the field's current ethical position. In particular it will seek to explore the two dominant ethical frameworks that have evolved over the last half century in American public affairs and administration and the ethical codes that have been derived from these frameworks by established public affairs professional associations. This chapter will also comment briefly on the implications and limitations of these frameworks and codes for education in the public service and on why there is a need to move beyond the current position to new ethical frontiers.

As has been noted elsewhere, professions in and of themselves are generally identified as sharing a set of common traits or characteristics that distinguish them as such, thus setting them apart from other occupations. Included in this litany are (1) a cast of mind (for example, self-awareness), (2) a corpus of theory and knowledge, (3) a social ideal, (4) a formal organization to promote its interests, (5) a "national academy" to recognize outstanding leaders, and (6) ethical standards (Pugh, 1989). To varying degrees of success American public administration has managed to exhibit each of these traits. Yet, of the professional traits identified above, ethical standards represent what many regard as the weakest link in

9

the case for professional public administration. Except for professional city managers (see below), until recently the field did not have a code of moral precepts that went beyond vague generalities or were concrete enough to serve as guidelines for scholars and practitioners.

However, despite this anemic condition, ethical frameworks of sorts were clearly discernable, and subsequent codes of ethics did evolve. Attention must be turned to a review of these ethical frameworks to yield better understanding of the limits to the field's frontiers of ethical reasoning.

Ethical Frameworks for Public Administration

Fortunately, thoroughly analyzing the last half century of public administration to identify dominant frameworks that drive ethical standards has been done with some apparent success (Fleishman and Payne, 1980). To date, two primary candidates have emerged as the principal frameworks for approaching public management ethics: bureaucratic ethos and democratic ethos. Below, each is described in terms of its apparent content values (standards), sources of origin (intellectual, social, and professional), and methodology.

Bureaucratic Ethos. Bureaucratic ethos has long been associated with the historical mode of modern public administration, particularly its mainstream organizational locus. Drawing on a continental tradition, this approach was extremely popular among early public administration theorists and remains so today (Waldo, 1948). Its influence over the entire field and its development are profound (Waldo, 1980). The content values of bureaucratic ethos are chiefly contained in five pervasive concepts: efficiency, efficacy, expertise, loyalty, and accountability. In one form or another these concepts and their inclusion as positive behavioral norms for public administrators have remained viable in both theory and practice (Hejka-Ekins, 1988, p. 886).

The origin of bureaucratic ethos is generally well known among students of public administration. Intellectually, this framework has been championed by several sources, including the

Weberian model of bureaucracy, where the rational principles underlying this ethos are clearly articulated (Weber, 1946); the Wilsonian dichotomy of politics and administration, where the rationalization is created for the adoption of the ethos as behavioral norms in a political context (Wilson, 1887); the theory of scientific management, where F. W. Taylor raises the utility of efficiency to the level of a moral imperative (Taylor, 1967); and the scholarly works of Frank Goodnow and William F. Willoughby, where the salience of bureaucratic ethos is found to be consistent with the study of comparative administration issues and the application of rationalism (for example, science) to public administration (Goodnow, 1903; Willoughby, 1937).

The social origins of bureaucratic ethos are numerous and cross-cultural. For purposes of brevity, only a few of the more salient forces in the American cultural context will be identified here. Certainly, some of the more profound social movements to advance bureaucratic ethos include social Christianity, the progressive political movement, the scientific management movement, and the social science movement.

The social Christianity movement of the late nineteenth century, in its close association with the early municipal reform movement and progressive political leaders, played an important role in fostering the development of bureaucratic ethos (May, 1963, pp. 224–225, 228–231). Spawned by a reaction to the plight of the poor, particularly America's urban poor, social Christianity sought to justify social change in terms of a Christian doctrine. Imbued with a "social gospel" that offered reform of social institutions as the key to personal moral salvation, this movement endorsed instrumental rationality and bureaucratic means in pursuit of the "heavenly city" on earth. The rhetoric of this movement was to have an influence on public administration's definition of the "good life" well into the twentieth century.

Similarly, the progressive political movement of the same period also contributed to the popularity of bureaucratic ethos by its fundamental acceptance of the utility of bureaucratic principles in quest of improved public planning and service delivery. The progressive political movement embraced bureaucratic principles along several dimensions, namely efficiency, hierarchy/centralization, and expertise. It did so because the movement was fixed on no less a goal than the replacement of the "market system" model of political decision making, in which groupings of influence freely compete in a larger political system, with a model that grounded political decision making in modern science and technology (Hays, 1959, pp. x–xiii). The need to gain control of the widening scope of public affairs generated by the complexities of industrialization required a system of centralized power and placed a premium on expertise that could acquire and manipulate information while developing overall techniques that would improve efficiency. As Dwight Waldo noted about the progressives, "These persons believed that democracy must rethink its position and remold its institutions; particularly it must create a strong right arm for the State in the form of an efficient bureaucracy" (1948, p. 18).

Almost on a parallel track to the progressives, the scientific management movement also pushed bureaucratic ethos to the forefront of early American business administration. Launched by the work of Frederick Winslow Taylor, the Taylorites who followed showed a keen, sometimes zealous, acceptance of rational principles of organization and the concomitant values with which they were infused. This new "philosophy" sought to place economic activity on a scientific basis by eliminating tradition and convention in favor of measurement and codified knowledge. To facilitate this objective, scientific management embraced bureaucratic values such as efficiency, hierarchy (especially as it relates to the need for centralized planning of the work effort and the need to organize along functional lines), and expertise (Taylor, 1967, pp. 37–38).

Taylor's philosophy became an attractive alternative for organizing among American progressives and subsequently had tremendous influence on the development of public administration. The effects of scientific management reached from the U.S. Army's Watertown Arsenal in Massachusetts to the chambers of the United States Supreme Court. For example, in 1909, General William Crozier, head of the Army Ordnance Department, used Taylor's approach in the area of armament manufacturing, and in 1911, Louis D. Brandeis relied on the theory in building his case before the Interstate Commerce Commission (ICC) against freight rate increases (Schachter, 1989, pp. 53, 60–61).

Another origin was the American social science movement, particularly with the turn-of-the-century development of political science. The movement to organize the social sciences was a pre- and post–World War I phenomenon tied to both the successes and the failures of progressives, especially those intellectuals directly linked to the academy (Karl, 1974, pp. 100–105). Disillusioned over the drift of American politics during this time, many of these intellectuals sought to dissociate progressivism from the earlier reform and social gospel movements. To accomplish this, leading intellectuals such as Charles E. Merriam (political science) and Wesley C. Mitchell (economics) sought to imbue their respective disciplines with objective instruments of social observation and analytical techniques and to provide a mechanism for organizing research and coordinating it among allied fields (Karl, 1974). In the context of this movement, the idea of a science of government became an attractive objective. Moreover, the values associated with bureaucratic ethos—efficiency, efficacy, and expertise—placed well in the framework of this new "science" and its methodologies, since those involved regarded these values as subject to quantification and empirical verification.

Finally, the rise of bureaucratic ethos has one other important tributary, namely, the professional stream of public administration itself. Explicit examples of those associations that sought to embrace the tenets of bureaucracy's instrumental approach included the Civil Service Assembly, the Municipal Reform League, the Society for the Advancement of Management, and, although not an association, the Maxwell School of Citizenship and Public Affairs. With their collective emphasis on efficiency, efficacy, and expertise, these professional associations and their members were steadfast proponents of this particular framework.

A final issue to be addressed with respect to this framework is what may be regarded broadly as its methodology (that is, the systematic process by which the framework ensures its continuity and consistency). Here, content values are assessed against established rational goals and objectives using instrumentalism and utilitarianism as the criteria for action. Perhaps no better articulation of this methodological approach can be found than in Herbert Simon's seminal work *Administrative Behavior*. In it, Simon clearly explicates the process of vertical value integration that should take place in the organizational context against a backdrop of instrumental rationality. He notes, "Through the hierarchical structure of ends, behavior attains integration and consistency, for each member of a set of behavioral alternatives is then weighed in terms of a comprehensive scale of [organizational] values—the ultimate ends" (1947, p. 63).

The evolution of bureaucratic ethos has had a tremendous influence on American public administration, perhaps the dominant influence. Yet, the impact of this attitude has been tempered to a degree by the existence of another more broadly based framework. The next section of this chapter will examine this second framework, democratic ethos.

Democratic Ethos. The framework labeled by scholars as democratic ethos is considerably less precise than its bureaucratic counterpart. It is, to say the least, eclectic and broadly based. One can surmise from its content values that it is an evolving framework, often grafting on valuative ideals as they emerge in succeeding periods. Consequently, its origins are several and spaced over time. Yet despite an apparent ambiguity and patchworklike appearance, its methodology has remained largely unchanged. Content values for democratic ethos include (1) regime values, (2) citizenship, (3) public interest, and (4) social equity, a set of values that clearly places the framework in the realm of political theory.

The intellectual origins of this framework, unlike those of its bureaucratic alternative, are both historical and recent. They include the antifederalists and federalists, who are generally viewed as being responsible for the formulation of what John Rohr has identified as *regime values*. The sources of regime values are supposedly those manifest in the Constitution of the United States and include but are not limited to personal liberty, property, and equality. According to Rohr, they represent "the values of the American people" (1976, p. 399). Although it would be difficult to supply an exhaustive list of these values, they can be discovered in a wide variety of works ranging from political writings, major speeches, and papers of leading American statesmen, historical treatises, and of course the decisions of the United States Supreme Court. In theory, these values are to serve as general guides to ethical reasoning in public administration.

The ideas of citizenship and public interest have played an important role in the general democratic framework, and they are particularly significant for public administration. The notion of *citizenship*—the ideal of a citizenry informed about government and active in its operation—has American roots as deep and as distant as the Revolution. Its influence on modern public administration dates back to the municipal reform and efficient citizen movements of the late nineteenth and early twentieth centuries—although those who studied administration during this period had ideas slightly different than that of the "ideal" (Wilson, 1887, pp. 204-214, 217). As Chester Newland has duly noted, citizenship and public service were considered coterminous in the early practice of public administration (1984, p. 41). Even today, this value remains the focus of much discussion ranging from theories of governance to concrete proposals for the coproduction of public services (Frederickson, 1974).

The public interest as well has added to the blend of democratic ethos, extending our administrative vocabulary and giving new meaning to an understanding of action and motivation. Although there may be a lack of precision in defining the term, perhaps one can accept Walter Lippman's characterization of *public interest* as "what men would choose if they saw clearly, thought rationally, and acted disinterestedly and benevolently" (1955, p. 42). This notion has had a profound effect on public administration, if not always in practice, then at least rhetorically. As the President's Committee on Administrative Management observed in 1937, "Our government rests on the truth that the general interest is superior to and has priority over any special or private interest, and that final decisions in matters of common interest to the Nation should be made by free choice of the people of the Nation" (1937, p. 1). Although called into question as a viable representation of reality by the dominant pluralist (competing interests) paradigm of American political science, the notion of public interest remains a fundamental component of the democratic framework.

A final content value that has emerged in the democratic framework is the concept of *social equity*, which, according to David K. Hart, may be defined as follows: "In its broadest and most general signification . . . [equity] denotes the spirit and the habit of fairness, justness, and right dealing which would regulate the intercourse of men with men,—the rule of doing to all others as we desire them to do to us; or, as it is expressed by Justinian, 'to live honestly, to harm nobody, to render to every man his due [*sic*].' . . . It is therefore the synonym of natural right or justice. But in this sense its obligation is ethical rather than jural, and its discussion belongs to the sphere of morals. It is grounded in the precepts of the conscience, not in any sanction of positive law" (1974, p. 3).

As Dwight Waldo documented in 1948, equity has been a chief ingredient of a sense of justice for students of public administration since at least the beginning of this century, particularly with respect to the enjoyment of material things (1948, p. 73). Legislatively, social equity emerged after World War I and again following World War II with the various legislation that dealt with the preferential treatment of veterans and was extended to other groups through initiatives such as the Equal Pay Act (1963), the Civil Rights Act (1964, 1972), and the Equal Employment Opportunity Act (1972). In the 1960s and 1970s, social equity took on additional importance and dimension in the scholarship of the "new" public administration theorists, who based their work with social equity on philosopher John Rawls's treatise *A Theory of Justice* (Frederickson, 1971, 1974, 1990). The many orientations to social equity lend the concept a sense of complexity, perhaps even ambiguity; however, it underlies numerous significant actions (such as equal employment opportunity and representative bureaucracy) that are now permanently entrenched in the field.

The social origins of the democratic ethos framework are as eclectic and diverse as its intellectual origins. In brief, contributions have streamed from American political institutions, particularly the courts; political movements, especially rural populism and progressivism; the urban reform movement; and the American civil rights movement. Professionally, this framework has benefited from numerous organizations, including governmental research bureaus; educational institutions, particularly the University of Chicago; and associations such as the American Political Science Association and the American Society for Public Administration.

Lastly, the methodology of democratic ethos is different from that of its bureaucratic rival. Specifically, its method is deductive (reasoning from a general truth to a particular instance of that truth), dialectical (whereby questions and their answers lead to their logical conclusion), and deontological (where the rightness or wrongness of a moral action is determined by referencing formal rules of conduct rather than the action's results or consequences). Thus the framework requires a thorough grounding in history and political philosophy. Furthermore, there is a heavy, if not exclusive, reliance on the case study as a means by which to analyze and test ethical propositions.

In sum, these two frameworks represent the major ethical approaches open to public administrators over which discussion takes place and behavior is assessed. Therefore, it is not surprising that they should have had an influence on the development of ethical codes that deal directly with the practice of public administration. Ethical codes, because they are intended to provide guidance to practitioners, can be important precursors to behavior as well as formal measures by which behavior can be judged. What these codes contain in terms of standards and how these standards relate to either the bureaucratic ethos or its democratic alternative become essential parts of understanding the field's current ethical bearing. Consequently, it is to an assessment of these codes that one must turn.

Codes of Ethics

Codes of ethics that provide recommendations or guidelines for professional conduct for public administrators are relatively recent phenomena. The first such standard was adopted in 1924 by the International City Managers' Association and has been amended five times (International City Management Association, 1987a). The International Personnel Management Association adopted its code in the 1970s, and the American Society for Public Administration approved its code of ethics in 1984, after ten years of deliberation. In government, the first federal-level code was adopted in 1958 by congressional concurrent resolution; executive order 10939, the "Guide on Ethical Standards to Government Officials," was issued by President Kennedy in 1961; and, of course, many are familiar with the passage of the Ethics in Government Act of 1978 (National Academy of Public Administration, 1974; Ethics in Government Act, 1978).

Although such codes exist, they are widely regarded as offering little hope of serving as effective supports of ethical behavior. Reasons for their limited utility include the diversity of public service, their vague and general nature, their tendency to dwell on proscribed rather than prescribed behavior, and their inability to answer specific behavioral questions (Wakefield, 1976, p. 663).

Despite these limitations, many advocates cite the value of such codes. For example, Ralph Chandler has identified three principal virtues of codes: (1) objectivism—the belief in external transcendent values; (2) community—the notion that moral behavior is not simply a matter of private preferences and personal integrity but is and should be subject to the community's judgment; and (3) courage—the idea that codes can promote courageous behavior (1983, pp. 33–34). Exhibits 1 and 2 show the two codes of ethics from major public administration associations, discussed in detail below.

The International City Managers' (now Management) Association (ICMA) adopted its code of ethics in 1924—the same year that Calvin Coolidge was elected president in his own right, having survived the Teapot Dome scandal; Hitler was in jail writing *Mein Kampf;* and Al Capone was getting rich running illegal whiskey from Canada across Lake Michigan into Chicago's lower east side. There were no Council of State Governments, no county administrators, and no American Society of Public Administration. Public administration education had just begun at Syracuse University's Maxwell School, and its first textbook was still two years away from publication (White, 1926). Yet ICMA had taken the professional lead on public service ethics.

Since its adoption in 1924, the ICMA code has been amended no less than five times. The ICMA executive board revised the code most recently in 1987 (International City Management Association,

Exhibit 1. ICMA Code of Ethics.

The purpose of the International City Management Association is to increase the proficiency of city managers, county managers, and other municipal administrators and to strengthen the quality of urban government through professional management. To further these objectives, certain ethical principles shall govern the conduct of every member of the International City Management Association who shall:

1. Be dedicated to the concepts of effective and democratic local government by responsible elected officials and believe that professional general management is essential to the achievement of this objective.

2. Affirm the dignity and worth of the services rendered by government and maintain a constructive, creative, and practical attitude toward urban affairs and a deep sense of social responsibility as a trusted public servant.

3. Be dedicated to the highest ideals of honor and integrity in all public and person relationships in order that the member may merit the respect and confidence of the elected officials, of other officials and employees, and of the public.

4. Recognize that the chief function of local government at all times is to serve the best interests of the people.

5. Submit policy proposals to elected officials, provide them with facts and advice on matters of policy as a basis for making decisions and setting community goals, and uphold and implement municipal policies adopted by elected officials.

6. Recognize that elected representatives of the people are entitled to the credit for the establishment of municipal policies; responsibility for policy execution rests with the members.

7. Refrain from participation in the election of the members of the employing legislative body, and from all partisan political activities which would impair performance as a professional administrator.

8. Make it a duty continually to improve the member's professional ability and to develop the competence of associates in the use of management techniques.

9. Keep the community informed on municipal affairs; encourage communication between the citizens and all municipal officers; emphasize friendly and courteous service to the public; and seek to improve the quality and image of public service.

10. Resist any encroachment on professional responsibilities, believing the members should be free to carry out official policies without discrimination on the basis of principles and justice.

11. Handle all matters of personnel on the basis of merit so that fairness and impartiality govern a member's decisions, pertaining to appointments, pay adjustments, promotions, and discipline.

12. Seek no favor; believe that personal aggrandizement or profit secured by confidential information or by misuse of public time is dishonest.

Reprinted by permission of the International City Management Association, 777 N. Capitol Street, NE, Washington, D.C. 20001.

Exhibit 2. ASPA Code of Ethics.

The American Society for Public Administration (ASPA) exists to advance the science, process, and art of public administration. ASPA encourages professionalism and improved quality of service at all levels of government, education, and the not-for-profit private sector. ASPA contributes to the analysis, understanding and resolution of public issues by providing programs, services, policy studies, conferences, and publications.

ASPA members share with their neighbors all of the responsibilities and rights of citizenship in a democratic society. However, the mission and goals of ASPA call every member to additional dedication and commitment. Certain principles and moral standards must guide the conduct of ASPA members not merely in preventing wrong, in pursuing right through timely and energetic execution of responsibilities. To this end, we, the members of the Society, recognizing the critical role of conscience in choosing among courses of action and taking into account the moral ambiguities of life, commit ourselves to:

1. demonstrate the highest standards of personal integrity, truthfulness, honesty and fortitude in all our public activities in order to inspire public confidence and trust in public institutions;

2. serve the public with respect, concern, courtesy, and responsiveness, recognizing that service to the public is beyond service to oneself;

3. strive for personal professional excellence and encourage the professional development of our associates and those seeking to enter the field of public administration;

4. approach our organization and operational duties with a positive attitude and constructively support open communication, creativity, dedication, and compassion;

5. serve in such a way that we do not realize undue personal gain from the performance of our official duties;

6. avoid an interest or activity which is in conflict with the conduct of our official duties;

7. respect and protect the privileged information to which we have access in the course of official duties;

8. exercise whatever discretionary authority we have under law to promote the public interest;

9. accept as a personal duty the responsibility to keep up to date on emerging issues and to administer the public's business with professional competence, fairness, impartiality, efficiency and effectiveness;

10. support, implement, and promote merit employment and programs of affirmative action to assure equal opportunity by our recruitment, selection, and advancement of qualified persons from all elements of society;

11. eliminate all forms of illegal discrimination, fraud, and mismanagement of public funds, and support colleagues if they are in difficulty because of responsible efforts to correct such discrimination, fraud, mismanagement or abuse;

12. respect, support, study and when necessary, work to improve federal and state constitutions, and other laws which define the relationships among public agencies, employees, clients and all citizens.

Reprinted by permission of the American Society for Public Administration.

1987a). In all the code contains twelve specific principles that encompass three broad categories of behavior: personal honesty, politics, and professional conduct. Specifically, articles 3, 9, and 12 fall in the first category; articles 1, 2, 4, 5, 6, and 7 address the second; and articles 8, 9, 10, and 11, constitute the third (see Exhibit 1).

In addition to the code, the ICMA also has established rules of procedure to provide a reasonable process for investigating and determining whether members have violated its code and to afford members who are being investigated due process (International City Management Association, 1987b). All members of ICMA fall under the jurisdiction of its code, and the executive board is responsible for enforcement with the assistance of ICMA's Committee on Professional Conduct (CPC). However, every member assumes responsibility for enforcing ICMA's code and may bring a complaint alleging violation of the code by a fellow member. Once such a complaint is registered, ICMA's executive director reviews the alleged conduct to determine if it violates the code; if so, the director forwards the complaint to the CPC for investigation. Should the CPC determine that a member's behavior has violated its code, the committee may impose sanctions against the member after holding a formal hearing. These sanctions include private censure, public censure, and expulsion. This elaborate mechanism of self-policing has prompted one public ethics scholar, Ralph Chandler, to comment that "the ICMA Code has been one of the most successful to be adopted. One reason for its effectiveness . . . is that managers are tried by their peers" (quoted in Jaben, 1986, p. 24).

In contrast to the ICMA code stands the ethical code of the American Society for Public Administration (ASPA) (see Exhibit 2). Adopted in 1984, exactly sixty years later than the ICMA code, ASPA's code of ethics represents a skein of behavioral guideposts tempered by the moral ambivalence and ambiguity of the six interceding decades. The struggle to adopt a code of ethics for ASPA was carried out over a ten-year period from 1974 to 1984, and it met with considerable resistance from those in the organization who felt that (1) public administration was too diverse an enterprise for a code, (2) such a code was unenforceable, and (3) codes were "too preachy" (Chandler, 1983, p. 33). In fact, a code of ethics for ASPA was originally rejected by that organization's national council, who instead opted for "a statement of ethical behavior" (Pugh, 1988, p. 104). The ambivalence of ASPA's leaders over the enactment and content of such a code is perhaps best exemplified by the code's article 11. This article appeared in its first form by ASPA's Professional Standards and Ethics Committee in 1981; in its second, modified form as a part of ASPA's Statement of Ethical Behavior in 1982; and in its final form as a part of ASPA's official code in 1984:

> We will neither commit nor condone the commitment of fraud, waste, abuse of government funds or property, or mismanagement of government programs. When it has been established that wrongdoing has occurred, and an innocent colleague is in difficulty because he or she exposed it, we will take appropriate steps to defend that colleague's interests. We will call attention to those agencies which demonstrate a pattern of harassment of persons who attempt to maintain high ethical standards or which ignore wrongdoing when it has been responsibly exposed.
>
> Efficient and effective management is basic to public administration. Subversion through misuse of influence, fraud, waste, or abuse is intolerable. Employees who responsibly call attention to wrongdoing will be encouraged.
>
> Eliminate all forms of illegal discrimination, fraud, and mismanagement of public funds, and support colleagues if they are in difficulty because of responsible efforts to correct such discrimination, fraud, mismanagement, or abuse [Chandler, 1983, pp. 38–39].

The substantive changes in this single standard indicate movement away from a clear behavioral norm (a prohibition against committing or condoning fraud, waste, or abuse of government funds, property, or programs and an explicit call to action in condemning such behavior) to simply a negative statement that fails to provide any explicit direction.

Like the ICMA code of ethics, ASPA's code has twelve articles (see Exhibit 2), but here they can be reduced to two behavioral categories: personal honesty (articles 1, 5, 6, and 7) and professional conduct (articles 2, 3, 4, 8, 9, 10, 11, and 12). ASPA's code manages to avoid the several political issues squarely addressed by that of the ICMA.

In addition, the ASPA statement lacks any formal, published rules of procedure to ensure code enforcement. No mechanism exists for accusing a member of violating the code, determining his or her culpability, and finally employing sanctions. To date, there is no evidence that anyone has ever been accused of violating ASPA's code or certainty that a "trial by ones' peers" would be the course taken in resolving such a claim. Consequently, ASPA's code in practice remains largely "a statement of ethical behavior."

Although the historical differences and practical contrasts of these two major codes of ethics are interesting, perhaps the most enlightening aspect of each is the apparent similarity of substance they both share: namely, an overwhelming concern with bureaucratic ethos. As Ralph Chandler has pointed out, these codes seem more content to deal with behavioral criteria that address issues of efficiency, economy, and administrative principles than to agonize over criteria of morality such as justice, equity, and the public interest (Chandler, 1983, p. 34). There is good reason for this condition. The bureaucratic mind-set that holds it moral to avoid morality still prevails as sound moral reasoning among many practicing public administrators. Once again, as Chandler noted, "The politics-administration dichotomy appears to be alive and well" (1983, p. 34). This time, however, the mythology is used to embrace the very real construct of Weberian social theory known as *zweckrational,* or instrumental rationality.

Instrumental rationality has for some become synonymous with bureaucratic ethos, legitimizing "the conversion of the good into the functional [instrumental] and the ethical into the a-ethical" (Ventriss, 1990, p. 779). According to social theorist Alberto G. Ramos, instrumental rationality is a direct distortion on classical reasoning or "substantive rationality" found in democratic ethos, which "enables the individual to distinguish between good and evil, false and genuine knowledge, and accordingly, to order one's personal and social life" (1981, pp. 4–5). *Consequently, bureaucratic ethos has a strong ideological overtone that substitutes for—not complements—democratic principles.* Moreover, Ramos argues, the dominance of instrumental rationality in modern bureaucratic organizations continues to distort the moral behavior of the individual, and it obscures the fact that these types of organizations are historically recent institutional inventions "required by the imperative of capital accumulation and the enhancement of processing capabilities characteristic of the market system" (1981, p. 105). *In short, the bureaucratic ethos is the consequence of modern capitalism and not that of republican, constitutional self-governance.*

The idea that our sense of correct ethical behavior may have run amok because of the overpowering influence of instrumental rationality is not a popular argument among many administrative scholars, particularly the pluralists, who argue that the degree of diverse interests precludes a concept of shared ethical reasoning (Chandler, 1983, pp. 32–33). However, despite the appearance that the codes discussed above may fail to have much impact on the behavior of public administrators, they nonetheless carry a powerful ideological message regarding what the field considers "ideal" behavior. If this is the message being conveyed to public administration practitioners, then what message is being given to students of American public administration based on these frameworks and codes? It is to this question that the remainder of the chapter turns.

Ethical Frameworks and Codes: Implications for Public Service Education

The fact that today in public service education we are confronted by these two distinct ethical frameworks is well known among academicians but surprisingly not well understood. Recent research indicates an ambivalence among those who purport to teach ethics, leading the majority of them to offer both frameworks as either complementary to or subsets of rather than alternatives to one another. April Hejka-Ekins documents this tendency toward cumulativism (that is, simply adding new theory to existing theory) rather than substitutivism (that is, replacing outdated or inaccurate theories with new theory) in her study on ethics instruction in public administration (1988). She found that over 72 percent of instructors emphasize both frameworks in their courses. It seems as if instructors prefer to view the frameworks as effective analytical tools that permit students to acquire different angles of understanding on the same ethical problem rather than to acknowledge that these frameworks may be at the core of those problems.

This confusion compounds itself in the classroom and ultimately in the squad room or the council chambers or wherever students of public administration and affairs apply their craft. Students not only remain ignorant of the historical, sociological, and ideological meanings of these frameworks but also appear to be left unaware of how differently these approaches frame reality, call for different behavioral responses, and limit views of the ethical frontiers of public management.

Furthermore, although there is general agreement on the ethical frameworks that dominate, academicians seem to be more interested in the pedagogics of their ethics courses than in the substance of these frameworks. As Dalton Lee has observed, the teaching of ethics has been misunderstood as a pedagogical problem (Lee, 1990): for example, the debate in the literature between Mark Lilla, Joel Fleishman, and Bruce Payne over whether to teach "moral judgment" or "moral behavior" and the epistemological dispute between deontological and teleological (utilitarian) approaches to ethics (Lilla, 1981; Fleishman and Payne, 1980). Consequently, we know what is being taught and how it is being taught but at the expense of understanding why.

As far as ethical codes are concerned, among those who teach public service ethics, not much progress is being made. Teachers are simply ignoring established codes in their instruction. As Hejka-Ekins found in her study, fewer than 8 percent of instructors refer to these codes in the classroom, and fewer still regard them as important (1988). Although the reasons for the attitude toward these codes have not been studied, it seems likely that those who teach ethics to students of public administration consider ethics to be irrelevant.

The implications of these conditions do not augur well for public service education. If allowed to persist, ethics education will continue to suffer from the appearance of being misperceived, misunderstood, and irrelevant. Yet there is hope for improvement if salient matters are addressed: namely, the significance of these frameworks and their assumptions and the place of ethical codes in the practice of public administration. Each of these is briefly explored below.

Significance of the Frameworks. Despite the way in which bureaucratic and democratic ethos apparently are being presented, they are not complementary to one another. Neither is one a subset of the other. In fact, they are alternatives, perhaps even threats, to one another (Mosher, 1982, pp. 231–232). As Paul Appleby noted in *Morality and Administration in Democratic Government,* "There is no single problem in public administration of moment equal to the reconciliation of the increasing dependence upon [bureaucratic] experts with an enduring democratic reality" (1952, p. 145). Reconciliation may have been an unreasonable expectation. After all, the two are so different. Bureaucratic ethos is teleological, employs instrumental rationality, and is predicated on the values of capitalism and a market society. Democratic ethos, in contrast, is deontological, is based on substantive rationality, and emanates from classical values of the state and higher law (Waldo, 1980).

That the original political theory of American public administration embraced the bureaucratic ethos over the democratic one cannot be denied. As the President's Committee on Administrative Management wrote in its report in 1937, "There is but one grand purpose . . . in our National Government; that is to make our Government an up-to-date, efficient, and effective instrument for carrying out the will of the Nation" (1937, p. 3). Or, as another scholar in the same year remarked, "Without results we know that democracy means nothing and ceases to be alive in the minds of men" (Bates and Field, 1939, p. viii). Moreover, academicians in the field continue to believe that bureaucratic ethos dominates public administration (Hejka-Ekins, 1988). Scholars as diverse as Dwight Waldo, Alberto Ramos, and Ralph Chandler recognize the preeminence of bureaucratic ethos in public organizations and among public administrators. Although the field has claimed to reject the politics/administration dichotomy—replacing its emphasis on the word *administration* with an emphasis on the word *public*—the operational values have remained bureaucratic.

The consequence of this is far reaching. Despite what may be said about the merging of politics and administration, as long as the field's assumptions are shaped by bureaucratic ethos the politics we speak of will not be democratic. Even Max Weber recognized that "the distinctive characteristics of a problem of social policy is indeed the fact that it cannot be resolved merely on the basis of purely technical [bureaucratic] ends. Normative standards of value must be the objectives of dispute in a discussion of a problem of social policy because the problem lies in the domain of general cultural values" (1974, p. 75). This should be cause for concern, unless, of course, bureaucratic and not democratic ethos truly represents American "general cultural values."

Work is needed in this area to ferret out the historical, sociological, and ideological differences between the two frameworks. Much has been done, but much more remains to be done to explore the ethical frontiers of public management. Rather than continue the preoccupation with pedagogical issues, resources should be channeled in another direction. For example, an explanation of the historical disjunction between the rise of political and administrative self-awareness and its implications for democratic ethos and bureaucratic ethos would be extremely useful. Also, a survey of related social science disciplines, such as economics, anthropology, and sociology, should be conducted to assess any contributions toward the conduct of inquiry into ethical administration. The field needs a body of literature that can guide us through these differences and explain the implications of these frameworks for ethical problems in public administration. The field needs a lot more mapping of the terrain. As Dwight Waldo has noted, "If we are going to talk about ethics in public life, it would be useful to know what we are talking about" (1980, p. 107).

Role of Ethical Codes. The place of ethical codes is another important matter that needs immediate attention. The widespread reports of failure to use ethical codes of public administration organizations in educating students of public administration is a serious problem. Criticisms from the academic community include the beliefs that these codes tend to trivialize ethical behavior, reduce ethical behavior to simply "staying out of trouble," fail to intellectually challenge and inspire those for whom they are written, and finally are simply irrelevant (Streib, 1987, p. 16).

Obviously not all ethical codes fail as miserably as those in public administration. An important example of an effective code can be found in the field of medicine. Here, the institution of codes through established medical societies has played an important role in enhancing the image and prestige of medical doctors (Streib, 1987, p. 17). Moreover, the code has served to inspire professional conduct and improve the integrity of peer and patient relationships.

What, then, is wrong with the codes found in public administration organizations? Although the answer to this question is complex and deserves careful thought and investigation, perhaps some tentative answers can be given. First, the evidence on codes of ethics indicates that successful codes have three common characteristics: these codes provide at least a modest level of behavioral guidance, they are written to be applicable to a variety of occupations in the same profession, and they have an effective mechanism that ensures compliance.

The results of applying these characteristics to public administration codes are scattered. For example, although ICMA's code seems to meet the second and third characteristics, it is arguable whether it has achieved the first one. As for ASPA, even more seems to be missing, especially an appropriate enforcement mechanism. As Ralph Chandler observed not long ago: "The American Society for Public Administration cannot control even one of its members who may be convicted of fraud, embezzlement, or mismanagement of any kind. There is no legal tender, no commonly agreed-upon currency, the counterfeit of which is the legal basis for expulsion from the society. The current by-laws provide no standards of professional behavior against which a member can be judged unprofessional" (1983, p. 38). If you add to this the proposition that these codes have been based on bureaucratic ethos at the expense of democratic values, you may begin to understand the reluctance among those who teach ethics courses to include these codes as a part of instruction or to regard them as relevant.

Again, with respect to ethical codes, work needs to be done. Organizations such as ICMA and ASPA should seriously reevaluate their codes in light of the characteristics identified above. Attention to the type of behavioral guidance offered by these codes is needed. Are they specific enough to help the individual? Are they broad enough to foster a sense of professional community? Are they bold enough to inspire and challenge members to higher ideals? Compliance needs to receive more emphasis, particularly by ASPA. Some kind of enforcement mechanism needs to be adopted now. Finally, the substance of these codes, the origin of the values that they embody, needs to be investigated to assess the type of moral behavior the codes are modeling. Initiating steps such as these could ensure a place for these codes in public service ethics education.

Conclusion

The historical origins of ethics for public administration are diverse and integrally entwined with the motifs and movements in American political thought. To be sure, the dominant ethical approaches have centered on bureaucratic ethos and democratic ethos. Between these two, the field of public administration has largely coalesced around the values of efficiency, efficacy, expertise, loyalty, and accountability found in the bureaucratic character. This has been particularly true for the practice of American public administration.

Public management professional associations, such as ICMA, ASPA, and the International Personnel Management Association (IPMA), through their actions, particularly their ethical codes of conduct, have furthered the advance of bureaucratic ethos. Consequently, these codes, because they serve as "ideals" for proper conduct, may be modeling behaviors that have clear ideological overtones that run independent of and contrary to democratic principles. Furthermore, to the extent that these associations gain in influence among professional public administrators, the significance of these codes may become far more extensive.

The implication of the direction taken by the "professional stream" regarding ethics may be far reaching for public administration education as well. Although, as the data indicate, those who teach ethics are encountering many problems, from pedagogical to epistemological, the most salient one remains the conflict felt by educators over the content values of these two frameworks (Hejka-Ekins, 1988). Furthermore, as far as personal attitudes are concerned, public administration instructors are particularly troubled by bureaucratic ethos. Academicians, who may view their field differently than their professional counterparts, may be operating on the horns of a dilemma: namely, the ethical directions taken by the practice of public administration may be at odds with the desired direction for public administration education. In some measure, this may explain why so few instructors use professional codes or regard them as important.

What, then, can one conclude from the conditions discussed thus far? Perhaps the most elementary response one can offer is that the issue of ethics for public administration, and by extension public management, is inherently a broader issue of political theory and the role of the administrative state in contemporary society. To a significant extent the profound uneasiness that persists among practitioners and academicians alike stems from a failure to appropriately address this broader issue. Despite what some may argue, to engage ethics is to engage our theory of politics. The limitations to our ethical frontiers can be overcome when reason brings us to ask the right questions.

American public administration is in the midst of a search for understanding and reasonableness with respect to the issues of ethics and ethical behavior. It is not a search initiated by the recent flood of negative publicity surrounding public servants and their actions. Its origins are far deeper and richer. In fact, much has been written on the topic, especially during the last decade, as scholars and practitioners have struggled to better understand the meaning of their behavior. Yet much work remains to be done, especially in relation to furthering our understanding of our political theory and the broad constitutional democracy that we serve. That responsibility belongs to all who labor in this field.

References

Appleby, P. H. *Morality and Administration in Democratic Government.* Baton Rouge: Louisiana State University Press, 1952.

Bates, F. G., and Field, O. P. *State Government.* New York: Harper Bros., 1939.

Chandler, R. C. "The Problem of Moral Reasoning in American Public Administration: The Case for a Code of Ethics." *Public Administration Review*, 1983, *43*, 32–39.

Ethics in Government Act. Public Law 95-521, S 555, 1978.

Fleishman, J. L., and Payne, B. L. *The Teaching of Ethics, Vol. 8: Ethical Dilemmas and the Education of Policymakers.* Hastings-on-Hudson, N.Y.: Institute of Society, Ethics and the Life Sciences, Hastings Center, 1980.

Frederickson, H. G. "Toward a New Public Administration." In F. Marini (ed.), *Toward a New Public Administration.* Scranton, Pa.: Chandler, 1971.

Frederickson, H. G. (ed.). "A Symposium: Social Equity and Public Administration." *Public Administration Review,* 1974, *34,* 1-51.

Frederickson, H. G. "Public Administration and Social Equity." *Public Administration Review,* 1990, *50,* 228-237.

Goodnow, F. J. *Comparative Administrative Law.* New York: Burt Franklin, 1903.

Hart, D. K. "Social Equity, Justice, and the Equitable Administrator." *Public Administration Review,* 1974, *34,* 3-10.

Hays, S. P. *Conservation and the Gospel of Efficiency: The Progressive Conservation Movement 1890-1920.* Cambridge, Mass.: Harvard University Press, 1959.

Hejka-Ekins, A. "Teaching Ethics in Public Administration." *Public Administration Review,* 1988, *48,* 885-891.

International City Management Association. "ICMA Code of Ethics with Guidelines." *Public Management,* 1987a, *69,* 9-13.

International City Management Association. "Rules of Procedure." *Public Management,* 1987b, *69,* 14-17.

Jaben, J. "Preventing Corruption." *American City and County,* 1986, *101,* 24-30.

Karl, B. *Charles Merriam: The Study of Politics.* Chicago: University of Chicago Press, 1974.

Lee, D. S. "The Difficulty with Ethics Education in Public Administration." *International Journal of Public Administration,* 1990, *13,* 181-205.

Lilla, M. T. "Ethos, 'Ethics,' and Public Service." *The Public Interest,* Spring 1981, *63,* 3-17.

Lippman, W. *The Political Philosopher.* Boston: Little, Brown, 1955.

May, H. F. *Protestant Churches and Industrial America.* New York: Octagon, 1963.

Mosher, F. C. *Democracy and the Public Service*. (2nd ed.) New York: Oxford University Press, 1982.

National Academy of Public Administration. *Watergate: Implications for Responsible Government*. New York: Basic Books, 1974.

Newland, C. A. *Public Administration and Community: Realism in the Practice of Ideals*. McLean, Va.: Public Administration Service, 1984.

President's Committee on Administrative Management. *Report with Special Studies*. Washington, D.C.: U.S. Government Printing Office, 1937.

Pugh, D. L. *Looking Back Moving Forward: A Half Century Celebration of Public Administration and ASPA*. Washington, D.C.: ASPA Press, 1988.

Pugh, D. L. "Professionalism in Public Administration: Problems, Perspectives, and the Role of ASPA." *Public Administration Review*, 1989, *49*, 1–8.

Ramos, A. G. *The New Science of Organizations*. Toronto: University of Toronto Press, 1981.

Rohr, J. "The Study of Ethics in the PA Curriculum." *Public Administration Review*, 1976, *36*, 398–405.

Schachter, H. L. *Frederick Taylor and the Public Administration Community*. Albany: State University of New York Press, 1989.

Simon, H. A. *Administrative Behavior*. New York: Free Press, 1947.

Streib, G. "Ethics and Expertise in the Public Service: Maintaining Democracy in an Era of Professionalism." Unpublished conference paper, 1987.

Taylor, F. W. *The Principles of Scientific Management*. New York: Norton, 1967.

Ventriss, C. "Organizational Theory and Structure: An Analysis of Three Perspectives." *International Journal of Public Administration*, 1990, *13*, p. 777–798.

Wakefield, S. "Ethics and the Public Service: A Case for Individual Responsibility." *Public Administration Review*, Nov./Dec. 1976, *36*, 661–666.

Waldo, D. *The Administrative State: A Study of the Political Theory of American Public Administration*. New York: Ronald Press, 1948.

Waldo, D. *The Enterprise of Public Administration.* Novato, Calif.: Chandler & Sharp, 1980.

Weber, M. "Bureaucracy." In H. H. Gerth and C. W. Mills (eds.), *From Max Weber: Essays in Sociology.* New York: Oxford University Press, 1946.

Weber, M. "Objectivity in Social Science and Social Policy." In G. Riley (ed.), *Values, Objectivity and the Social Sciences.* Reading, Mass.: Addison-Wesley, 1974.

White, L. D. *Introduction to the Study of Public Administration.* New York: Macmillan, 1926.

Willoughby, W. F. "The Science of Public Administration." In J. M. Mathews and J. Hart (eds.), *Essays in Political Science: In Honor of Westel Woodbury Willoughby.* Baltimore, Md.: Johns Hopkins University Press, 1937.

Wilson, W. "The Study of Administration." *Political Science Quarterly,* 1887, *2,* 197–222.

2   How Public Managers
View Their Environment:
Balancing Organizational Demands,
Political Realities, and Personal Values

Harold F. Gortner

Starting with Watergate, continuing through the Defense Department procurement scams and the Iran/Contra caper, and culminating most recently in the savings and loan bailout and the Department of Housing and Urban Development scandal, there have been continuing problems in the federal bureaucracy as well as at the highest levels of government. Interest in improving the ethical level of the public service is high. The question of how to develop ethical sensitivity, thereby improving public servant behavior, has invigorated research by public administration scholars over the last decade. The research has led to a literature addressing many important ethical problems in public administration; it has led to a broadening of the frontiers of administrative ethics. However, there is a question whether the research and literature address the world of the particular civil servant known as the *public manager.*

This chapter reports on research focusing on the significance, or relevance, of current ethical discussion for midlevel managers in the federal bureaucracy. After defining who is included as a "public manager" and briefly describing the assumption about what level of ethical discussion addresses the needs and interests of individuals fitting this definition, the chapter categorizes the current literature on ethics in public administration according to five common themes. Then, based on the described methodology, an attempt is made to determine the importance and utility of the five common themes for public managers. The conclusion considers ways to increase the impact of discussion about administrative ethics on the lives of public managers in their daily attempts to balance organizational demands, political realities, and personal values.

Discussion of the governmental bureaucracy requires the recognition of at least three levels of public administrators (executives, managers, and supervisors), and that categorization does not account for the fourth, "yeoman" level of individuals who work as nonsupervisory employees (Gortner, Mahler, and Nicholson, 1987). Thus, the world of public administration has more than one audience, more than one level of ethical perception and analysis, more than one set of skills that must be applied before arriving at a satisfactory answer to ethical dilemmas.

Public managers (and the professionals who often fit into this discussion) are defined here as individuals at the GS-12 to GM-15 levels of the federal bureaucracy. They usually hold merit system positions, supervise other supervisors (individuals at the GS-12 level may not be supervisors), and answer to a superior inside the organization. Managers' functions tend to focus on solving problems related to organizational goals, resources, processes, and structures. The goals are "given," and the manager strives to guarantee predictable procedures, efficient resource allocation and time usage, and other elements leading to effective achievement of the given goals. All of these functions must be carried out in an environment that differs from that of the private sector: public administration is nonprofit, oriented toward public service, based on a legal framework emphasizing fairness and due process, carried out under the scrutiny of varied interests all convinced that they are in danger of being mistreated, and performed in a volatile political atmosphere.

Individuals fitting this description of a public manager make up a significant portion of the public administrative ranks. Many public servants will complete useful and rewarding careers having risen no higher in the civil service. These individuals perform critical functions for and often guarantee the success or failure of the government. The question examined in this research is: "How often are the needs of these individuals, who are critical to successfully running the government, directly addressed in the literature on ethics?"

Ethical discussion, in a similar manner, involves a continuum between "policy ethics" (macroethics) and "individual ethics" (microethics). Macroethics is concerned with the impact of decisions on society as a whole, in both the material and spiritual senses of the word *impact*. Such decisions involve large numbers of people, indeed, complete institutional systems; thus any decision at the macroethical level has both positive and negative impacts on society. At the extreme, macroethics generates what Harmon and Mayer (1986) call "wicked problems" that will not go away or that Calabresi and Bobbitt (1978) call "tragic choices" where there is no way to avoid, for instance, deciding who will die while others live. Public officials, usually elected or appointed, operating at this level of ethical decision must base their roles and the decisions they make on loyalty to democratic ideals and other basic social values to arrive at the best possible solution. They also use quantitative and political analytic skills to understand "what ought to be" and "what is possible."

At the other end of the continuum, microethics tends to relate to the bureaucrats—often careerists—who operate from the middle or lower levels of the public service and whose power seldom extends beyond their immediate environments. These individuals are the public managers on whom this chapter focuses. Their decisions influence their perceptions of themselves and their personal worth. In addition, their decisions have an impact on the effectiveness of a segment of their organization; however, it is doubtful that the success or failure of the agency is in the balance (although it can certainly be affected), since organizations have built-in redundancies that guarantee overall success even though single elements fail in their mission. Therefore, the scope of ethical consideration is relatively limited and usually includes the values of the decision maker and a recognizable set of factors surrounding the individual and the situation. While the dilemma may be quite complex, it is more likely to be comprehensible and, to a certain extent, calculable because of its recognizable limits.

People in the middle levels of the bureaucracy seldom have great influence on the policies of their organizations; instead they are expected to carry out their preordained tasks in an efficient and effective manner. The primary conflict they face is one of personal integrity versus pressures to conform, to overlook, to keep quiet, or to perform wrongful acts; the results of these conflicts usually cause only minor ripples on the sea of public policy, although a large number of such cases will have a deleterious effect on the overall morale and sense of values among public employees and on the trust and respect for government held by the citizenry at large. After looking at the common themes of the literature, it is necessary to determine how that literature addresses the dilemmas of public managers.

Literature: The Recurring Focuses of Ethical Research

The literature on public administration ethics takes many forms; however, for the sake of discussion and analysis, it is necessary to categorize these treatises in a reasonable way. It appears that the material can be grouped under five major themes, which move from broad approaches to relatively specific ones; the relevance of these themes to public managers varies depending on how applicable the subjects are to the world in which these individuals work.

The five themes into which the literature on public administration ethics can be divided, from most general (based on relevance to public managers) to most specific, are (1) treatises on philosophy, culture, and the public interest; (2) discussions on the role of the professions in maintaining ethical behavior; (3) studies on individual personality and character; (4) essays on organizations and their impact on individuals; and (5) discourses on the law in its broader and narrower forms.

Discussions about *philosophy and culture* tend to be drawn primarily from the Western, Judeo-Christian background and point out important factors in our basic philosophical and cultural heritage that determine how we and others perceive what is right and wrong, good and bad (Burke, 1989; Kaplan, 1963; Leys, 1968; Roelofs, 1976; Ventriss, 1989). The search for comprehension of terms such as *justice, right, the good,* and *the public interest* and how these concepts apply to democratic theory as developed by our nation's founders and later interpreters is central to these writings. Kaplan and Roelofs, for example, address the economic, social, and political values of our American democracy (Kaplan from an optimistic and Roelofs from a pessimistic viewpoint) and attempt to show

how public values get interpreted as they are applied to public policy issues by both politicians and public servants. Leys, in contrast, attempts to interpret the general tenets of political philosophy to fit the needs of policy analysts as they address the major political issues facing government today. Such basic questions must be addressed at some level; however, for this research the question is: "How directly relevant are these general discussions of issues facing society to the concrete decisions being made by bureaucrats?"

The role of the *professions* and the values held by professionals in the making and carrying out of public policy is the central theme of the second category of writing (Mosher, 1982; Mosher and Stillman, 1982; Rainey and Backoff, 1982). The major question asked about professions is whether they contribute to the achievement of the public interest, with a secondary question being the extent to which the professions improve ethical behavior through education, socialization, and specific artifacts such as codes of ethics. Mosher argues that, for better or worse, professionals play a major role in the policy process, while Stillman sees the professional city manager (one important type of public professional) as the "best [political] hired gun in town." Other literature attempts to address the role of codes of ethics and the ethical values of the professions in guaranteeing that the public is properly served by its servants. This discussion would appear to be of special interest to public managers; however, the central question to be asked in the case of managers is: "To what extent do your professions play an important role in helping you deal with ethical dilemmas that you face?"

Studies of the influence of *personal characteristics and personality* on the ability of individuals to deal with ethical dilemmas as they arise have become increasingly important to students of ethics (Hrezo, Harmon-Brown, and Robertson, 1987; Marini, 1971; Schott, 1986). This literature, focusing on the impact of personality, intellectual maturity and sophistication, management style, and other similar factors as they are related to an individual's ethical behavior, has helped scholars to better understand the variables that must be taken into consideration as judgments are made about the moral stance of public managers. Do managers, however, ever consider these matters as they attempt to deal with the ethical dilemmas they face on a daily basis?

Organizations, the usual home of public administrators, have become the fourth focus of studies about ethics because organizations have a tremendous impact on what people perceive, how they act, and what recompense—positive or negative—comes about as a result (Barnard, 1938; Downs, 1967; Hummel, 1982; Mahler, 1988; Weisband and Franck, 1975). Some of these authors, for example, Hummel or Weisband and Franck, see the bureaucracy as a detrimental force in maintaining personal ethics. Others examine the organization as an important but not omnipotent, and sometimes a positive (Goodsell, 1983), force in framing ethical questions and determining responses. The important issue is to determine which of these views is more correct and how central the knowledge of their organizations is in the thought process of managers as they wrestle with ethical dilemmas.

Finally, discussions of the *law* usually start with an explanation of how the law, in its broadest sense, defines what values are involved in a just political and social system. Rohr (1989), for example, approaches this issue from a general level, referring to "regime values" and pointing out how these values can be best understood by examining issues argued before the Supreme Court. Other authors, especially those operating in the governmental bureaucracy, move to the more concrete level of discussion about how specific statutes, rules, and regulations place parameters on the possible interpretations and actions of public servants. All public managers agree on the centrality of the law, albeit often at the more concrete level, in their daily public bureaucratic lives.

In each of these five categories, writers have attempted to apply, both descriptively and prescriptively, the knowledge and wisdom gained in that area of the recognition, definition, analysis, decision making, and actions required by public servants as they work in the public interest. In many cases, and in spite of the simplification presented here, the literature crosses boundaries and includes material from several of these five fields. In fact, that is probably the only way to adequately deal with the complexity that is ethics. For example, two recent books—Cooper's *The Responsible Administrator* (1990) and Denhardt's *The Ethics of Public Ser-*

vice (1988)—attempt to deal with the fields described here in a comprehensive way. To carry out the current research, however, it is necessary to recognize the existence of these categories and the tendency for writing in them to be more or less germane to the needs of public managers.

Methodology: Interviewing Public Managers

In an attempt to determine what part of the discussion on ethics addresses the needs of public managers in the middle of the federal public bureaucracy, a case study approach was taken. This approach was especially appropriate to the question being examined. Quantification of response was not the goal; instead, it was essential to delve into the contextual understanding of managers' attitudes and behaviors in a real-world setting. It was important to understand the episodes themselves with their accompanying encounters, roles, relationships, meanings, practices, and settlements as seen by those experiencing the ethical dilemmas under consideration.

Forty-two senior or retired federal employees, chosen from nearly as many agencies, were interviewed. Each individual was asked to describe a critical ethical dilemma she or he had faced while serving as a middle manager (defined as the time worked in the range from GS-12 to GM-15). After describing, in a nondirected way, the chosen dilemma in its entirety, each individual was asked a set of questions that covered the areas usually included in writing about public administration ethics and related to the categories described above. This approach to the interviews guaranteed that the individuals would describe their ethical dilemma without the introduction of researcher bias. After they had described their dilemma, and how they had handled it, the researcher was able to find out, through his questions, if all the categories of ethical discussion were involved in the manager's analysis of his or her situation (Babbie, 1986; Lofland and Lofland, 1984).

This use of the "critical incident" approach was geared to getting the public managers' responses about what influenced their decisions and actions when they faced an ethical dilemma. (As defined by the participants in this research, an *ethical dilemma* is a situation where two or more competing values are important and in conflict, yet one *must* be chosen.) The answers suggested that all five categories mentioned above are of interest to individuals at this level of the bureaucracy; however, a definite "hierarchy of relevance" came to light in the interviews. In the next section, those five categories are examined in their order of importance, or relevance, to the interviewed public managers.

The Results: Diffuse to Converging Elements

The five general categories of writing about public administration ethics are ranked according to their centrality to the thought of the interviewed public managers. The more central the topic, the larger the role it played in the definition and analysis of ethical dilemmas as they were described by public managers. The managers understood the importance of the central issues, were relatively familiar with the concepts used by ethicists, and used these concepts (or very similar terms) in their thought processes and their descriptions of their critical incidents.

The less central (or more diffuse) categories are sometimes included in the descriptions of critical incidents given by the public managers, but when these categories appear, they usually exist as "rules of thumb" or concepts that are much less sophisticated than those used by ethicists in their analysis. The meanings of less central categories are less clear to practitioners. This concept of "diffuseness" and "centrality" will be made more clear by discussions of the five categories, starting with the most diffuse and moving to the most central in the thoughts and actions of midlevel managers.

1. *Philosophical or cultural values.* Philosophical or cultural concepts were never raised by any of the interviewees as they described their ethical dilemmas. When later asked about such concepts and whether they had any influence, few of the interviewees could discuss these principles on a familiar level, especially in relation to their specific cases; however, they were aware of the basic influence that philosophical, social, economic, and political principles had in forming their environment and their own general beliefs. As one of the interviewees commented, most successful managers are aware of the impact of culture on actions, but "culture

does not usually impinge on one's thinking. Instead it creates an environment, a milieu, in which alternatives are imagined and analyzed. We are aware of it only if we stop and think specifically of it. Obviously, to the extent that general values, principles, and perceptions do apply, they must then be translated so they become relevant to the specific issue about which we are concerned."

Two areas of philosophical and cultural values did arise. The first area was the economic values under which the government worked. In most cases the change in economic values that had occurred over the last decade was recognized but had nothing directly to do with the kinds of ethical dilemmas interviewees described. They recognized a change in general economic "doctrine" or belief, but those matters were handled at a policy level not directly involving them.

The second set of values that arose related to "religion," because several of the recurring themes of political debate over the last decade have been related to that subject. The respondents, when placed in decision-making roles related to issues with religious overtones, had no difficulty recognizing that element of the joint personal-cultural milieu, and they felt relatively comfortable in dealing with it as managers running specific programs, even though the people with whom they had to relate often did not separate personal religious views from policy stances and program activities.

The rule of thumb used by public managers that most related to the philosophical and cultural underpinnings of public life was a check of actions against the three concepts of *fairness, openness,* and *due process.* (*Fairness* appears again when we discuss the importance of personal characteristics in resolving ethical dilemmas. The term has a personalized meaning there, whereas its use in this case refers to the appearance of procedures to the populace at large.) They did not go back to philosophical tenets for the justification of such action, but they recognized the political implications of their procedures and decisions. These terms were simplifications of the ethicists' complicated philosophical debates that public managers could use in their daily lives. As noted by one manager at a relatively high level of his organization, "I think that government ought to be sensitive to notions of fairness. When you are dealing with public business, it is important to make sure nothing undercuts confidence because people see business being done for personal benefit. One of the best ways to achieve that confidence is through openness, so there can be no perception of shady deals or special arrangements. I will not argue that policy always should be made in the sunshine, but its implementation must occur in an environment of sharp shadows."

This individual continued by noting that public bureaucrats are aware "that the public sector is a world of perception; perception is often equal to, if not more important than, issues of legality." Therefore, due process is important so that all appears proper. Successful public managers have an instinctive understanding of the milieu in which they work, but they do not spend much time analyzing the philosophical bases of that environment.

2. *Professions.* Perhaps the failure to comprehend more general philosophical and cultural values is not too astonishing; however, the second most diffuse area was unexpected. Surprisingly, the managers seldom mentioned the professions (for example, medicine, law, accounting, engineering, and psychology) and the codes of ethics related to those professions as having any influence on their actions. In a few cases *where the individuals acted in professional capacities* (for example, as lawyers or accountants), the codes of the relevant professions played a central role in their decisions and actions, but *when interviewees were acting as managers,* the professional mores and ethical codes became much less relevant. Each of those interviewees who had started their public careers in one of the professions but had moved into managerial positions recognized that they had moved from the particularized environment of the professional to the more general milieu of the manager, and they found the demands made upon them, and therefore the mores and values of their new positions, different from those of their original professions. Most of them found the ethics of their profession either irrelevant or inadequate for dealing with the problems they faced as managers. One manager in the Department of Commerce noted the situation and clearly reacted to the dichotomy between professional and management values: "My profession as accountant has had little to do with my *management* function. It applies to those few actions I still take as an accountant, but my much greater role as manager primarily deals with organizational structure, planning and implementing programs, and dealing with personnel issues. While it sets a proper general tone for behavior, the accounting code of ethics does not deal with those issues."

In his last sentence this manager addressed the interesting issue that related "professional*ism*" and management ethics. The connection between these two intellectual constructs became clearer among managers who did not come from a professional background. For those managers the question of professional values and ethics was important but was addressed differently. Many of the management fields of these individuals (for example, personnel, budgeting, planning, and policy analysis) have developed codes of ethics, but the emphasis on that code was much less, nor could the professional organizations to which they belonged control actual member behavior. Codes of ethics were "advisory" rather than having formal teeth through a means of policing action and reprimanding code violators. These individuals made no pretense of being professional in the traditional sense; however, they were sensitive to the values and attitudes attached to the professions, and they strove to apply and fulfill the appropriate professional values (obligation to service, commitment to the work as a "calling," autonomy in decision making and actions, protection of the public interest, and so on) in their more general world.

Thus, the way that the professions had an impact on public managers was through the constant thread of consideration or thought about the concept of *professionalism* and its meaning in the context of management. This effort to wrestle with the ideals and values surrounding the concept was important to the maintenance of an objective approach to ethical problems across the board. When the public managers faced an ethical dilemma, they consistently tried to act in a "professional" way.

3. *Individual characteristics.* In Western culture we accept the idea that an individual is responsible for his or her own actions. We also attempt to understand better what makes the individual tick and how personal characteristics influence the perception and resolution of all kinds of problems. Ethicists have drawn heavily on this body of literature, much of it from psychology, as they have discussed the impact of individual qualities on public administration ethics, and this dialogue appears to address questions that are of importance to public managers. Although they had little or no training in "self-analysis or -understanding," the public managers interviewed were aware of and sensitive to their personal character-istics and understood that these factors played an important role in how they handled any ethical dilemmas that arose. These discus-sions regularly included three categories of influences: individual background, personality characteristics, and levels of ethical matur-ity. The managers applied these concepts both to themselves and to those around them. While their terminology was often unsophisti-cated, examples of knowledge about these factors appeared in al-most all of the cases discussed by the public managers.

It is argued that *personal background,* such as family influ-ence, religious beliefs, educational experience, and peer pressure, have an impact on the way individuals perceive the world, but these factors are not seen by managers as primary movers in their public life. Only when an ethical dilemma was directly related to issues such as racial discrimination or religious beliefs did interviewees recognize that their personal background influenced their decisions, and in those cases they tried to make sure that their predispositions did not affect their ability to act fairly and equitably. When ques-tioned about such factors, they recognized the presence of their "per-sonal background" and admitted they occasionally had to control their first reactions.

Education was an important element in the way managers dealt with ethical problems. Graduate and professional education was cited as the specific location of training in ethics; managers who came from professional areas had often had classes or segments of classes addressing ethical issues related to the profession, and several others noted that their graduate work in public administration (none in business administration) had included such material. Typ-ical of comments by managers was that of an individual who had completed a graduate public administration program shortly before being faced with the problem he described: "Eighteen months be-fore this situation arose, I had taken a course on ethics in graduate school. It helped immensely because it helped me to think through my responsibilities as a public manager, and it forced me to con-sider my own personal values within the public context." Because of that training he knew what drove him as an individual and understood his management style: "My own personal values informed me as I went along. My style was very open and driven by a pretty literal interpretation of the laws, rules, and regulations; however, I wanted to be recognized as fair, generous, honest."

Personality characteristics compose the second general area related to the individual. Much work has been done on how individual perceptions, thinking processes, temperaments, and action modes affect one's ability to deal with problems involving other individuals (Keirsey and Bates, 1984)—as is almost always true in ethical dilemmas. People want different things and have different motives, purposes, values, needs, drives, and impulses in everyday life. People cognize, conceptualize, understand, believe differently; therefore, they act and emote differently. Ethicists have found this area pregnant with information and theories useful to their study.

Very few of the interviewees had participated in any formal kind of "personality analysis" such as having taken the Myers-Briggs test. Likewise, over two-thirds were not familiar, except through the popular press, with much of the literature or many of the tests for "management style" in vogue among management trainers. Still, these individuals demonstrated an understanding of "what made them tick." An amazing level of self-understanding was present, although responses to questions did not elicit the jargon of the professional analyst. Interviewees generally knew how they were perceived, both managerially and personally, by those around them—superiors, subordinates, and peers—and took those kinds of factors into account as they dealt with the particular problems they faced. The kind of understanding that existed is represented by one individual's description of himself in which he said, "I had a reputation for being 'hard-nosed,' but people agreed that I was hard on myself also. As one of my cosupervisors put it, 'You are seen by your subordinates as firm but fair.'"

The public managers also applied personality and management style concepts to individuals above and below themselves. When political actors were involved in the cases, the managers understood the personalities of these individuals and how their temperaments led them to define, and often misdefine, political forces with which they had to deal. As public managers, working in an organization in a political milieu and having as one of their primary functions the handling of people, these individuals were immersed in the actualities of "personality and management style" even if they were not up to date on the latest vocabulary used by academics to describe the phenomena.

The third factor, *ethical maturity*, drawn from Kohlberg's (1976) work on human intellectual development and its impact on one's ability to conceptualize about moral or ethical problems, was very useful to the interviewer. (Kohlberg argues that individuals develop through six stages [two at each of three general levels] of moral maturity, starting at the preconventional level with an orientation to punishment, reward, and power, moving to a conventional level where morality is defined by group acceptance and respect for law and order, and finally moving to a postconventional moral order based on principles established by society or, ultimately, by the application of self-chosen principles that are applied universally.) In more than one case the interviews had to be pitched at a particular level of maturity to communicate meaningfully with the interviewee. The most interesting finding, however, was that managers, while not aware of the formal theory, also thought in this way. The idea of a hierarchy of moral maturity was something generally understood by the public managers. These concepts were used—often employing terms surprisingly near to those developed by Kohlberg—as rules of thumb about how and when a person could be trusted to carry out specific kinds of assigned tasks.

Perhaps the best way to describe the value of this theory is to note the individual in the interviews who, in describing his "ethical dilemma," fell at level three of Kohlberg's hierarchy (the lower of the two conventional levels described above). Interestingly, this was the only individual who described a case where he felt he had failed in his attempt to deal with his ethical dilemma. It was impossible to recognize the ethical dilemma he was describing until it became clear he was operating at level three on Kohlberg's scale. Briefly, he believed he failed in his assigned mission of "selling" his agency's special budget request to representatives of the Office of Management and Budget *because he was not able to win the personal approval of important individuals on both sides of the case.* He desperately wanted the approval of his significant peers, but he was in a situation where he believed significant peers existed in both of the agencies involved—his own and the Office of Management and Budget—and he felt a sense of failure because he could not find a way to gain approval for his actions from both groups. He did not seem worried about the outcome of the budget request.

When the details of this case were presented to a retired Senior Executive Service official who had spent his entire career in the merit system, he immediately understood what was going on, and he responded to the description of the case by saying,

> I have known several individuals like that in my time. They are almost useless to their superiors, because that kind of individual always tries to give you what he thinks you want rather than dealing with the facts and giving you good objective analysis and advice. He will go to any length to endear himself to you, but what you need is someone who will help you to understand the world. These kinds of individuals get you into real hot water because they will not tell you that you are about to make a mistake; instead, they will go so far in trying to do whatever you want that you end up in trouble with everybody—the president's office, Congress, constituents, other agencies—because no one is satisfied with the convoluted results of this mistaken effort to please.
>
> Oh, by the way, as an aside, if this individual has risen to the highest level of middle management (GM-15), usually he desperately wishes to become a member of the SES, since he sees that as the ultimate symbol of acceptance. However, such individuals almost never make it because of this fatal flaw. They try so hard, fail, never understand why, and often become bitter.

This manager came very close to using Kohlberg's terms because he understood that people operate at different levels of maturity and sophistication in their general work and in facing ethical situations. He also understood the pitfalls present in dealing with such individuals. The kinds of assignment given to individuals under him, and the way he supervised them, varied according to the qualities and abilities of the person involved. While he did not use any specific theories or refer to any scholars on the subject, this public manager supervised individuals working for him according to the levels of maturity they represented in their actions. He looked for subordinates who "understood the world and would tell him the facts," who, therefore, operated at the higher levels of Kohlberg's hierarchy.

This type of individual is also described in Stephen Bailey's (1965) classic article on the mental attitudes (the recognition of moral ambiguity in all people and public policies, contextual forces that condition or affect moral priorities in the public service, and the paradoxes of procedures) and moral qualities (optimism, courage, and fairness tempered with charity) of the successful public administrator. When, in the latter part of the interviews, the literature on these areas of individual characteristics and background was mentioned, there were a warmth of response and an eagerness to discuss that showed a deep interest in better understanding the personal characteristics that make the managers, and their surrounding coworkers, function in what they recognize as a world fraught with ethical dilemmas.

Organizational Dynamics. Public managers work in the middle of the bureaucracy; therefore, central to the decisions and actions of all successful managers is the sense of the importance of "the organization" to everything they do. The aspects of organization that had an influence on the managers can be grouped into three categories, although the variety of factors in each category is immense.

External groups play a central role in determining the perceptions, alternatives, and actions considered acceptable in an organization. The public managers recognized that the political environment of public organizations colors almost everything that occurs related to goals and processes. For example, the type of clients served (politically powerful versus unorganized, wealthy versus poor, receivers of services versus submitters to regulation) and the kind of activities carried out (defense, regulation, human services, science support) have tremendous impacts on the strength and vitality of the programs and the prestige, power, independence and morale of the civil servants working in a specific public bureaucracy

(Rourke, 1976). Even in a specific bureaucracy it is recognized that certain parts of the clientele have power, while others are helpless before the onslaught of the bureaucratic juggernaut, and these kinds of factors influence what can and should be done by public servants.

Public managers often found their ability to deal with ethical dilemmas limited because the clients they were helping were either politically powerful or, conversely, powerless. In one case, minority groups were excluded from receiving federal funds and professional help even though such discrimination was illegal. When the individual describing the case tried to correct the problem, she ran into strong opposition from those comfortable with the present situation, and included in that group were both members of the bureaucracy and politically powerful clients. Her politically weak constituents were not able to help her, so she had to almost singlehandedly battle for change. In other situations, some of the individuals the managers had to deal with from outside the agency were politically powerful and were operating in positions that enhanced their ability to gain the ear of authorities at the highest levels of the executive branch. Such situations often cannot be resolved in a manner satisfactory to everyone, especially the manager who has to put her or his job on the line.

Given the cycles in which the political process works, always with some programs gaining in popularity and political support and others dropping, the only sure thing is that the cycle will change and programs will trade places. For example, the "defense juggernaut" of the 1980s becomes "defense in retreat" of the 1990s with the changing of the international environment. Ethical issues that were glossed over during the heyday of the defense establishment may become central sore issues in a period of retrenchment and weakened political clout. In this world public servants see their freedom of and support for action changing over time. Public managers are aware that the kinds of ethical dilemmas faced and the possible solutions to those problems change as inevitably as do the tides of popularity for and public attention to specific programs and organizations.

The *structure and function* of the organization help determine what ethical dilemmas public managers face and what the possibilities for resolving them are. Such structural factors as (1) the size of the bureaucracy, (2) the type of hierarchy that exists, (3) the dispersion or centralization of decision making in the overall organization, and, of course, (4) the location of the individual in the organization all have a tremendous impact on the kinds of ethical problems faced and the possible alternatives for resolving them. Likewise, such functional issues as the type of output (service or product) generated and the kind of specializations required to do the work must be balanced against the demands of general managerial tasks as public managers attempt to deal with ethical dilemmas— which always occur at the most unpropitious moment.

Finally, one of the most salient organizational factors when we are talking about ethical dilemmas is the *organizational culture*. Organizational culture has received a considerable amount of attention from scholars over the last three decades, and there is still much to learn about how this phenomenon influences individual ability to resolve ethical problems. Culture includes values, mores, attitudes, and perceptions developed through the history of the organization based on the interactions of group members with one another. Central to the culture, of course, are the values and mores of the organization's leaders.

Again, this was an area with which public managers were quite familiar. Almost every interviewee spent some time discussing such factors and the limitations they placed on possible actions. In this area academic work and the world of the practitioner seem to be in close conformity because an understanding of this phenomenon develops in sensitive managers as they gain experience and maturity. This was noted by one well-traveled manager when he said, "There is a vast array of values that come into play in your consciousness. Part of being a success in such a variety of agencies are individual growth, new inputs with experience, and insights that come with each new environment. Not only does the successful manager adapt to the values, mores, and goals of each organization, but he or she adds each new experience to his or her bank of knowledge, and that hopefully leads to greater sensitivity and sophistication in handling the ticklish situations."

This increasing storehouse of knowledge about organizational culture is used constantly by public managers in most of their decisions and activities; however, it becomes extremely important when ethical dilemmas arise because, by definition, in these situations there are competing values at stake, and different values will be held by the various actors in the dilemma.

Organizational dynamics (environment, structure, function, and culture) play a central role in many if not most ethical dilemmas. These factors, in the right combination, may lead to *systemic corruption* in organizations that make it risky to be ethical and lead to actions such as whistle-blowing and resignation from an apparently comfortable job. These organizational problems are recognized by public managers, and they take such factors into account constantly as they attempt to deal with the ethical problems they face.

The Law and Legal Issues. At the higher (philosophical) level, laws are the official designation of the hopes and desires of society. At a statutory (political) level, laws show who has won and who has lost in the constant battle to influence society's choices and actions. Rules and regulations (the level of the law with which public managers work most) describe what is to be done in implementing the law and the parameters in which action must take place. In the managerial environment, statutes, rules, and regulations take on disproportionate importance. The legal analysis has usually been done by someone else; public managers see themselves as simply trying to live in the confines of the law while getting their jobs done. As noted by one interviewee, "It is important to separate the ideas of legality and ethicality. A legal conflict cannot be an ethical conflict because in case of any legal question you can get some legal advice or ruling on what you are required to do. You are expected to obey the law, you are told what the law means, and if you do not follow the law you are performing an illegal act. Whether or not it is an ethical act is another question."

All of the public managers regularly mentioned the law— usually referring to specific statutes, rules, or regulations—as they described the ethical situations they faced and the actions they took. The public managers understood the larger implications of the law as an interpretation of social goals, but the cases with which they were dealing seldom related to such lofty issues. They were dealing with specific problems for which rules and regulations had been established, although their interpretation was often in question.

Implementation, the Law, and Ethics. The managers generally faced one or more of three situations related to the law and *implementation.* First, the law served as a delimiter—managers had to deal with ethical situations where the law was a limiting factor. They wanted to accomplish a specific goal and stay within the rules and regulations. Often the current rules and regulations kept them from efficiently or effectively achieving the goal that seemed most desirable. Substantive and procedural goals of the law conflicted, yet a decision had to be made and action had to be taken. (Remember that managers are often in the uncomfortable position of having to act. They cannot, in many cases, take the easy way out by doing nothing. In their situations, doing nothing is doing something to someone.)

What often occurs here is that public managers operating at Kohlberg's "postconventional" stages of moral maturity (noted above) gain a sense of the ambiguous relationship between the spirit and intent of law and the implementation of law (Bailey, 1965). They can even identify laws that are poorly drafted and contain loopholes that thwart the original purpose of the statutes (for example, Section 8 housing laws, which were criticized by many HUD employees after the revelations of misconduct in that department).

At the same time, these public managers have to work with conventional-stage individuals who see the unswerving and literal application of rule and regulation as ethics defined. For example, the Civil Service Reform Act of 1978 contains a noble "statement of purpose" and some very useful "merit principles" to which the civil service system should adhere along with a set of statutory "prohibited personnel practices" that are to be avoided. However, federal managers often have their attempts to adhere to these higher principles frustrated by staffs who regard any deviation from cumbersome and sometimes outdated procedural requirements as illegal. Flexibility is essential but prohibited; a conflict in interpretation of what is "ethical" limits the public manager's ability to be efficient, effective, and "successful."

One of the managers interviewed had a different but equally

frustrating problem with his personnel office when trying to deal with a troublesome handicapped employee. When the manager went to the personnel office for advice, they always quoted "the book" to him, stating that "the performance standards are the same for all individuals in all positions. If she cannot do the job, fire her." After giving him this advice, they would always look at him and say, "The bosses are not going to like it if you make any waves." The personnel staff hid behind the rules but refused to help the manager follow them.

The second situation faced by managers during implementation was a positive one where the law served as protection and support when managers were pressured to do things that they felt were not appropriate or in the strict interpretation of the law as it applied to a case. In many cases managers were asked not to "make waves" when rules appeared to be broken, or they were implicitly or explicitly asked to "shave the rules for us." In some cases the managers were able to resolve the issue by clearly stating the rules and regulations related to a specific situation and refusing to carry out the desires of superiors or peers. In other cases the problem became one of clearly understanding the rules and regulations in order to know what was an appropriate compromise that remained in the letter and intent of the law. Compromise, after all, is central to politics (the world in which most of these decisions are made) and an honorable resolution of many conflicts. Therefore, York Willbern's dictum that "it is necessary upon occasion to rise above principle and make a deal' (1984, pp. 107–108) is correct, but one must understand the law in its broader sense in order to compromise in meaningful yet principled ways.

The third type of problem related to the law involved those situations where the law served as the point of contention—managers had to deal with a problem where others were ignoring, misinterpreting, or misapplying the law. In such a case the expected response is to attempt to correct the situation, and if it can be corrected there is probably no ethical dilemma. However, in many cases, rather than being able to correct the situation, the individuals who become aware of such problems are faced with threats, intimidation, or active efforts to guarantee that nothing changes and they keep their mouths shut. From these situations arise the whistle-blowers and other individuals who often become sacrifices on the altar of ethics. (These individuals are described as sacrifices rather than martyrs because in most cases they disappear without a trace or a ripple in the business of government. Encouraging such action should be done with great caution. It is important to remember that while a few whistle-blowers become saints, most become statistics.)

It must be understood that the law demands appropriate actions but seldom protects those who fulfill their obligations. This points out one of the weaknesses of law that is often commented upon by practitioners: the law cannot regulate or overcome the informal set of mores that develops in an organization or a society. As one manager noted, "Where there is a wile, there is a way." If powerful organization members wish to punish a whistle-blower or nonconformer, they can usually do so.

Two interesting and unique cases further stressed the centrality of the law in public managers' ethical dilemmas. In one case the individual, along with members of her immediate work group, decided to break one law—a specific statute regarding budget procedures—because she and her group believed that higher, more comprehensive laws required action denied to the group in the specific statute. The decision was not taken lightly; however, an action was required, and delay could cause serious repercussions. The group ultimately acted outside established statutory authority to meet what they considered the public interest as spelled out in laws and treaties established by the political system. The action, whether or not one agrees with it, was symbolic of the sophisticated understanding of the law held by the group. They recognized the differing levels of generality existing in the legal code and that laws may come into conflict when one attempts to do what is best for everyone concerned.

In only one case did the individual being interviewed fail to refer to the law. That individual was also the only one to describe a situation (noted above) where he felt he utterly failed to achieve his goal. This individual was so involved in attempting to satisfy peer groups that he failed to recognize that a standard from a higher level of generalization, namely, the law and the substantive and procedural goals it established, might be relevant to his case. His thinking was not sophisticated enough to recognize more general standards of that type; therefore, he attempted to satisfy or impress two competing groups, both of which he saw as valuable peers, and his efforts were doomed to failure from the beginning. This individual failed to understand the environment in which he worked, and his thought processes and actions were therefore inappropriate from beginning to end.

The law, usually defined as rules and regulations, was the most central and pervasive element in the thought processes of public managers. Given the fact of public scrutiny and the problem that the media and the citizenry in general always focus on what does not work instead of on what does, it is not surprising that public administrators looked for justification for their actions by attempting to "work within the law." However, the organizational and individual elements of ethical dilemmas were also constantly in the minds of these individuals, so the difference in level of importance of these three focuses should not be stressed too greatly. The centrality of these three elements in the thought processes of public managers is important to remember as we move to our discussion of the conclusions drawn from this study.

Conclusion: Directions for Future Research and Action

Public managers are generally sensitive to and interested in ethical issues. The all-too-typical stereotype presented by politicians, the public, and, unfortunately, many academics of bureaucrats as "faceless, shiftless, amoral automatons" is nonsense. The public's image of the public service is "created by the exception" rather than by the norm. Public servants in the middle of the bureaucracy are as sensitive (or more so) to questions of values and ethics as are the people they serve. Therefore, discussion of public administration ethics is a useful, important activity.

The group interviewed cannot be classified as typical of the larger service, nor were the cases shared guaranteed to represent a cross section of the types of problems faced by public managers across the field (although in both instances the samples probably are not that far from reality). However, analysis of the interviews delivers an important message to those wishing to address public administration ethics in ways that will "speak directly to managers." Several important lessons can be learned from the experiences and words of the management practitioners.

The interviews of these public servants make it clear that if one wishes to speak directly to managers and to influence their thinking and behavior, the message must be addressed to them in a way that "connects" with their reality. That is not a world-shattering finding, but it tends to be forgotten all too often. Material about ethics must be brought down to a level of conceptual specificity or tangibility that represents the ongoing world of the public manager—a world of politics, organizations immersed in a system of rules and regulations, and people holding many views and immensely differing levels of power. Any discussion that helps to show how these various elements play important roles in ethical dilemmas and helps individuals to understand how to comprehend, analyze, and deal with these elements is welcomed by public managers. This is discussion about ethics at the primary, direct, relevant level for public management.

Is this an argument that discussions about ethics at the professional and cultural-philosophical levels are useless? No. But if one's goal is to influence *public managers,* one must focus, or "translate," discussions about these general subjects in ways that are more directly related, or useful, to managers. As one interviewee noted, "It really doesn't matter to me what Confucius said—unless I am dealing with a problem in the Chinese community." In other words, managers are interested in philosophical and professional issues only if they help to answer questions related to concrete dilemmas of the workaday world.

There must be an understanding of and commitment to democratic values, especially to the concept of individual worth and dignity. Public service must be understood as service "in the public interest." However, if public managers are to participate in this dialogue, those values and concepts must be translated into images, situations, and actions that are pertinent to actions taken while serving the larger polity in the context of organizational life. Cases that present meaningful ideas about how individual dignity can be developed or maintained in the environment of the public organization and how actions in the organization can achieve these goals for clients and the citizenry at large are critical to developing and maintaining ethical sensitivity. Such cases may often lead to debate about what is proper action; however, what must be remembered is that *the debate is what is important.* When dealing with public administrative ethics, finding "right" answers is often not as important as asking the "right" questions.

The same attempt to bring lofty ideas down to practical levels appears in discussing the professions. Public managers appear to be searching for "the essence of professionalism" in an attempt to apply that set of values to ethically related actions. Conversation tends to move from discussions of ethics in specific professions to an attempt to create a broader theoretical base useful to public managers. Public managers want to develop an understanding of what it may mean to be a "professional public manager." Is it possible to combine the essence of these three words—*professional public manager*—in a way that will allow us to develop a single code of conduct applicable to everyone in this vital set of positions that have so many different actualities? Probably not. The concept of the professional public manager has to remain a situational idea related to the specific environment of the organization being considered. Success in finding a general definition of professionalism that can be applied to specific managerial situations may be central to the development of "the ethical public manager."

A final, special question to be considered in this instance is whether this desire for a "profession of public management" opens the door for organizations such as the American Society for Public Administration to try to develop a code of ethics for public managers. The efforts of ASPA and other professional management groups did not seem to have had any impact on the individuals interviewed in this research. In some cases, the incidents described may have occurred prior to ASPA's focus on the development of a code of ethics, but that was certainly not true in all cases. It should be noted that the same situation arose for other similar organizations in areas such as personnel, budgeting, planning, and policy. For instance, a personnel specialist commented that "the professional [personnel] code of ethics, although on my wall, I perceived as a motherhood statement without all that concrete meaning for me. It belabored the obvious." Although the codes of ethics were occasionally used as vehicles for avoiding conflict or confrontation, *not once did one of the interviewees refer to any of the codes of ethics developed by these organizations as an influence in how they arrived at their decisions or actions.*

What public managers are looking for is an understanding of the *values* that are central to the idea of professionalism. To the extent that codes address these issues, those codes will have increasing relevance and value to public managers; to the extent that the codes prescribe or proscribe specific actions and do not address the more fundamental reasons behind the prescriptions, they will remain useless to practitioners.

When looking at the other three areas of ethical discussion, it becomes clear that public managers have a direct, immediate interest in the discussions that combine concepts and theories about the individual, organizational, and legal aspects of life with the resolution of ethical dilemmas. Public managers feel that researchers of public administrative ethics have been on the mark in these areas of study. These subjects are proximate to the everyday lives of public managers. The insights and ideas generated from this discussion can be taken to work and applied tomorrow. The problem in this area of discussion is to make sure that practitioners know about it and can get to it easily.

Availability of information about ethics is a special problem that apparently has not been faced by the federal government. In a few cases ethics had been subsumed in some other larger training program; however, none of the public managers interviewed had participated in a formal training program sponsored by the government specifically focusing on ethics. What training had been given primarily emphasized rules and regulations designed to keep employees out of trouble; it seldom if ever dealt with preparation for dealing positively or proactively with ethical dilemmas.

It is not enough to pass laws requiring ethical behavior. Laws usually deal only with what *cannot* be done and do not help to resolve ethical dilemmas positively. Public managers need knowledge about what cannot be done but also, especially, knowledge about how to achieve the larger goal of positive, proactive ethical behavior. In fact it is necessary to go further than "making the knowledge available"; as a first step in helping to create a more ethically sensitive public service, training in ethics should be made easily available to everyone. Training will not help those who have no interest in ethics, but for those who care (and this is the *vast* majority of civil servants at all levels of government), such training will help them to improve both their ethical sensitivity and understanding.

Ethics training will require extensive effort. "Generic" ethics training fails in exactly the same way that discussion of general philosophy does: it does not address the real world of the public manager. Instead the training must take into account the diversity of the organizations, goals, functions, and cultures faced by the public manager. Useful ethics training will be tailored to the organization, laws, environment, and to the individuals receiving the instruction. Tailored training can also take many forms; it can occur from the moment of orientation until one leaves the organization and can involve discussion groups, regular communication from superiors both orally and in writing, and more formal classes and conferences.

If top management supports such an effort, the entire environment can be made sensitive to ethical issues. One of the interviewees noted that her superior was constantly commenting on the need for "the implementation of statutes not only to fall within the defined parameters but also to meet the larger test of serving the public interest." Her actions, accordingly, were always considered in those terms. Success requires support from the top.

This appears to be an area where the Office of Management and Budget, the Office of Personnel Management, Congress, and others in charge of the federal civil service system are penny wise and pound foolish. Any reasonable investment in helping to raise the ethical sensitivity and sensibility of public servants will achieve multiple returns. However, since a clear dollar figure cannot be attached to those returns, it is unlikely that such an investment will occur in the foreseeable future unless someone is willing to champion the cause.

Over the last couple of decades there has been a movement toward a calculus of politics and a definition of "good government" that considers only measurable, usually economic, attributes. ASPA and the National Association of Schools of Public Affairs and Administration, as organizations interested in the public service, and especially those of us who study public administration ethics, must reclaim our "good government" mantle, held in the early days of the public administration field, and ardently advocate the inclusion of ethics in the calculus of government and politics.

References

Babbie, E. *The Practice of Social Research*. (4th ed.) Belmont, Calif.: Wadsworth, 1986.

Bailey, S. K. "The Relationship Between Ethics and Public Service." In R. C. Martin (ed.), *Public Administration and Democracy: Essays in Honor of Paul Appleby*. Syracuse, N.Y.: Syracuse University Press, 1965.

Barnard, C. *The Functions of the Executive*. Cambridge, Mass.: Harvard University Press, 1938. (A fortieth-anniversary edition was published in 1979.)

Bayles, M. D. *Professional Ethics*. (2nd ed.) Belmont, Calif.: Wadsworth, 1989.

Blake, E. C. "Should the Code of Ethics in Public Life Be Absolute or Relative?" *Annals of the Academy of Political and Social Science*, Jan. 1966, *363*, 4-11.

Burke, J. P. "Reconciling Public Administration and Democracy: The Role of the Responsible Administrator." *Public Administration Review*, Mar./Apr. 1989, *49* (2), 180-185.

Calabresi, G., and Bobbitt, P. *Tragic Choices*. New York: Norton, 1978.

Cooper, T. L. *The Responsible Administrator: An Approach to Ethics for the Administrative Role*. (3rd ed.) San Francisco: Jossey-Bass, 1990.

Denhardt, K. G. *The Ethics of Public Service: Resolving Moral Dilemmas in Public Organizations*. Westport, Conn.: Greenwood Press, 1988.

Downs, A. *Inside Bureaucracy*. Boston: Little, Brown, 1967.

Fragola, A. T. "Professions: Have They Become Un-American?" *Vital Speeches of the Day*, July 1984, *50*, 555-557.

Goodsell, C. T. *The Case for Bureaucracy: A Public Administration Polemic*. Chatham, N.J.: Chatham House, 1983.

Gortner, H. F., Mahler, J., and Nicholson, J. B. *Organization The-*

ory: A Public Perspective. Pacific Grove, Calif.: Brooks/Cole, 1987.

Harmon, M. M., and Mayer, R. T. *Organization Theory for Public Administration.* Boston: Little, Brown, 1986.

Hrezo, W. E., Harmon-Brown, M., and Robertson, D. L. "Public Administration: A Personalized Approach." *Virginia Social Science Journal,* Spring 1987, *22,* 25–35.

Hummel, R. P. *The Bureaucratic Experience.* (2nd ed.) New York: St. Martin's, 1982.

Jackall, R. *Moral Mazes: The World of Corporate Managers.* New York: Oxford University Press, 1988.

Kaplan, A. *American Ethics and Public Policy.* New York: Oxford University Press, 1963.

Keirsey, D., and Bates, M. *Please Understand Me: Character and Temperament Types.* Del Mar, Calif.: Prometheus Nemesis, 1984.

Kohlberg, L. "Children's Perceptions of Contemporary Value Systems." In N. B. Talbot (ed.), *Raising Children in Modern America: Problems and Prospective Solutions.* Boston: Little, Brown, 1976.

Leys, W.A.R. *Ethics for Policy Decisions: The Art of Asking Deliberative Questions.* Westport, Conn.: Greenwood Press, 1968.

Lofland, J., and Lofland, L. H. *Analyzing Social Setting: A Guide to Qualitative Observation and Analysis.* (2nd ed.) Davis: University of California Press, 1984.

MacIntyre, A. *After Virtue: A Study of Moral Theory.* Notre Dame, Ind.: University of Notre Dame Press, 1981.

Mahler, J. "The Quest for Organizational Meaning: Identifying and Interpreting the Symbolism in Organizational Stories." *Administration and Society,* Nov. 1988, *20,* 344–368.

Marini, F. (ed.). *Toward a New Public Administration: The Minnowbrook Perspective.* Scranton, Pa.: Chandler, 1971.

Mosher, F. C. *Democracy and the Public Service.* (2nd ed.) New York: Oxford University Press, 1982.

Mosher, F. C., and Stillman, R. J., II (eds.). *Professions in Government.* New Brunswick, N.J.: Transaction, 1982.

Rainey, H. G., and Backoff, R. W. "Professionals in Public Organizations: Organizational Environments and Incentives." *American Review of Public Administration,* Winter 1982, *16,* 319-336.

Roelofs, H. M. *Ideology and Myth in American Politics: A Critique of a National Political Mind.* Boston: Little, Brown, 1976.

Rohr, J. A. *Ethics for Bureaucrats: An Essay on Law and Values.* (2nd ed.) New York: Marcel Dekker, 1989.

Rourke, F. E. *Bureaucracy, Politics, and Public Policy.* (2nd ed.) Boston: Little, Brown, 1976.

Schott, R. L. "The Psychological Development of Adults." *Public Administration Review,* 1986, *46* (6), 657-667.

Thompson, D. F. "The Possibility of Administrative Ethics." *Public Administration Review,* Oct./Dec. 1985, *45* (5), 555-561.

Ventriss, C. "Toward a Public Philosophy of Public Administration: A Civic Perspective of the Public." *Public Administration Review,* 1989, *49* (2), 173-179.

Weisband, E., and Franck, T. M. *Resignation in Protest: Political and Ethical Choices Between Loyalty to Team and Loyalty to Conscience in American Public Life.* New York: Grossman, 1975.

Willbern, Y. "Types and Levels of Public Morality." *Public Administration Review,* Mar./Apr. 1984, *44* (2), 102-108.

3 Taking Ethics Seriously in Administrative Life: Constitutionalism, Ethical Reasoning, and Moral Judgment

Bruce Jennings

When the study of the ethical dimensions of a professional practice reaches a certain degree of sophistication, metalevel questions begin to be raised about the purposes and effects of "ethics talk" in the profession. What is ethical analysis for? Why should it be included in the curriculum of professional training? Is a state of ethical self-consciousness a better mind-set for professionals to have than a prereflective sense of custom, habit, and tradition or than an explicitly amoral, technique-oriented attitude? If so, then in what terms and in what way should professionals think about their own "moral agency"? That is, how should they think about the constraints they face and about their ethical responsibilities in decision making and in the exercise of power?

One important path along the frontiers of ethics in public administration will be to press these methodological and metalevel questions about ethics itself in the context of the bureaucratic institutionalization and practice traditions of the field. Doing so will lead us to raise two questions that most work in applied ethics disregards. The first has to do with how various ethical discourses shape the texture of the moral life of the profession, the second with the ways in which ethical discourse shapes the place of the profession in the broader society and legitimates (or delegitimates) the

The author is grateful to James Bowman, Patrick Dobel, Kathryn Denhardt, and especially John Forester for their comments on an earlier version of this chapter.

profession's power. For public administration these have been—and should be—perennial questions.

Public administration seems now to be in a mood to look at these questions afresh, as evidenced, among other things, by the recent revival of interest in casuistry (Jonsen and Toulmin, 1988) that has captured the imagination of many in the field. In general, this is a healthy and a hopeful sign. It suggests that ethicists in public administration, as in many other professions, are attentive to important debates and shifts of perspective now taking place in moral philosophy and ethical theory (Clarke and Simpson, 1989). It also suggests that the field's interest in ethics is deepening as it comes to be motivated by fundamental concerns about the nature and future health of public service in America and not simply by the pressure of scandal, media attention, and short-term political expedience.

This chapter explores three different ways of taking ethics seriously in the professional practice of public administration. The traditional perspective on ethics has emphasized obedience to higher political and constitutional authority. Recently, under the influence of work in applied ethics, a perspective has emerged that focuses on ethical reasoning and the guidance of general moral principles and rules. In contrast to legalism and an ethics based on moral reasoning, this chapter defends yet a third perspective, one that gives pride of place to the exercise of moral judgment.

Functions of Ethics

Ethics talk is neither neutral, nor transparent, nor merely referential. It is not simply about the values, the obligations, the rules, the rights and the wrongs that are somehow out there in the real world of public administration, antecedent to and independent of discourse about them, just waiting to be discovered and described. On the contrary, ethical discourse has many different voices, and each provides a communicative framework in which norms, values, and obligations are constituted by the human agency, interaction, and institutional practices that such communicative frameworks make possible. Put differently, ethical discourses do not simply describe; they interpret the reality of the moral life of public administration.

It is through them that the texture and meaning of moral life are expressed, and when they change that texture and meaning change as well. For these reasons it is important to consider with some care what competing ethical languages or frames offer and what is at stake when one operates in the conceptual and semantic confines of any one of them.

This framing function of ethical discourse has largely to do with the internal moral life and ethos of the profession—or particular sectors of the profession. A second function, which may be called the civic or legitimating function, pertains to the external civic role of the profession in the broader society. Ethics (especially "practical ethics" or "applied ethics") can be looked at from a political point of view; it can be seen as a form of discourse in which a symbolic, cultural politics of authority and legitimacy is played out. Adopting this perspective makes us more attentive to the civic functions of ethics and to what is at stake when public administration (or any field) struggles with the ethical dilemmas of its practice. Questions about how best to accommodate ethical analysis into settings of professional education or how to integrate stricter ethical standards into the professional workplace are not finally resolvable unless they are connected with much broader questions about the moral and political legitimacy of the profession as a whole and the legitimacy of the institutions through which it works.

Norms such as justice, equity, accountability, individual rights, and the common good are the *lingua franca* of legitimacy in a liberal democratic society. The discourse of ethics is one venue where these norms receive a public interpretation and where specific policies or specific instances of conduct are evaluated in light of them. Moreover, debates over substantive standards in applied and professional ethics often involve, at bottom, questions about how much trust the public ought to bestow on a profession, how much discretion professional practitioners ought to enjoy, what degree of oversight and regulation ought to be imposed on the profession, and the like. Are professionals and decision makers in bureaucratic institutions trustworthy moral agents? What is reasonable to expect from them, and how can they be made more trustworthy and responsible in the future?

These considerations suggest that different ways of framing

the study of ethics in public administration can be distinguished by asking what these frames *do* rather than what they *say*—by looking at the styles of ethical understanding and agency they tend to promote (or inhibit) rather than by looking at their substantive normative content and the philosophical grounding of that content. This perspective also suggests that it will be fruitful to move away from epistemological questions toward political questions when evaluating competing modes of ethical discourse. Questions about the nature of moral knowledge and attempts to determine which ethical framework offers the true, most rationally justified account should be put on hold. Instead we should pursue a critical inquiry into the forms of power and the institutional structures that a particular style of ethical discourse reinforces or disables. Ethics reinforces or disables power as much by *how* it makes us think as by *what* it makes us think.

Frames of Ethics in Public Administration

In what follows I propose to explore how this political and pragmatic perspective on ethical discourse can be developed in relation to the problem of moral agency in bureaucratic settings. The argument will develop two strands, which I hope to weave together as I go along. The first strand turns on a contrast between three different frames of ethics in public administration: (1) ethics as authoritative obedience, (2) ethics as the logic of moral reasoning, and (3) ethics as the practice of moral judgment. The second of these frames, ethics as the logic of moral reasoning, is the dominant paradigm today in the academic ethics of public administration. In characterizing it here I am particularly concerned with highlighting the ways it contains a response to and a critique of some fundamental assumptions in the first frame, ethics as authoritative obedience. For at least a century authoritative obedience has been—and probably remains—the dominant ethical orientation in the field of public administration as a whole.

In the future of public administration ethics the interesting contest will be between ethics as moral reasoning and ethics as moral judgment. The distinction between these two frames obviously turns on a particular usage of the words *reasoning* and *judgment* that I somewhat reluctantly employ as terms of art in this chapter. By ethical reasoning I mean the identification of general covering principles or rules appropriate to a given circumstance and the derivation of a morally justified choice of a course of action from those covering principles and rules. By ethical judgment, in contrast, I mean the capacity to discriminate among available courses of action on the basis of an interpretive understanding of shared values embedded in an ongoing institutional practice and in a broader form of communal life.[1]

The second strand of the argument examines the constraints on moral agency in a bureaucratic environment, the form and style of ethical thinking and understanding that life in bureaucracies tends to foster. Bureaucratic settings—and more particularly the reflexive self-understandings that bureaucratic settings promote in the individual agents who act in them—are selective in terms of the forms of ethical thinking they facilitate and inhibit. In breaking with the traditional frame of authoritative obedience, the appeal of mainstream applied ethics to a certain logic or structure of moral reasoning has done many good things, but it has not created an ethical consciousness that is critical, let alone subversive, of the bureaucratic ethos. Indeed, ethics as moral reasoning privileges a form and style of ethical thinking that is well adapted—too well adapted, in my estimation—to our received understanding of bureaucratic life and the legitimation of bureaucratic power.

This, then, is how the two strands of the argument fit together. My claim is that the received understanding of what bureaucracies are and of how people should think and act in them promotes ethical reasoning and inhibits ethical judgment. Instead of explicitly identifying this aspect of bureaucratic life and critically assessing it, applied ethics has helped to disguise and reinforce it. With its focus on the logic of moral reasoning, applied ethics has perfected an adaptive moral mentality for an advanced bureaucratic polity and economy. My interest in moral judgment, as I use the term here, and in a frame of ethics for public administration that emphasizes the practice of exercising moral judgment, comes from the hope that this frame may eventually give us a more critical purchase on the possibilities and the problems of moral life and the exercise of public power in bureaucracies.

Authoritative Obedience

In 1887, four years after the Pendleton Act initiated a process of progressive civil service reform that would continue for several decades, Woodrow Wilson ([1887] 1978) published an article entitled "The Study of Administration." Although it was not widely read at the time, in retrospect it can be regarded as an important turning point in the development of public administration as a profession in the United States (Rabin and Bowman, 1984). Persuaded that "[i]t is getting to be harder to *run* a constitution than to frame one," Wilson called for the development of a science of administration to complement and to complete the nascent reform movement. The transformation of the civil service from a system based on partisanship and patronage to one based on merit and objective qualification was, in Wilson's view, but a "moral preparation" for the improvement of the organization and methods of government; it established the basis in law for an ethics of public service but did not create the conceptual or organizational foundations for that ethics.

In this Wilson was clearly anticipating the rise of a profession of public administration whose practice would be grounded in a body of specialized knowledge and expertise and informed by a sense of ethical responsibility finely tuned to the values and processes of American democracy. His intellectual reference point was the great nineteenth-century German public law tradition, out of which Max Weber's work also grew, but his ethical and political sensibilities clearly lay on this side of the Atlantic. In the course of his discussion Wilson introduced two ideas that have proved to be pivotal in the subsequent development of professional ethics in public administration. These ideas are the establishment of professional autonomy through professional neutrality on the one hand and the preservation of democratic accountability on the other.

To develop these ideas Wilson first introduced the distinction between politics and administration:

[A]dministration lies outside the proper sphere of *politics*. Administrative questions are not political questions. Although politics sets the tasks for administration, it should not be suf-

fered to manipulate its offices. . . . Public administration is
the detailed and systematic execution of public law. . . . The
broad plans of governmental action are not administrative; the
detailed execution of such plans is administrative. . . . This is
not quite the distinction between Will and answering Deed,
because the administrator should have a will of his own in the
choice of means for accomplishing his work. He is not and
ought not to be a mere passive instrument. The distinction is
between general plans and special means. . . . Self-government
does not consist in having a hand in everything, any more
than housekeeping consists necessarily in cooking dinner with
one's own hands. The cook must be trusted with a large discretion as to the management of the fires and the ovens [(1887)
1978, pp. 10-13].

Next Wilson drew a distinction between "a distinct, semi-
corporate body" of bureaucrats insulated and withdrawn from "the
common political life of the people" and a body of professional but
democratically subordinate and accountable public administrators—"a corps of civil servants prepared by a special schooling and
drill, after appointment, into a perfected organization with appropriate hierarchy and characteristic discipline" ([1887] 1978, pp. 13-
14). The ideal for America, he concluded, "is a civil service cultured
and self-sufficient enough to act with sense and vigor, and yet so
intimately connected with the popular thought, by means of elec-
tions and constant public counsel, as to find arbitrariness or class
spirit quite out of the question" ([1887] 1978, p. 14).

Wilson believed that there are several different but mutually
reinforcing ways to ensure that a professional civil service would
remain democratically accountable. The first of these is implicit in
the distinction between politics and administration itself. If administrative practice should be relatively autonomous and insulated
from political bias in its own sphere, that practice nonetheless pertains only to the instrumental means of pursuing politically determined ends. Administration remains constitutionally subordinate
to the authority and direction of democratic representatives. The
second democratic safeguard against the development of an insular
and arbitrary bureaucracy is reminiscent of James Madison's rea-

soning in *Federalist* 51. It lies in creating an organizational structure that will fuse democratic responsibility and accountability with the personal self-interest of public administrators. Finally, Wilson somewhat vaguely appeals to the higher sense of conscience, honor, and integrity that he hopes will be inculcated in civil servants. This looks to the internalization of democratic values as a part of the professional self-identity and the professional ethics of public administrators: "The question for us is, who shall our series of governments within governments be so administered that it shall always be in the interest of the public officer to serve, not his superior alone but the community also, with the best efforts of his talents and the soberest service of his conscience? How shall such service be made to his commonest interests by contributing abundantly to his sustenance, to his dearest interests by furthering his ambition, and to his highest interests by advancing his honor and establishing his character?" ([1887] 1978, pp. 16–17).

During the first three decades of the twentieth century Wilson's prescient and nuanced ideas were popularized and carried forward in basic textbooks of public administration that dominated thinking and research in the field. In particular, Frank Goodnow's influential *Politics and Administration* (1900) was an uncompromising expression of the distinction that Wilson had suggested. Wilson had cautioned against using this distinction to make the public administrator a merely passive instrument of the popular will expressed through the directions of elected officials. He wanted the professional civil servant to retain some discretion in how to serve not just his superior but also the community as a whole. Goodnow and later administrative theorists were much less subtle and nuanced on these points. They purchased professional autonomy for public administrators at the price of extreme moral passivity. Obedience to superior constitutional authority became the regulative, authoritative cornerstone of administrative ethics. Obedience not out of prudence, or careerism, or self-interest but out of principled moral commitment was the central ethical frame that both shaped the internal life of public bureaucracies and served to legitimate the considerable de facto power that administrators exercised. Over time the ethics of authoritative obedience came to so dominate public administration and to seem so self-evident that explicit discussions of ethics fell largely into abeyance as attention turned in the work of such figures as Leonard White, W. F. Willoughby, Luther Gulick, and Herbert Simon in developing scientific principles of public management.

How was it that so much of the nuance and the richness of Wilson's original concerns could be lost in the ethical frame that eventually emerged in American public administration? For surely what had emerged by midcentury, as Dwight Waldo and other critics of the administrative state observed, was something far closer to the insular German or French bureaucracies that Wilson warned against than to what Wilson himself envisioned as a democratically responsible and responsive profession of public administration (Wolin, 1960, pp. 352-434). Part of the explanation may be that Wilson was trying to hold together too many antithetical elements in his vision of public administration so that both conceptually and practically his center could not hold and his framework had to fly apart.

Another reason, especially germane to understanding how the ethical frame of moral reasoning has come to challenge if not wholly supplant the frame of authoritative obedience, is that later theorists of public administration simply could not maintain the same philosophical hold on the rational adequacy of basic democratic values that Wilson took for granted. Part of the reason they could not share his faith is that the influence of logical positivism in public administration tended to undermine the rational basis of any values, democratic or otherwise. This leaves one with little to cling to in Wilson's legacy but the formalistic, legalistic distinction between political (read arbitrary) ends and administrative (read technical, instrumental) means.

Logical positivism holds that all claims that cannot be operationalized and empirically tested lack cognitive significance. A closely related view, ethical emotivism, maintains that normative and prescriptive claims are meaningful only as expressions of the subjective preferences held by individuals making or assenting to those claims. Together these two perspectives put all normative discourse outside the arena of rational, public, and intersubjectively meaningful (objective) deliberation and assessment. (*De gustibus non est disputandum:* Matters of taste are not subject to dispute.)

It is now widely recognized that the metatheoretical and metaethical strictures of positivism and emotivism lead by a short route to a technocratic orientation (Tribe, 1972; Tong, 1986).

Looked at in conjunction with the background intellectual influences of logical positivism and emotivism, the ethical frame of authoritative obedience in public administration can be seen to rest on two basic suppositions. The first is that ultimate values or ends cannot be defined by a rational analysis or consensus but must be accepted as arbitrarily given. (Whether these values come from cultural tradition, the formulation of democratic opinion from below, or the imposition of elite fiat from above does not make much difference since each of these sources is equally arbitrary from a "rational" point of view.)

The second supposition is that scientific knowledge and technique can determine the most rational (optimal) means for achieving abitrarily selected ends and that the justification of means is logically separate and distinct from the justification of ends. Hence professional-technical decision making and the technical design and implementation of policy "instruments" are to be judged strictly by the value-free criteria of efficiency and efficacy. No room is left for reasoned ethical deliberation on either side. It has no place in the selection of ultimate ends, for they are arbitrary, or in the selection of means, for they are technical and scientifically chosen.

The only thing in this vision standing in the way of utter nihilism was the hope that the bounded domain of scientific expertise and instrumental rationality could sustain social order and legitimate authority even in the face of inherently subjective and arbitrary ultimate ends. Max Weber, in whose work this hope finds its most systematic and sophisticated expression, singled out the bureaucracy as the most important institutional locus of this bounded domain of rational means; for him it represented the principal bulwark against the forces of unreason in modern times (Weber, [1922] 1978, vol. 2, pp. 941-1006). Nothing stands between the prophet and the engineer. In a nice reversal of tradition, for Weber it is the latter, not the former who will deliver us, if only into an iron cage.

Ethics as the Logic of Moral Reasoning

Applied ethics is on the front lines of the current cultural and philosophical backlash against the legacy of positivism and emotivism. In the context of public administration, this means that applied ethics offers an alternative to the ethical frame of authoritative obedience, a frame that presents a different image of public administration's public purpose and professional vocation. With its emphasis on the structure and logic of moral reasoning—the derivation of justified decisions and courses of action from covering ethical principles applied to specific factual situations—applied ethics goes beyond the restricted notions of efficiency and instrumental rationality offered by ethics as authoritative obedience. In this way it reempowers public officials as responsible moral agents charged with the pursuit of principled ends and not solely the devising of efficient means and aims to provide sufficient moral guidance for the exercise of power by professional experts and political elites.

There is now a growing literature on the ethical duties of public and corporate officials who make and manage policies in bureaucratic settings. The bureaucratic context of corporate management, for example, is a central theme in Richard DeGeorge's *Business Ethics* (1982); on the public management side one thinks of John Rohr's *Ethics for Bureaucrats* (1989), John Burke's *Bureaucratic Responsibility* (1986), and Dennis Thompson's *Political Ethics and Public Office* (1987). Each of these fine works and others in the same genre focus almost exclusively on general moral or political principles and the corresponding ethical role obligations incumbent on bureaucratic officials and managers. The basic aim of this body of work is to bring ethical theory to bear on concrete and practical issues of public policy and decision making in institutional and professional practice settings.

Applied ethics has no single ideological or political orientation. Methodologically, most of the work in the field grows out of the analytic tradition in professional academic philosophy. It draws its water from many different wells in contemporary ethical theory—consequentialist and duty-based (deontological) theories, utilitarian and contractarian theories, theories of natural rights and

natural law. It is sometimes libertarian in outlook, sometimes egal-
itarian; some analysts stress respect for individual autonomy and
the duties of justice; others stress individual well-being and the
duties of beneficence.

The policy approaches to a given problem growing out of
the discourse of applied ethics are similarly diverse. They range
across the normal spectrum of policy strategies. Here one finds an
emphasis on market approaches and voluntarism, there a stress on
regulatory solutions; here an appeal to private duties of charity and
philanthropy, there a call for public, governmental obligation for
social welfare provision; here a reliance on proactive, conscientious
action by public officials or professional elites to protect vulnerable
clients, there an emphasis on informed democratic opinion and
pressure from below. In fact, applied ethics, drawing on what is (to
my mind) a philosophically richer theoretical base, calls for about
the same range of practical policy options as that called for by the
policy sciences, drawing as they do on cost-benefit analysis, decision
theory, macro- and microeconomic models, and the like.[2]

So, one might ask, given this substantive diversity, just what
is distinctive about the discourse of applied ethics? What sets it
apart from other available ethical languages and frames? Here, as
was suggested earlier, one needs to look behind a diversity of substantive content to a commonality of style, an approved and privileged form of moral thinking. This common emphasis on the logic
or structure of moral reasoning gives applied ethics in public administration a coherence, and it supplies its most powerful challenge to the rival frame of authoritative obedience.

Ethics as the logic of moral reasoning rests on three basic
propositions:

First, ethical theory or moral philosophy provides a distinct
body of knowledge comprising fundamental moral principles,
middle-level principles, and ethical rules. Accounts of how these
principles are grounded differ, but most philosophers now agree
that some principles are sufficiently grounded to be given rationally
justified belief.

Second, the application of ethical theory takes place through
the logical derivation of action-guiding conclusions (reasonable assessments, ethical prescriptions and proscriptions) in specific situa-

tions from general principles and rules in light of relevant empirical facts about the situation.

Third, the reasoning process involved in deriving specific ethical conclusions from general principles and rules should be impartial and disinterested. In other words, the application of ethical theory is itself a metalevel and theory-neutral form of reasoning. The rational warrant for this mode of reasoning is not logically dependent on the validity of the substantive moral perspectives contained in the principles that are being applied.

Armed with this intrepretation of the situation of the moral agent and reasoner (for that is what these propositions amount to), applied ethics systematically attacks the two suppositions of ethics as authoritative obedience mentioned earlier: the rational arbitrariness of ultimate ends and the logical distinction between the justification of ends and the justification of means. The attack on the second of these suppositions need not detain us. Again and again, the means-end separation has been called into question, and the hidden "value slopes" of purportedly neutral technical criteria have been brought to light in many areas—a significant literature on cost-benefit and risk-benefit analysis now shows this, as do specific case studies of regulatory decision making (Tong, 1986; Sagoff, 1988).

More interesting is the response that applied ethics has made to the first supposition: the inevitably arbitrary and nonrational character of fundamental values. The key to the applied ethics critique of this supposition (and to Weber's parallel acceptance of ethical decisionism) lies in the availability of rationally grounded ethical principles—such as respect for persons, individual self-determination, beneficence and nonmalfeasance, equality of opportunity, equality under the law, and justice, to name a few of the most salient moral principles appealed to in the recent literature of applied ethics. Now, to be sure, not all applied ethicists (or the ethical theorists they tend to follow) give the same interpretation of these principles. Some are neo-Kantians (John Rawls, Ronald Dworkin, Thomas Nagel), while some are much closer to the utilitarian tradition (R. M. Hare, Peter Singer). But however they think the principles are to be grounded and metaethically justified, they all maintain that practical concerns of moral agency can be rationally discussed, adjudicated, and decided on the basis of appeal to general moral rules and even more general moral principles that cover specific cases.

Ethical Reasoning in Bureaucratic Life

Consider now the link between the frame of moral reasoning offered by mainstream work in applied ethics and the traditional normative self-understanding of bureaucracies—our received understanding of how the bureaucratic organizational form is supposed to order and discipline official thinking, decision making, and action. To avoid misunderstanding, it should be emphasized that we are not concerned at the moment with the descriptive question of how bureaucrats actually do think, decide, and act but only with a certain normative conception of how they should think, decide, and act. Insofar as this normative conception has been internalized into the self-understandings or professional ideals of bureaucratic officials and into broader social and cultural expectations and demands placed on bureaucracies from the outside, actual behavior may reflect the normative conception. (I think that in fact it does, but this is not the place to pursue the topic.)

Bureaucracies are such a central and important aspect of modern society, and our political culture has been so self-conscious about the presence and effects of bureaucracies in it, that bureaucracies have been subjected to an almost constant process of interpretation. Thus there are, of course, many normative conceptions available, not all of which have the fit with applied ethics I want to single out. Above all, however, two normative conceptions are especially influential. These conceptions are in considerable tension with one another; interestingly, both can be found in Weber, who never reconciled them in his work.

One conception of what bureaucracies and bureaucrats should be is closely related to the ethical frame of authoritative obedience and is registered in the literature of scientific management and codes of public and administrative law. On this account, by now familiar, public managers should not usurp the democratic authority of elected officials; they should only provide efficient technical means for achieving ends set by their political superiors. If this were the only available normative conception of bureaucratic authority and the legitimate moral agency of civil servants, then it might well have been the case that applied ethics would not have been able to supplant the ethics of authoritative obedience to the extent that it has. What we are dealing with here are really two variables, two discursive formations, so to speak—an ethical frame for bureaucrats as moral agents (and of course as public servants also) and a normative frame for bureaucracies. There must be some symbiosis between these two frames, I suppose; as our perspective on the ethics of bureaucrats shifts, so too must the aspects of bureaucracies we emphasize.

In any case, there is a second normative conception, which is also of long standing in our understanding of bureaucracy and is thoroughly compatible with the ethical frame of moral reasoning. This conception places its stress on the fact that bureaucracies are the vehicles for achieving uniformity, impartiality, equality under the law, and procedural justice in the administration of laws and rules. Here duties lie in the office or role rather than in the person. Officials must be able to abstract their thinking from their own self-interest and personal bias. They must be able to act "on principle," in accordance with uniform and presumably impartial rules. Bureaucracies eliminate what Weber called Kadi justice; they eliminate—or should eliminate—arbitrariness, caprice, and personal idiosyncrasy in the administration of public policy.

This normative conception of bureaucracy does not call for officials to adopt an attitude of moral neutrality or to be amoral, purely instrumentally rational technicians. Quite the contrary. But the moral attitude or mentality that officials should adopt and practice must take a particular form if it is to be legitimate. This is where ethical reasoning and the fit with applied ethics come in.

To see this more clearly, consider the type of moral agent the ethical reasoner must be and what is called for morally when such an agent finds him- or herself in a situation of moral quandary and choice. In one sense, compared to the purely technical agent, the moral reasoner is a moral agent in a much fuller and robust sense. Nonetheless, it is not so much the reasoner's qualities as a moral personality—aside from an intellectual ability to identify and weigh moral principles and apply them in specific situations—that gives moral force and legitimacy to the reasoner's decisions and choices made and actions taken. Instead, that moral force comes from the rightness of ethical principles, rightly applied. Ethical reasoning is not so much interested in the reasoner as in the reasons; it is fundamentally committed to what Richard Rorty (1989) has called an orientation of "objectivity" rather than "solidarity," seeing in morality a connection between the moral agent and something transcendent (truth, reason, nature, God's will) rather than a connection among human agents. Similarly, the equitable, impartial bureaucrat as a moral agent is essentially an empty self, whose actions and decisions count ethically not because they were made by a particular, thickly encumbered self but precisely because they were not. They are the reflection of rational rules and procedures applied to like cases alike.

Moreover, to make sense of an ethical quandary, the ethical reasoner must begin a process of working backward—or better, upward—through a chainlike series of steps seeking moral guidance. From the specific options of the choice situation to existing guidelines or maxims, to general rules, to more general covering principles, and to some basic assumptions contained in a moral theory or, depending on the account one follows, some process of reflexive equilibrium to reach some coherence among conflicting principles. Each step upward in the chain of reasoning is motivated by indeterminacy or conflict between inconsistent guidelines, rules, or principles. Each higher level is assumed to be able to resolve conflict at the lower levels (Fox and DeMarco, 1990). I need not belabor the fact that this same model of pushing upward to reach more general authority in cases of uncertainty or conflict is the essence of the bureaucratic type of organization.

Ethics as the Practice of Judgment

It is not easy to say precisely what conclusion should be drawn from these affinities between ethical reasoning and bureaucratic equity and impartiality. I have been at pains to stress that in exchanging one ethical frame for another, it is problematical to maintain that unambiguous progress has been made. It is rather like walking west: you may get to someplace good, but you have to give up going north, south, and east. This is not to say that ethics as the logic of moral reasoning does not have a distinct superiority over ethics as authoritative obedience for the field of public administration. It does. But as work in public administration ethics moves ahead, it may become less important to assess applied ethics in terms of its advantages over what it has replaced and more important to assess it in terms of its own characteristic blind spots and its limitations compared to some other perspective we could develop.

Nor would I want to draw the conclusion that applied ethics is incapable of taking a critical orientation toward bureaucratic decision making and practice. For example, applied ethics can always criticize any bureaucratic action or decision for adhering to midlevel ethical rules (that have been turned into legal and administrative rules) when those rules should be overridden by appeal to higher level ethical principles. In fact, one sees this kind of critical analysis all the time in the literature of bureacratic ethics, as, for example, in numerous discussions of whistle-blowing (Glazer and Glazer, 1988).

Still, this sort of critique does not challenge the fundamental normative orientation of bureaucratic life, which is itself an orientation to general, impartial principles and rules. It merely challenges a particular application of that orientation. For a more far-reaching critique, we must look elsewhere.

To develop the notion of ethics as a practice of moral judgment, let me return to the definition of judgment I have provisionally crafted for the purposes of this essay. Ethical judgment is the exercise of a capacity to discriminate among available courses of action on the basis of an interpretation of shared values embedded in an ongoing institutional practice and in a broader form of communal life. This formulation can be explicated by pulling out several themes for more detailed discussion: (1) the contextual and personal nature of moral judgment, (2) its interpretive or hermeneutical character, (3) the way the notion of judgment gives a dialogic account of the situation of moral agency, and, finally, (4) the sense in which the notion of judgment is a "conservative" orientation. I will close with some brief thoughts about how these ideas could relate to the ethics of public administration and bureaucracy.

1. Judgment is context sensitive. It does not seek to make

global and ultimate determinations but rather provisional, local ones—decisions for the here and now. In saying that it involves discrimination among *available* options, I mean to underscore the fact that the options are immediate, tangible, doable. Since the options are real, not hypothetical, and since the social world normally offers a rather narrow range of effective options at any time, the options are not usually grossly different from one another. They present instead subtle, fine-grained differences of meaning and implication. Catching the nuance, "discriminating" aptly, is highly sensitive to present attitudes, understandings, and probable reactions by others, and these others are often arrayed in concentric circles radiating outward in terms of how they will be affected by the choice made by judgment. The best metaphor that springs to mind is to say that judgment always relies on the moral agent's "reading" of the situation. Perhaps we should simply say that judgment is that reading.

Because judgment, on this account, is something that can be done only by a person closely embedded in a situation—someone who knows how to read the signs, who can hear the intimations—judging is a more personal conception of moral thinking than moral reasoning is. Ethical reasoning holds that the content and meaning of principles can be specified prior to and independently of their application to specific situations. Reasoning subsumes the particular to the general, the local to the universal. It gives definition and resolution to moral quandaries attached to the here and now by reference to what Thomas Nagel has called the "view from nowhere"—the realm of detached covering principles and rules whose validity comes from objective reason rather than socially and historically encumbered tradition, circumstance, and practical experience. Judging, by contrast, is always done by somebody somewhere. The act of judging cannot be cordoned off from the individuality of the person's moral character, imagination, and sensibility.

This fact makes judgment dangerous, particularly when circumstances are such that there is no opportunity or mechanism for reconsideration, review, or appeal. But this does not make judgment a purely private or subjective thing, because those personal characteristics to which judgment is sensitive are not themselves purely private. They are the products of the individual's past history in a culture of shared meanings and a common life world. Character, imagination, and sensibility are characterizable using publicly available and understood categories and concepts; they can be understood and recognized by others even in the unique form they take in a particular individual. Because they can be understood, they can also be taken account of and compensated for, so that one person's judgment is not totally incomprehensible or inaccessible to others.

2. Judgment—or perhaps better, judging—is active, not contemplative. It involves a dialectical interplay of the meaning-seeking/meaning-making mind (or imagination) and the meaningful world, a relationship of reciprocal constitution between the self and its relationships with other agents, institutions, and cultural traditions. This hermeneutical dimension of judgment also protects against the dangers of radical subjectivity. Judgment is not a narcissistic act of projecting the self onto a plastic, silent world. Judgment always takes place in medias res, where meanings, customs, traditions, and standards of appropriateness are already in place. Judgment can always be challenged by these "facts"; their reality, their solidity resists the imposition of judgments that are wildly out of keeping with the situation. Where there is no impersonal method or logic to use to guide judgment, it is not the case that good judgment cannot be distinguished from bad judgment or that the interpretations of the values embedded in a common form of life, which judgments represent, cannot be challenged as unsound.

3. Judgment requires a space for open dialogue and room for maneuver. It posits the moral situation as being one in which some degree of equality and mutual understanding exists among the parties, at least enough so that some movement of ideas can take place, and dialogue is not a sham. (This condition holds both when the dialogue is an actual social one and when it is a virtual internal dialogue in the deliberations of a single moral agent.) The final judgment is not predetermined in advance of the process of mutual dialogue and judging; although the parties may come to the dialogue with some initial judgment in mind, it is inherently and rightfully subject to change. This is because altering one's judgment is never tantamount to self-betrayal or giving up one's principled convictions; it is more like changing one's perception.

4. Finally, judgment tends toward accommodation, consensus, and compromise precisely because of its dialogic and communally embedded character. Judgment is conservative in this, and only this, sense: it tends to conserve, preserve, and repair the fabric of norms, ideals, and values that binds the community together. The opposite of this kind of conservatism is not liberalism but utopianism—the willingness to rend existing communal fabrics in order to realize an abstract, universal ideal. Moral reasoning may be at times utopian in this sense, but moral judgment by its nature cannot be. This too makes judgment dangerous, for it cannot easily disengage itself from its moorings in ongoing practices and forms of life and thus may be unable to detect and respond to profound injustice under its own nose. This danger is mitigated somewhat in a pluralistic society by the fact that judgment must reach its own kind of reflexive equilibrium because it must guide moral agency not only by reference to the values embedded in one localized practice or one institution but also by reference to the values embedded in the polity as a whole (Walzer, 1987). Judgment tends to err mainly when it suffers from too narrow a compass, when it fails to integrate the values of wider communities and social practices.

How might the notion of moral judgment, developed further along lines like those mentioned above, reorient work in the ethics of public administration? Its first consequence, I think, would be to focus more attention on those aspects of the practice of public administration that involve creatively and proactively shaping the political situation rather than reactively applying the rules or carrying out the policies of political superiors (Forester, 1989). Our images of the exercise of bureaucratic discretion are too polarized at present: too filled with stories of civic disaster, cover-ups, captive regulators blatantly indifferent to the public interest, conflicts of interest and waste, fraud, and abuse on the one side, and too filled with heroic stories of whistle-blowers and dauntless investigators on the other. Much of the moral reality of the day-to-day practice of professional public administration falls out of these narratives, for it is neither scandalous nor heroic. Most exercises of discretion and professional autonomy by public administrators and civil servants are precisely cases of the bounded exercise of judgment—neither making up whole new rules nor passively, impersonally applying them as they are, but actively using them, fitting them to messy human particularity. It is my impression that this is done in quiet ways that almost never get described in the literature of public administration ethics but that form a part of the folklore of every agency and are the stuff of the stories that public administrators tell each other when they gather over drinks.

Another thing to which a focus on ethical judgment in a bureaucracy might lead is a greater moral appreciation of the value of compromise (Benjamin, 1990). To take judgment seriously as a genuine frame of moral understanding and as a valid mode of moral agency is to reexamine the reasons principle-based and rights-based ethical theories give for rejecting compromise as an immoral or at best a nonmoral activity. Compromise is such a central feature of actual political and bureaucratic life that this could open up a whole domain of cases and decisions for a kind of moral analysis that would see in them not simply instances of cowardice, tragic choice, or dirty hands.

Talking the communitarian, dialogic, and hermeneutic values built into the conception of moral judgment offered here seriously as a point of departure can finally lead to some concrete questions about the organization and management of bureaucratic settings. If departures from legalistic obedience to higher authority or principled impartiality are inevitable and sometimes ethically justifiable in any case, should we just condemn them as dangerous deviations? Or can we use the texture and particularity of real bureaucratic life to good effect? After all, bureaucracies are cultural formations, too, places where individuals express themselves and make and follow meanings as well as rules. We should be able to tell the difference between healthy and pathological agencies in terms other than cost-efficiency, absence of indictable crime, burnout rate, and so on.

A more fundamental critique of bureaucracies than that offered by ethics as moral reasoning is to fault them for their failure to become spaces of dialogic moral agency and institutions supportive of professional public administrators who serve, in Wilson's words, not only their superior but also the community. As we develop this kind of critique framed by ethics as the practice of judgment, we will return afresh to the large questions about bureaucracy and modern democracy that Woodrow Wilson raised over a century ago but that public administration has not yet answered.

Notes

1. I am not particularly happy with this terminology for making what I think is an important distinction, especially because this is an admittedly idiosyncratic use of the term *judgment*. In employing it I have been influenced by kindred discussions in Arendt (1968, 1982), Beiner (1983), and Bernstein (1983, pp. 210-230).
2. This ideological spectrum shows up in different ways and in regard to different issues in various fields of professional ethics. In business or corporate management ethics it shows up on various sides of the debate over corporate social responsibility (Beauchamp and Bowie, 1983). In journalism few discussions of professional ethics proceed very far before clashing interpretations of the First Amendment emerge (Lichtenberg, 1990). In bioethics and health policy the libertarian–welfare rights spectrum is well represented by Engelhardt (1986) and Daniels (1985).

References

Arendt, H. "The Crisis in Culture: Its Social and Political Significance." In *Between Past and Future.* New York: Viking, 1968.

Arendt, H. *Lectures on Kant's Political Philosophy.* Chicago: University of Chicago Press, 1982.

Beauchamp, T., and Bowie, N. (eds.). *Ethical Theory and Business.* (2nd ed.) Englewood Cliffs, N.J.: Prentice-Hall, 1983.

Beiner, R. *Political Judgment.* Chicago: University of Chicago Press, 1983.

Benjamin, M. *Splitting the Difference: Compromise and Integrity in Ethics and Politics.* Lawrence: University Press of Kansas, 1990.

Bernstein, R. J. *Beyond Objectivism and Relativism.* Philadelphia: University of Pennsylvania Press, 1983.

Burke, J. P. *Bureaucratic Responsibility*. Baltimore, Md.: Johns Hopkins University Press, 1986.

Clarke, S. G., and Simpson, E. (eds.). *Anti-Theory in Ethics and Moral Conservatism*. Albany: State University of New York Press, 1989.

Daniels, N. *Just Health Care*. Cambridge, Eng.: Cambridge University Press, 1985.

DeGeorge, R. T. *Business Ethics*. New York: Macmillan, 1982.

Engelhardt, H. T. *The Foundations of Bioethics*. New York: Oxford University Press, 1986.

Forester, J. *Planning in the Face of Power*. Berkeley: University of California Press, 1989.

Fox, R. M., and DeMarco, J. P. *Moral Reasoning: A Philosophic Approach to Applied Ethics*. Fort Worth, Tex.: Holt, Rinehart & Winston, 1990.

Glazer, M. P., and Glazer, P. M. "Individual Ethics and Organizational Morality." In J. S. Bowman and F. A. Elliston (eds.), *Ethics, Government, and Public Policy*. Westport, Conn.: Greenwood Press, 1988.

Goodnow, F. J. *Politics and Administration*. New York: Macmillan, 1900.

Jonsen, A. R., and Toulmin, S. *The Abuse of Casuistry: A History of Moral Reasoning*. Berkeley: University of California Press, 1988.

Lichtenberg, J. (ed.). *Democracy and the Mass Media*. Cambridge, Eng.: Cambridge University Press, 1990.

Rabin, J., and Bowman, J. S. (eds.). *Politics and Administration: Woodrow Wilson and American Public Administration*. New York: Marcel Dekker, 1984.

Rohr, J. A. *Ethics for Bureaucrats: An Essay on Law and Value*. (2nd ed.) New York: Marcel Dekker, 1989.

Rorty, R. "Solidarity or Objectivity?" In S. G. Clarke and E. Simpson (eds.), *Anti-Theory in Ethics and Moral Conservatism*. Albany: State University of New York Press, 1989.

Sagoff, M. *The Economy of the Earth*. Cambridge, Eng.: Cambridge University Press, 1988.

Thompson, D. F. *Political Ethics and Public Office*. Cambridge, Mass.: Harvard University Press, 1987.

Tong, R. *Ethics in Policy Analysis.* Englewood Cliffs, N.J.: Prentice-Hall, 1986.

Tribe, L. "Policy Science: Analysis or Ideology." *Philosophy and Public Affairs*, 1972, *2*, 66–110.

Walzer, M. *Interpretation and Social Criticism.* Cambridge, Mass.: Harvard University Press, 1987.

Weber, M. *Economy and Society.* 2 vols. Berkeley: University of California Press, 1978. (Originally published 1922.)

Wilson, W. "The Study of Administration." In J. M. Shafritz and A. C. Hyde (eds.), *Classics of Public Administration.* Oak Park, Ill.: Moore, 1978. (Originally published 1887.)

Wolin, S. S. *Politics and Vision.* Boston: Little, Brown, 1960.

PART TWO
Seeking New Meanings
and Values

4 Unearthing the Moral Foundations
of Public Administration:
Honor, Benevolence, and Justice

Kathryn G. Denhardt

Despite recent attention to ethics in the field of public administration and many improvements in the effort to teach ethics in public administration and affairs programs, a significant problem remains. Every recent study of ethics education and even a "state-of-the-discipline" report on ethics in public administration have concluded that the field is marked by diversity bordering on chaos, a lack of clarity about what ethics in public administration means, and ambivalence about teaching or approaching a subject with such a lack of coherence (Rohr, 1990; Lee and Pugh, 1987; Hejka-Ekins, 1988). Public administration strives to be a profession (or at least to act professionally), yet exhibits uncertainty about the values and standards that should be a part of socializing new members into that profession. As others have suggested, this leaves public administration somewhat closer to being a loosely formed association than to being a true profession (Lee and Pugh, 1987).

Numerous factors contribute to this situation, but perhaps the most important is an unwillingness or inability to specify clearly the moral principles on which the ethics of public administration should be based. As the study, application, and critique of moral principles, ethics demands a clear understanding of the moral foundations of the profession. Without this, meaningful development in ethics research, practice, and education will be limited. The period of intense interest in governmental and administrative ethics cannot be sustained if met with a confusing disarray of responses regarding the meaning of ethics. A profession unable to agree on and articulate the central values to which its members are expected to adhere will find its legitimacy eroding and its identity deteriorating.

Public administration stands at this crossroads, but it is suggested in this chapter that consensus can replace chaos. The discipline has been built on a coherent set of moral principles and virtues. By articulating and embracing those moral foundations, public administration may experience a strengthened identity and renewed legitimacy as it faces the challenges of the twenty-first century.

The following analysis suggests, first, that there are identifiable barriers impeding the articulation and advancement of a moral foundation of administrative ethics, yet there is also reason to believe those barriers can be overcome. Second, a review of the literature serves as a reminder that ethics and moral virtue are themes present throughout the history of public administration. Over the decades many authors have presented their views on the moral principles and virtues that exemplify public administration. An analysis of this literature reveals a significant pattern—something suggesting a consensus, but a consensus that has been obscured during years of critique, change, and revitalization in the field. It will be argued that the moral foundation of public administration consists of three elements: *honor, benevolence,* and *justice.* As moral guideposts these have the advantage of encompassing many other principles, virtues, and ideals associated with public administration while still maintaining the clarity of focus necessary for a meaningful professional identity. And rather than have one overriding imperative for the profession (and risking the excesses inherent in the overzealous pursuit of any one ideal), these three together provide a necessary balance—one offering good reasons for limiting the potential excesses of another.

Public administration ethics faces a new frontier, one in which members of the profession take seriously the demand for high ethical standards in every facet of public service. To meet the challenges of this new era, however, public administration must develop a rough consensus about the moral foundations of the field. An argument is offered in support of honor, benevolence, and justice as the guiding principles, an argument intended to provoke dialogue in the profession, perhaps helping achieve the consensus on moral foundations needed by any discipline that aspires to be or act like a profession.

Barriers to Consensus on Moral Principles

Discussing Morality. A major barrier to achieving consensus on the foundations of public administration is an unwillingness to talk about morality directly for fear of being accused of moralizing. As Chandler pointed out in his discussion of the development of the code of ethics of the American Society for Public Administration, "The tradition of American public administration came to be that we ought to live with a moderate degree of immorality and condemn the occasional self-righteous moralist who forgets that men and women are not angels" (Chandler, 1983, p. 32). Chandler himself had been the object of such condemnation in response to an earlier piece on ethics: "I often have the feeling that those who most loudly proclaim the need for 'moral standards' really are seeking authority for themselves" (Thayer, 1982, pp. 17–18).

MacIntyre points out in *After Virtue* that moral arguments in the context of our society are structured logically in that they follow from the moral premises on which they are based. But at the point where the moral premises (or moral principles) of two opposing viewpoints conflict, argument becomes shrill and interminable because in our society there is no established way of deciding between the two moral claims (1981, pp. 6–21). MacIntyre suggests that we are reduced to emotivism and thus lose any real notion of what morality as a concept means.

If, as a society, we have lost the ability to decide between competing moral principles, then it follows that individuals who assert their point of view about which moral principles should guide a profession will be accused of moralizing, seeking authority for themselves, or (in the educational setting) moral indoctrination. In an effort to avoid those accusations, many avoid committing themselves to or promoting a particular moral point of view—and the ability to have a dialogue about moral issues is eroded further.

This state of affairs has drawn much criticism, especially as it is manifested in the educational system. Mark Lilla argued several years ago that "ethics education" as it is being approached in recent times has emphasized a method of analysis rather than moral principles and that "students preparing for public service today are not receiving what can be called moral education . . . they are learning a rather peculiar sort of philosophical discourse which allows them to make sophisticated excuses for their actions without preparing them to act responsibly in a democracy" (1981, p. 4). More recently, Bloom (1987) accused educators of taking tolerance to such an extreme that nothing more than moral relativism is being taught to students.

While an analysis of the ethics courses taught in public administration graduate programs did not discern a single course that appeared to promote ethical relativism (Catron and Denhardt, 1988), it cannot be denied that the line between identifying the moral foundations of a profession and "moralizing" or "moral indoctrination" is a line that most practitioners and academics resolutely avoid crossing. In avoiding accusations of imposing one's own moral principles on others, individuals sometimes err on the side of making no moral statements at all. Thus, moral discourse in public settings has become increasingly rare.

This reluctance or inability to engage in moral discourse may also be due to the increasing reliance on "reason" rather than a belief in *virtue*. Indeed, language associated with virtue came to be avoided because it seemed too moralistic. As noted earlier, MacIntyre has suggested that moral arguments are interminable because rationalized argument provides no acceptable solution to a conflict between competing values. He argues that a belief in and pursuit of virtue would be more in keeping with a meaningful concept of morality than the stilted and incomplete concept of morality found in practice today.

Practitioners, academics, and the profession as a whole are, in fact, overcoming this barrier today as terms such as *virtue* are returned to currency. For several years, discussions of virtue at academic meetings have been commonplace. Recent scholarship has begun to explore the meaning of virtue in both the theory and practice of public administration (Cooper, 1987). But practitioners and the general public have also begun to reincorporate the language of virtue. For example, in the wake of the Iran/Contra hearings, there were considerable discussion and debate about what *honor* means and whether the Iran-Contra participants were *honorable* people. These and other terms are being taken out of the closet and returned to the language used to discuss people, policies, and practices in public administration and affairs. While MacIntyre might have been correct that *morality* has lost its meaning in modern society, the problem appears to be reversible. In public administration, that process of reversal has begun.

Teaching Ethics. Arriving at a consensus about the moral foundations of public administration is hindered by a second major barrier: the acute problem of ethics education in public administration given the concern over moral indoctrination. Good professional education necessarily involves a socialization process whereby new members are introduced to the values and ethical commitments of the profession. It is generally the role of the professor to select the topics, design the process for deliberating over these matters, and evaluate the performance of the student. In a profession experiencing ambivalence about its moral commitments, however, even the choice of topics can be problematical. The greater problems arise, though, in determining what (if anything) to present as the definitive ethical commitments of the profession and how to evaluate whether students have "learned" the material. This is the arena in which questions of moral indoctrination can arise.

If educators are to fulfill their obligations to address the ethical dimensions of the field but at the same time avoid crossing over into the arena of moral indoctrination, some fairly clear guidance from the profession is needed. In the absence of at least an "emerging consensus" from the profession, it would be inappropriate for professors to claim for themselves special authority regarding the moral principles or commitments of the profession, judging students' ethics according to the particular principles held by the professor. But the *profession* has greater latitude in establishing the ethical standards according to which members will be judged. The professions of law, medicine, public accounting, and city management have taken on this role of establishing ethical standards to which members will be held. While individuals cannot assert that kind of authority, professions *can* and do. Where professions do not exercise this prerogative, the meaning of ethics in the profession is likely to be ambiguous and interpretations so diverse as to appear chaotic.

The American Society for Public Administration (ASPA), as a professional association, has adopted a code of ethics, and the National Association of Schools of Public Administration and Affairs (NASPAA), as an accrediting body, has adopted accreditation standards requiring that ethics be a component of professional education. Though each of these actions communicates the commitment of the profession to ethics, thus placing demands on practitioners and educators, each falls short of specifically articulating the moral foundations of the profession. Another step is needed to identify and acknowledge the moral principles on which the ASPA code is based and to be more specific about the content of the ethics component of professional education required by NASPAA. The ability to develop a code of ethics suggests a widely shared commitment to certain moral foundations, and it is these deeper, foundational principles and virtues that define the real character of a profession, on the basis of which the public grants that profession legitimacy. By explicitly acknowledging these implicit moral principles and virtues, the profession infuses *meaning* into the code of ethics and *guidance as to content* into curriculum standards. Academics and practitioners can more confidently discuss and pursue those moral principles and even evaluate the actions of others according to the moral principles because the profession has given guidelines and parameters within which members can act with some confidence.

The primary reason a profession can assert moral leadership among its members is that the moral principles that guide the profession are not just self-serving values. Society expects and perceives that professional ethics are grounded in moral principles that are in the best interest of society, not just the profession. While both Goldman (1980) and Bok (1978) point out that professions often take too much license with what is in the best interest of society (becoming paternalistic, among other things), they do not question the basic argument that professions can and should provide some kind of ethical leadership to their members. Thus, the pressures to adopt a morally relativistic approach to professional ethics education to avoid charges of moral indoctrination can be overcome by a profession through its ability to arrive at some authoritative consensus via the actions of professional associations. Even if the actions are controversial and short lived, they are authoritative and serve as a legitimate departure for action and debate—a claim that the individual preferences of an educator or practitioner might not be able to make.

Promoting Ethics Through Institutions. A final barrier to identifying the moral foundations of public administration is that in a pessimistic reaction to human failure and frailties, public administration has come to rely on *institutions* rather than individuals to promote the public good and ensure "correct" action. Laws, accountability mechanisms, hierarchies, assertion of constitutional principles, and even offices such as the inspectors general have been put into place, often without a complementary effort to improve the capacity of individuals to make morally defensible decisions. Such institutional approaches implicitly assume that the "correct" action is known in any given case and that institutionalized mechanisms can carry out this mandate. These external control mechanisms are widely accepted as an essential element of public administration accountability (Chandler, 1983; Stewart, 1985), but they cannot substitute for human judgment and the taking of personal responsibility for one's actions.

Putting too much faith in institutional arrangements and processes for the resolution to problems of bad decisions, unethical conduct, or abuse of administrative authority encourages us to lose sight of the real purposes of those institutions and instead to focus only on perfecting rules, regulations, and control mechanisms that will yield more ethical outcomes. If the goal of ethics reform is to achieve the strongest moral response to any given situation, then strict reliance on rules, procedures, and other external control mechanisms falls at least one level short of full moral development (Kohlberg, 1969; Gilligan, 1982). In ambiguous situations where rules are not clearly applicable, the person with an underdeveloped understanding of general moral principles and underdeveloped capacities of discernment and judgment will be unable to make a good decision.

An example of this shortcoming can be seen in the frequently administered oath to uphold the Constitution. Interpreted narrowly, that oath means little more than agreeing not to violate the actual words of the document. Since most of today's constitutional problems cannot be resolved with such a narrow interpretation, that oath can provide little ethical guidance to the practitioner or assurance to the public that high standards of ethical conduct will be met. However, if the commitment implied by the oath is not only to the institutional arrangements of the Constitution but *also* to the moral principles, virtues, values, and rights that underlie the institutional structures, then the individual has not only the institutional arrangements to work within but also a set of moral principles to be committed to and to apply in discretionary decisions where the words of the Constitution and Supreme Court interpretations provide no real guidance.

The same argument might be made when expressing commitment to upholding a democratic system. Emmette Redford argued that "when we write about democracy . . . we must write mainly about processes, but only because these have relevance to . . . three ideals that, compounded, produce democratic morality. The basic ideal is that persons are the units of value in social arrangements. . . . The second ideal is that all men have worth deserving social recognition. . . . The third ideal is that personal worth is most fully protected and enlarged by the action of those whose worth is assumed. . . . [L]iberty exists only through *participation either in decision making or in control of leaders who make the decisions*" (1969, pp. 5-6). It is to these ideals, and not just to the institutional arrangements of a democracy, that public administration must be committed. Because of overconfidence that institutional arrangements could solve our ethical difficulties, attention has been diverted away from the identification, explication, and adherence to the underlying moral principles of those institutional arrangements.

Twenty years of critique by organization theorists document the weaknesses of relying on institutional arrangements to promote moral relationships among people. The literature on ethics (for example, Stewart, 1985) is replete with calls for *both* the internal controls provided by individual responsibility and professionalism and the external controls of democratic accountability mechanisms.

Further, recent policy reversals by the federal government demonstrate that at some point external control mechanisms can do more harm than good. This evidence suggests the need for less reliance on (though never an abandonment of) formal institutional arrangements as solutions to ethical problems and greater attention to the moral principles that should serve as guides to individual and professional decision making.

For educators this implies a need to teach students respect for the institutions as protectors of values and as mechanisms of accountability but also to make them aware that individual virtue and the moral principles on which the institutions are based are the moral foundations of the profession. The institutions must not be seen as ends in themselves but as means to some other moral goal.

Perhaps the time has come, then, for the discipline to try again to achieve consensus on the core elements defining the moral foundations of public administration practice. The profession could benefit from asserting the moral identity and would in the process protect those who seek to practice or teach these moral principles from criticisms of moralizing and moral indoctrination.

Moral Foundations of Public Affairs/Administration:
An Emerging Consensus

Over the years, many scholars have proposed clear and explicit statements about the moral foundations of public administration. In reviewing these, there seems no particular reason that such efforts have not provided the kind of galvanizing statement that firmly anchors the profession to its moral roots, providing continuing inspiration and guidance to members. Perhaps the timing was not right, or the need for such an anchor was not recognized. Or perhaps maturing professions must go through an extended period of reflection and critique before being able to recognize and accept principles and virtues that define the essential character of that profession. Whatever the reason, public administration seems to lack the kind of pithy statement of identity that communicates the moral character of the public service, that conveys the nature of the "calling" in a way that inspires pride in the profession and confidence among those affected by public administration.

Public administration needs a definition of its foundational values that will help members come to terms with the changing nature of the discipline in which

- administrators become key policy-making actors because of and through the exercise of discretionary authority
- the ethics of "nonpartisanship" becomes increasingly unworkable in the upper reaches of administrations where career officials and political appointees must find a way to work together (Rohr, 1990)
- the city management profession recognizes that "neutral competence" does not serve as a useful guide in making decisions when it finds itself in the position of brokering among power centers.

Thus the ethics of neutrality, for many years the definitive guiding force in public administration, is an unworkable one. The "new public administration" scholars recognized the coming demise of the ethics of neutrality in the early 1970s (Marini, 1971). But by now both scholars and practitioners are *convinced* of that demise and are searching actively for some other principles to guide actions and to draw us together as a profession. Public administrators cannot leave it to political officials or to "the system" (or institutions) to achieve morally correct outcomes, just as they cannot leave it to these to achieve technically correct outcomes. As active participants in the the government, public administrators should have some moral center of gravity from which to act, one that helps shape decisions, focus on shared ideals, and establish priorities among competing values.

Such statements of moral purpose arise frequently in the literature of the past four decades. Reflecting on Paul Appleby's strong influences on public administration, Stephen Bailey suggested that honesty and other virtues such as loyalty are relevant moral qualities for public servants, but he took them to be so obvious and so basic to the legitimacy of public administration as not to require any discussion or explanation. He argues, instead, that a useful list of moral qualities "begins beyond the obvious and ends where essentiality ends" (1965, p. 293). For Bailey, the "three *essen-*

tial moral qualities in the public sector are optimism, courage, and fairness tempered by charity" (1965, p. 293).

York Willbern examined the issue of morality in public service and proposed that "six types, or levels, of morality for public officials can be discerned": basic honesty and conformity to law, conflict of interest, service orientation and procedural fairness, an ethics of democratic responsibility, an ethics of public policy determination, and an ethics of compromise and social integration (1984, p. 102).

Following Alasdair MacIntyre's distinction between an "internal good" and virtues necessary for achievement of internal goods, Terry Cooper (1987) suggests that justice is a central internal good in the practice of public administration, accompanied by popular sovereignty, accountability, due process, and the enhancement of excellence. Virtues that help bring about these central goods include benevolence, courage, rationality, fairmindedness, prudence, respect for law, honesty, self-discipline, civility, trustworthiness, respect for colleagues, responsibility for the practices, and independence (Cooper, 1987).

Worthley and Grumet (1983) suggest that the values of the public service system are rule of law, accountability, efficiency, responsiveness, competence, objectivity, and fairness. Frederickson and Hart argue for a model of the public service that they refer to as the "patriotism of benevolence." It is a "combination of patriotism (the love of the regime values) with benevolence (the love of others)" that is the ideal that public servants should seek to realize (Frederickson and Hart, 1985, p. 550).

In a recent treatise on balancing competing values in public administration, Charles Goodsell writes that "one can argue persuasively that government must be based not only on democratic responsiveness but also on the moral foundations provided by natural law, the Judeo-Christian ethic, or the founding fathers. Values such as equality, justice, honesty, fairness, and the protection of individual rights must prevail, despite election returns, the wording of statutes, or the orders of elected officials" (1989, pp. 576–577).

Many times (in fact, almost always) discussions of public service values and duties will contain a mix of institutional arrangements (for example, accountability), instrumental values (for example, efficiency), and fundamental or ontological values (for example, honesty, fairness). Obviously all of those do influence the administrator's decisions and make up the environment in which actions take place. But as a guide to action, as a method of stating the moral foundations of public administration ethics, such mixing of instrumental, institutional, and ontological values is more likely to give the impression of division and competing masters than to cause the profession to coalesce around a central definition of its moral foundations.

In addition, the various statements generally mix *principles* with the *virtues* necessary to carry out those principles. However, rather than splintering our understanding of the moral foundations of public administration, this combination adds a certain richness. Though virtues do not provide the substantive guidance of moral principle, they are necessary to bring moral principle into practice. Aristotle (1953) distinguished between virtues (qualities of character) and moral principles, concluding that knowledge of the greater good is insufficient without the virtue or character to carry out that good. Thus, in offering a core definition of the meaning and character of a profession, it is valuable to address both the core moral principles of the profession *and* the qualities of character necessary to interpret those principles and put them into practice, as one is insufficient without the other.

Though it is likely nothing was missing from previous statements about the core principles and virtues of public administration, somehow none captured the imagination of the field. None because the kind of ready and familiar definition of moral commitments needed by a profession at ease with its ethical identity. In an effort to capture the essence of public administration and inspire the profession to see itself in a more focused light, this chapter draws on the content of the above statements in an attempt to distill the basic core of tenets that together define the moral foundation of public administration. That essence, or core, it will be argued, are *honor, benevolence,* and *justice.*

Honor. Honor is adherence to the highest standards of responsibility, integrity, and principle. It is a term often used to mean being held in public esteem or being well thought of—in other words, a desirable by-product of virtue (MacIntyre, 1966, p. 60). But as interpreted here, rather than being a by-product of virtue, honor is the preeminent virtue in that it is understood as magnanimity or greatmindedness, presupposing excellence in all of the virtues (McNamee, 1960, pp. 1-7). Honor denotes a quality of character in which the individual exhibits a high sense of duty, pursuing good deeds as ends in themselves, not because of any benefit or recognition that might be accrued because of the deeds.[1] It is these high standards of personal integrity and this commitment to principled and responsible conduct that characterize the ideal of public service. Public service is often described as an honor, a privilege, even a calling. In recent times these words have been used most often to invoke a revival of this view of public service after years marked by scandal and widespread criticism of public servants. But public service as an honorable calling has remained the ideal, even during difficult times. It challenges public servants to exhibit honor as a most fundamental dimension of that calling.

Why are virtues, or qualities of character, associated with honor so essential to the moral foundations of public administration? For societies to function adequately, social interaction must be based on an assumption of honesty, truth, and the keeping of promises or commitments. This is particularly true of the relationship between members of society and their powerful institutions (especially government but also other institutions and professions). Therefore, the highest standards of honesty and integrity must be the cornerstone of any ethics of public service. Stephen Bailey (1965) argues that honesty is so obviously fundamental that it needs no explanation. Sissela Bok (1978) discusses honesty in detail in *Lying*. It is the basis on which public confidence rests. Without a fundamental commitment to honesty, public administration will have no legitimacy in the eyes of the public and will find its capacity to serve that public severely restricted.

But basic honesty does not sufficiently define what the public administration profession stands for. Beyond honesty, the highest standards of integrity, sincerity, and principle are demanded of us. To be *honorable* is to be known for exhibiting those high standards consistently. It is to put principle before self-interest. It is a standard to which few others are held, certainly a higher standard than that usually expected of business executives. But it nevertheless defines in part the moral foundation of public administration.

Honor involves truth telling, avoidance of deception, acknowledging the decisions and actions to which one was a partner, the fulfillment of duty, and holding oneself to a standard higher than self-interest. It requires a commitment to something beyond oneself—in the case of public administration this commitment is to the public interest, to the principles of democratic governance, and to the moral principles that define the commitments of our social contract.

Honor is a broadly encompassing tenet. It calls public servants to exhibit excellence in virtue. It is the failure to be honorable that raises the "character question" in the eyes of the public. The frequency with which the question of character has arisen in recent years (most often among elected officials and high-level appointees) testifies to the powerful presence of honor as a defining characteristic of the public service ideal. This ideal applies no less to career public servants. And while it might be claimed that it is an impossibly high standard, it nevertheless helps define the moral foundation on which the *ideal* of public service has been built.

Benevolence. In benevolence is found the other-regarding essence of public service. It is the disposition to do good and to promote the welfare of others. The very foundation of public administration is a commitment to service (both to the public and to the elected representatives of that public). But service is itself but an expression of the more fundamental moral principle of benevolence. Based on the Latin words *bene* (well) and *volens* (wishing), benevolence implies not only *actions* that promote good and the welfare of others but also *motivation* to pursue those ends. This point is important. Beneficence (performing acts of kindness and charity) is a somewhat lower standard in that the acts need only be kind and charitable, but no such motivation or concern is demanded of the individual responsible for the act. Benevolence, in contrast, requires not just doing good but also a driving motivation to do good *for the sake of others*.

It seems clear that in terms of acting on behalf of the welfare of others, public officials are held to a higher standard than those in private life. Private sector managers are expected by many to adhere to a standard of beneficence—expected to act in a socially responsible manner, doing things that provide some benefit (or at least do not harm) the society. But few would argue that social responsibility should be the primary purpose or motivation for businesses. It is generally accepted that the socially responsible actions of businesses will be motivated by the value placed on good public relations or profit maximization rather than benevolence, but from those in the public sector more is expected.

A recent Hastings Center report discusses the "public duties" of professions, counting public administration among those professions with an explicit public service orientation. Public duties, or "the obligations and responsibilities owed in service to the public as a whole" (Jennings, Callahan, and Wolf, 1987, p. 3), encompass an orientation toward both the *common good* ("that which constitutes the well-being of the community") and the *public interest* ("the aggregation of the private interests of individuals") (Jennings, Callahan, and Wolf, 1987, p. 6).

Benevolence is a moral principle that encompasses the public duties of the profession and also prescribes the motivation that should guide the pursuit of these public duties. Benevolence implies both sympathy and enthusiasm (regard for others and purposeful intent to help)—characteristics that Thompson (1975) suggests the public demands of bureaucracies but cannot get. Clearly it is a standard to which not all public officials adhere, but it nevertheless defines the moral foundation on which the profession rests and on the basis of which the public determines its level of trust in the profession.

Codes of ethics directed toward public administrators regularly invoke these notions of the public interest and the common good, describing a public service ideal dedicated to these public duties. The codes of ethics for the American Society for Public Administration and the International City Management Association both make references to the public interest, the good of all, and regard for the interests of others being more important than personal interests (Chandler, 1989). These aspects of the codes are often seen as cautions to avoid conflict-of-interest situations. However, it is important to understand that the fundamental moral principle reflected in these codes is benevolence as a moral imperative. Benevolence clearly requires avoidance of conflicts of interest, but more important, it enjoins public servants to act affirmatively on behalf of others, holding the public in highest regard.

Benevolence, then, encompasses the service organization and the other-regardingness of public administration and as a moral standard will help administrators recognize and balance obligations to various (and sometimes competing) groups. For example, benevolence requires that public administrators act as advocates for the interests of the public or particular subgroups of the public (client groups). Therefore, the administrator would be an advocate on behalf of certain policies and proposals, not merely a technician carrying out the instructions of elected officials.

But "service" in public administration also means to serve the particular administration in which one finds oneself, and a moral standard of benevolence provides support for that kind of service as well. By grounding a service orientation on the standard of benevolence rather than on institutional obligations to particular officials, however, the profession will be better able to discern the appropriate course of action on those occasions when service obligations to various groups come into conflict with one another. When serving the interests of a particular elected official coincides with acting benevolently to pursue the public interest, no conflict exists. But when service to the elected official comes in conflict with the interests of the public, the moral standard of benevolence should provide some guidance for the administrator in discerning the acceptable limits to serving either group.

Justice. Justice signifies fairness and regard for the rights of others. The rights of others include, most fundamentally, respect for the dignity and worth of each individual. This is the foundation of democratic morality as Redford (1969) has described it, but it is also the foundation of Kant's "categorical imperative" and Rawls's (1971) theory of justice.

Attendant to basic respect for the dignity and worth of individuals is a commitment to developing and preserving rights for individuals that will ensure that their dignity and worth will not be violated by others in the society. Such rights are essential to a just society. As Aristotle argues, "Political justice is manifested between persons who share a common way of life which has for its object a state of affairs in which they will have all that they need for an independent existence as free and equal members of the society," and "Justice can exist only among those whose relations to one another are governed by law" (1953, p. 156).

For public administration, then, a commitment to justice demands that public servants be committed to respecting the dignity and worth of every member of the society, to promoting a government of laws that protects the rights of those free and equal members of the society. Even though the role of the public administrator is not to make laws or to define rights for individuals, even applying and implementing the law properly are possible only for someone committed to the principle of justice.

Because justice can only be ensured through the virtuous acts of public servants *and* through a set of laws and other institutions that protect the rights of individuals, one can see the strong connection between the moral foundations of public administration and the institutions of democratic governance. Democracy, the Constitution, laws, and "regime values," then, are institutional means of achieving justice and are thus to be respected and upheld. But it is important to recognize that these institutions are means and not ends in themselves. *Justice* is a fundamental moral principle helping form the moral foundation of public administration. It is because they rest on this principle of justice that the law and regime values are to be respected and upheld. Only by putting justice first, followed by laws and regime values, will public administrators be able to identify and oppose unjust laws, interpretations of regime values that are unfair or inequitable, and other forms of injustice that are inevitable in any society. In contrast, if obedience to the law is identified as the primary moral imperative, then it is implied that even unjust laws are to be actively upheld by public administrators.

In the fundamental moral principle of justice we find the foundation needed to support public administration's commitment to democracy, individual rights, regime values, law, and the constitutional order. Justice requires that public administrators permit and promote informed participation in the governing process. It requires commitment to equality and fairness as rights that individuals can claim. It requires that administrators act to improve the decision-making process in their area of responsibility, giving full consideration to how current policies affect future structure of rights and legitimacy of institutions (Moore, 1981).

An argument for identifying justice as an essential element of the ethos of public administration is not new. For example, justice was the cornerstone of the ethics advanced by the new public administration (Hart, 1974; Henry, 1975). Where the argument of this chapter differs from earlier arguments is that justice is seen as one of *three* fundamental values—neither the single most important moral imperative nor only one of a long list of principles and virtues.

Honor, benevolence, and justice together delineate the moral foundations of public administration ethics. They offer the essence of the many ideals that characterize public service ethics and do so in a way that permits a ready answer to the question: What does public administration really stand for? Few of us could identify many of the components of commonly referred-to codes of ethics because the codes are relatively long and detailed. Honor, benevolence, and justice capture the essence of these longer codes, but with the advantage of providing a more easily articulated identity and moral focus to the enterprise of public administration.

Identifying a core of fundamental values (as opposed to a single most important principle) creates a situation whereby excessive zeal for any one of the moral principles will be tempered by the other two. As Aristotle argues, "It is the nature of moral qualities that they can be destroyed by deficiency on the one hand and excess on the other" (1953, p. 58). Thus defining the essence of public administration ethics as justice, or equity, or any other single moral principle opens up the possibility that the unbridled pursuit of that single moral good will result in unacceptable excesses that would then erode the very foundation on which public administration ethics rests.

A definition of the moral foundations of public administration that balances the complementary and competing values of honor, benevolence, and justice will lead to striking the mean in each. For example, benevolence in excess implies paternalism. Justice, in contrast, demands self-determination. Any tendency toward paternalism, therefore, could be "checked" by the principle of justice. Because justice tends to focus on individual rights, taken to the extreme it might stand in the way of working toward the *common good*. Benevolence, as it is oriented toward doing good for others, could be a check on excessive individualism. Whereas honesty associated with honor would appear to require telling the truth regardless of any harm that might result (as in some national security areas), both benevolence and justice would permit otherwise. Where benevolence requires extraordinary efforts to help others, justice offers a mitigating influence, as it compels consideration of the burden borne by those who must pay for the helping services (that is, taxpayers). Finally, while benevolence and justice articulate moral principles, it is honor that defines the virtue, or quality of character, necessary to put principle into action.

Conclusion

All three imperatives—honor, benevolence, and justice—make up the moral foundation of public administration, and this foundation should have a central place in the education of students of public affairs and administration. Teaching these moral imperatives is not moral indoctrination. It is instead the obligation and prerogative of a profession to impart its values to those seeking to enter the profession. Articulating, studying, and internalizing these moral commitments are essential steps in becoming a true professional.

Students of public administration can develop an awareness of these guiding principles and can be assisted in cultivating these principles and virtues in their own lives and actions. The education process can help students equip themselves with the skills needed to act virtuously. For example, Stephen K. Bailey suggested that there are three essential mental attitudes: "(1) A recognition of the moral ambiguity of all men and of all public policies, (2) a recognition of the contextual forces which condition moral priorities in the public service, and (3) a recognition of the paradoxes of procedures" (1965, p. 285). By helping students to develop these and other awarenesses and attitudes, educators help them to act in a principled and virtuous manner without being rigid, absolutist, or dogmatic.

For practitioners, the identification of the moral foundations of public administration ethics would help restore a meaningful identity to a discipline that has experienced an identity crisis during the past three decades. A strong foundation provides an anchor for resisting unreasonable demands felt during shifting political winds. It also helps practitioners readily articulate the meaning of public service, thus serving both as an essential guide to action and as a defense of the legitimacy of public administration when questioned by other entities.

A case has been made for honor, benevolence, and justice as the moral foundations of public administration ethics. Perhaps this can serve as a springboard to the next step of engaging in dialogue about these moral foundations, a dialogue involving critique, elaboration, and adjustment. Research in the discipline has already begun to examine the role of virtue in public administration ethics, and the continuation of this line of research will illuminate the meaning of honor in public service. Justice, as a central principle of public administration ethics, has been explored in some detail over the past twenty years, but the principle of benevolence has not. Discouraged about the possibility of defining "the public interest," scholars have generally abandoned the effort. By recasting the public interest question in terms of benevolence, perhaps the line of research could be resurrected—not in terms of defining the specific content of the public interest but in terms of the duty and motivation to be other regarding—and could *pursue* the public interest and the common good. Finally, research on the *interaction among and balancing of* multiple public service values might prove very fruitful. Arguments for any single moral principle serving as the focus of public administration ethics will be met with numerous examples of potential abuses. A response to this problem might be finding a combination of core principles with the potential of creating an equilibrium.

This chapter has attempted to open the door to dialogue and new directions in research. The desired outcome is building a broad consensus in the profession around a clear, concise moral identity. With such a consensus, the profession can address more powerfully the issue of professional ethics, both in educational programs and in the workplace. A reinvigorated public service ethics based on this moral identity can also help rebuild public confidence in government. This challenging new frontier for the profession holds great promise for supplanting an era of chaos and crisis in public administration, with an era of renewed moral understanding, commitment, and action.

Note

1. McNamee (1960) explores the changing concept of honor over the centuries. He describes a shift from the exaggerated individualism of the concept of honor among ancient Greeks to periods of exaggerated statism. He also describes "an attempt on the part of Christianity to check, elevate, and transform both exaggerations with the new virtues of humility and charity" (1960, p. 181). It is this latter concept of honor—one characterized by humility and charity—that influenced nineteenth-century liberalism and the birth of public administration as a profession.

References

Aristotle. *The Nicomachean Ethics* (J.A.K. Thomson, trans.). Middlesex, Eng.: Penguin, 1953.

Bailey, S. K. "Ethics and the Public Service." In R. C. Martin (ed.), *Public Administration and Democracy.* Syracuse, N.Y.: Syracuse University Press, 1965.

Bloom, A. *The Closing of the American Mind.* New York: Simon & Schuster, 1987.

Bok, S. *Lying: Moral Choice in Public and Private Life.* New York: Vintage Books, 1978.

Catron, B. L., and Denhardt, K. G. *Ethics Education in Public Administration and Affairs: Research Report and Recommendations.* Washington, D.C.: American Society for Public Administration, 1988.

Chandler, R. C. "The Problem of Moral Reasoning in American Public Administration: The Case for a Code of Ethics." *Public Administration Review,* Jan./Feb. 1983, *43,* 32–39.

Chandler, R. C. "A Guide to Ethics for Public Servants." In J. L.

Perry (ed.), *Handbook of Public Administration.* San Francisco: Jossey-Bass, 1989.

Cooper, T. L. "Hierarchy, Virtue, and the Practice of Public Administration: A Perspective for Normative Ethics." *Public Administration Review,* July/Aug. 1987, *47,* 320-328.

Frederickson, H. G., and Hart, D. K. "The Public Service and the Patriotism of Benevolence." *Public Administration Review,* Sept./Oct. 1985, *45,* 547-553.

Gilligan, C. *In a Different Voice: Psychological Theory and Women's Development.* Cambridge, Mass.: Harvard University Press, 1982.

Goldman, A. H. *The Moral Foundation of Professional Ethics.* Savage, Md.: Rowman & Littlefield, 1980.

Goodsell, C. T. "Balancing Competing Values." In J. A. Perry (ed.), *Handbook of Public Administration.* San Francisco: Jossey-Bass, 1989.

Hart, D. K. "Social Equity, Justice, and the Equitable Administrator." *Public Administration Review,* Jan./Feb. 1974, *34,* 3-10.

Hejka-Ekins, A. "Teaching Ethics in Public Administration." *Public Administration Review,* Sept./Oct. 1988, *48,* 885-891.

Henry, N. *Public Administration and Public Affairs.* Englewood Cliffs, N.J.: Prentice-Hall, 1975.

Jennings, B., Callahan, D., and Wolf, S. M. "The Professions: Public Interest and Common Good." *The Public Duties of the Professions,* A Hastings Center Report, Special Supplement, Feb. 1987, 3-11.

Kohlberg, L. "Stage and Sequence: The Cognitive-Developmental Approach to Socialization." In D. A. Goslin (ed.), *Handbook of Socialization Theory and Research.* Skokie, Ill.: Rand McNally, 1969.

Lee, D. S., and Pugh, D. L. "Codes of Ethics, Education, and the Making of a Profession." Paper presented at Western Social Science Association meeting, Apr. 1987.

Lilla, M. T. "Ethos, 'Ethics,' and Public Service." *The Public Interest,* Spring 1981, *63,* 3-17.

MacIntyre, A. *A Short History of Ethics.* New York: Macmillan, 1966.

MacIntyre, A. *After Virtue: A Study of Moral Theory*. Notre Dame, Ind.: University of Notre Dame Press, 1981.

McNamee, M. B. *Honor and the Epic Hero: A Study of the Shifting Concept of Magnanimity in Philosophy and Epic Poetry*. Orlando, Fla.: Holt, Rinehart & Winston, 1960.

Marini, F. (ed.). *Toward a New Public Administration: The Minnowbrook Perspective*. Scranton, Pa.: Chandler, 1971.

Moore, M. H. "Realms of Obligation and Virtue." In J. L. Fleishman, L. Liebman, and M. H. Moore (eds.), *Public Duties: The Moral Obligations of Government Officials*. Cambridge, Mass.: Harvard University Press, 1981.

Rawls, J. *A Theory of Justice*. Cambridge, Mass.: Belknap Press, Harvard University Press, 1971.

Redford, E. S. *Democracy in the Administrative State*. New York: Oxford University Press, 1969.

Rohr, J. A. "Ethics in Public Administration: A State-of-the-Discipline Report." In N. B. Lynn and A. Wildavsky (eds.), *Public Administration: The State of the Discipline*. Chatham, N.J.: Chatham House, 1990.

Stewart, D. W. "Professionalism vs. Democracy: Friedrich vs. Finer Revisited." *Public Administration Quarterly*, Spring 1985, *45*, 13–25.

Thayer, F. C. "Comments on Chandler's 'The Problem of Moral Illiteracy in Professional Discourse.'" *Dialogue*, Fall 1982, *5*, 17–18.

Thompson, V. A. *Without Sympathy or Enthusiasm: The Problem of Administrative Compassion*. Tuscaloosa: University of Alabama Press, 1975.

Willbern, Y. "Types and Levels of Public Morality." *Public Administration Review*, Mar./Apr. 1984, *44* (2), 102–108.

Worthley, J. A., and Grumet, B. R. "Ethics and Public Administration: Teaching What 'Can't Be Taught.'" *American Review of Public Administration*, Spring 1983, *17*, 54–67.

5   Reconstructing Government Ethics:
A Public Philosophy of Civic Virtue

Curtis Ventriss

In his Pulitzer Prize–winning book depicting the unstable pluralism that has characterized the history of the United States, Michael
Kammen (1973) argues that political and administrative ethics has
been beset by what he calls a troubling moral dualism. This dualism, Kammen observes, is "the conflict between high ethical standards and the ethos of the marketplace" (1973, p. 110). Kammen
concludes that this conflict has continued to manifest itself in our
incessant attempt to reconcile the tension between political morality and administrative expediency. While Kammen's observation
may strike us as hardly novel, he does make a compelling argument
that in the struggle to deal with this moral dualism, America's
political leaders and public institutions have not only tended to
hold such contradictory ideas in suspension but have also ignored
the salient intellectual and ethical implications of this tension.

   This moral dualism may, of course, be overdrawn. It could
be argued, for example, that most public administrators try to balance the adherence to high ethical standards with the pragmatic
considerations of their administrative and public duties. However
reasonable this may appear, the shifting back and forth from specific pragmatic concerns to normative ends relating to broad public
values may not be easy as it seems, given how entrenched the marketplace ethos is in the political process.

   The primary focus of this chapter is to explore the tension
between these two proclivities that have shaped, or helped to shape,
the prevailing ethos of our political and ethical character and to
propose a public philosophy of civic virtue. To be sure, this emphasis will not—and cannot—provide any applied ethical guidelines
concerning the moral ambiguity in the policy decision-making pro-

cess. Rather, the approach taken here is more basic: that any discussion of the frontiers of administrative ethics must be explored in the broader context of the body politic. In other words, before we start applying new ethical guidelines (and assessing their impact) and initiating institutional safeguards to ensure the public interest (as important as this is), we need—as Isaiah Berlin (Brodsky, 1989, p. 44) recently stated—to ask ourselves "in the name of what?" The significance of Berlin's rather simple point is that is forces us to more carefully examine the broader political landscape that we often take as a given.

Unfortunately, Berlin's suggestion has been largely ignored in public administration. By and large, public administration theorists have wrestled with administrative ethics by opting for an approach predicated on the premises of modern liberalism (a philosophy of government based on self-interest, competition, and individualism)—premises that are rarely examined, if at all. The salient question that needs posing is whether high ethical standards can be sustained when we may be captive in the interstices of a liberalism predicated on a market-centered approach to public affairs. Benjamin Barber (1984) has aptly called this approach thin democracy. Barber's analysis is worth quoting: "Oblivious to that essential human interdependency that underlies all political life, this democracy politics is at best a politics of static interest, never a politics of transformation; a politics of bargaining and exchange, never a politics of invention and creation; and a politics that conceives of women and men at their worst (in order to protect them from themselves), never at their potential best (to help them become better at what they are)" (1984, p. 25).

Following this same line of thinking, it will be argued that a public philosophy be formulated not on the tenets of liberalism but rather on the tradition of civic republicanism (Sullivan, 1986).[1] The intellectual legacy of this tradition dates back to Aristotle and is exemplified in works such as those of Alexis de Tocqueville (1956), Hannah Arendt (1958), Joseph Tussman (1960), Alasdair MacIntyre (1981), and Alberto Ramos (1981), to name just a few. Furthermore, it will be contended that such a public philosophy of civic virtue denotes an adherence to public interdependence, public learning, and a public language. The different aspects of this public philosophy have in turn been influenced by the theoretical contributions of Richard Flathman (1966) (what he calls the universalizability principle), John Dewey (1930), and Jurgen Habermas's (1970) notion of a communicative ethics.

In varying degrees, these thinkers contend that political (and administrative) theorists too often perceive ethics as merely a procedural approach of organizing and reorganizing the administrative apparatus, of applying new managerial safeguards to ensure the public interest, without ever seriously considering that perhaps it may be the body politic itself that needs revamping and revitalizing. Saying this, let us turn our attention to what has legitimized this moral dualism that is such an integral part of the American political ethos.[2]

Modern Liberalism and Administrative Ethics

The central concepts of liberalism were primarily forged as weapons for emancipating social and political life from the inequitable dominance of special privilege and monopoly that were, to a large degree, justified by the appeals to ecclesiastical and political tradition (Sullivan, 1986). Understandably, the emancipatory nature of philosophic liberalism associated the escape from injustice with individual freedom as an end in itself. From its philosophical beginnings, liberalism exalted independent reason, particularly in the scientific form, and sought the naturalness of a competitive, acquisitive stance in all spheres of social existence.

As laudatory as liberalism's contributions were in promoting individual freedom and the free exercise of rational faculties, it is a philosophy that is inherently dualistic in nature (Macpherson, 1964). A vivid example of this dualistic tendency is liberalism's portrayal of human nature as at once impulsive and deliberate, base and rational; an unsocial creature who is a calculating machine, yet at once too driven by desire and too reasonable (Barber, 1984). As a corollary, liberalism also drew a distinction between public and private realms and consequently restricted the public realm to governmental institutions in which the political conflicts of different interests in society could be umpired and appropriately negotiated (Sullivan, 1986; Walzer, 1980). Joseph Tussman (1960) has added another interesting twist to liberalism's dualistic propensity: while liberalism has successfully provided the individual with new rights and freedom, it ironically gave little if any incentive for citizens to act as morally autonomous agents. Tussman argues quite convincingly that in a political universe where possessive individualism, moral atomism, and competition and bargaining run rampant in our political veins, it should not surprise us that liberalism makes no claim for what might constitute the good of all. In other words, liberalism may have freed us from the dictates of a Leviathan, but it still forces us to wear the political clothing of Hobbes's philosophy.

As Alberto Ramos (1981) argues, it is Hobbes's philosophy (possessive individualism and self-interest) that continues to haunt us, since it was Hobbes who first provided the psychological requirements necessary for a marketplace polity and stripped reason of any normative role in shaping human affairs. According to William Sullivan, the cost of this liberal marketplace mentality carries a hefty price tag: "Philosophic liberalism, the set of beliefs common to the Liberal and Conservative tendencies of post–New Deal American politics, is deeply anti-public in its fundamental premises. Conceiving of human beings as exclusively and unchangeably self-regarding, liberal philosophy has viewed human association as a kind of necessary evil and politics as an arena in which the classes of individual and group interest can be more or less civilly accommodated. As a philosophy of government and social life, liberalism exalts both the supremacy of private self-interest and the development of institutional means for pursuing those interests. In its extreme forms, this philosophy denies meaning and value to even the notion of common purpose" (1986, p. xii).

Whether we like it or not, or even acknowledge it, in public administration we swim in these murky philosophical waters irrespective of the different theoretical swings we take at administrative ethics. Although many public administrative theorists may resent this frontal assault on liberalism as unduly cynical and misplaced, liberalism further demonstrates its inherent weakness by its relative silence on two important moral issues that cannot be so easily brushed aside: economic inequality and community.

Economic Inequality and Community:
The Moral Silence of Liberalism

Let us briefly discuss these points in turn. Liberalism has always regarded the market economy as part of the private sphere—a sphere that does not necessarily abide by democratic principles, since these principles might interfere with the conditions of liberty so necessary to the functioning of the market. For example, liberal social theory for the most part does not question the reasoning behind a company's desire to close a plant, since this is a private decision, regardless of its social and community implications. Not surprisingly, most liberal social theorists remain reticent on the moral implications of capital mobility and the growing disparity of economic wealth in the United States. According to Samuel Bowles and Herbert Gintis (1986), modern liberalism tends to legitimize the invisible power of capital and to shield the market economy, for the most part, from democratic accountability.

The latter point is even more perplexing. Liberalism tries to legitimize the role of the state as if it can represent community needs, particularly in the state's role to fill a social vacuum by the decline of what Robert Nisbet (1953) called local associative groups, for example, groups that reside between the individual and the state. Liberalism, in contrast, treats "the most powerful organization in contemporary capitalism—the modern business corporation—[as] stripped of its communal status" (Bowles and Gintis, 1986, p. 16). This is hardly surprising, since liberalism regards the notion of community as a fictitious body (Bentham, 1982). As uncomfortable as the implication may seem, the walls of liberalism and the ethical dichotomy it fosters only serve to obscure the existing power arrangements in society (Walzer, 1984). At a time when business interests are dominating more and more the tempo of politics, the potency of this power raises some alarming questions about how much the values of the democratic process are being corrupted (Dahl, 1985; Lindbloom, 1977).

As a result of these shortcomings of liberalism, the critical question is whether we can realistically address the issue of ethics when a marketplace ethos flows so unimpeded through the hallways of the body politic. As much as we may talk about the public interest and clothe our discussions in normative garments, we still have not come to terms with the "ghost in the machine" that forms the basis of the moral foundations of a marketplace politics that restricts substantive reasoning (Ramos, 1981; Wolin, 1960). The importance of substantive reasoning, writes Ronald Beiner, is that it "shapes the kind of person one is—making one, for instance, more reflective, more discriminating, more attentive—[for] it is only in this indirect way that [ethical judgment] has an influence upon practice" (1983, p. 144). In sum, we are reluctant to judge our marketplace politics by the character of the people it produces. An appropriate epithet to our reluctance is the inability to retrace critically the intellectual threads of our past and to rethink what we think. George Will put it well: "In politics, the place is a mental habitat, an intellectual and moral landscape. *To know clearly, perhaps even for the first time, the defective philosophic premises of our nation should not mean loving the nation less.* However, to know the thought that launched the nation is to know actions necessary to sustain the nation. Some actions, reflecting mature second thoughts, must compensate for the defects of the first thoughts. Because a nation is, to some extent, a state of mind, knowing a nation in a new way makes the nation into a new place. What is called for is a contemplative, a philosophic turn of mind" (1983, p. 164, italics added).

Simply put, if we are to retrace our intellectual steps, it is important to determine the "defective philosophic premises" that have shaped our state of public affairs.

Civic Virtue and Civic Commercialism

Following the logic of Will's argument, we might also ask ourselves—to use a phrase by Kant (Sullivan, 1989, p. 241)—whether it is "possible to build anything straight from such crooked wood?" That is, how can we develop a system of political and administrative ethics when we reify modern liberalism as a natural fact and thus leave unexamined the philosophical premises that legitimize the present underlying assumptions of politics?

Saying this, an unpopular notion will be proposed: that administrative ethics and the moral dualism in which it is encapsulated cannot be overcome by an adherence to regime values (Rohr, 1978) alone or by an intellectual grounding of civic virtue on the thoughts of our founding fathers, with their emphasis on "constitutional correctives, honor and education to assure that public administrators . . . be publically virtuous" (Richardson and Nigro, 1987, p. 369). Bluntly put, the most serious lacuna concerning our discussion of administrative ethics is that we still assume that the democratic character of liberalism (and the values it represents) provides the proper foundation for articulating an administrative ethic. We make this assumption, in short, without seriously questioning whether such a foundation is built more on cultivating what can be called "civic commercialism" than on "civic virtue" in the polity: "*Classical economics and liberal democratic political philosophy arise from the same psychological and epistemological doctrines. That is one reason why in bourgeois societies, political philosophy has had a tendency to disappear into economics, and economics has striven to become a comprehensive theory of social energy.* The shift in the focus of political philosophy, from concern for man's inner life to concern for his behavior and material well-being, has coincided with the rise of the social sciences, and capitalism. That is, the shift has coincided with growing confidence in man's ability to manipulate the natural and social worlds" (Will, 1983, p. 118, italics added).

Richard Krouse, arguing from a somewhat similar political angle, contends that it was none other than James Madison who espoused such a civic commercialism: "Madison himself occasionally supported [the view] that the virtue and intelligence of the citizenry must be the ultimate foundation of a republic. But the main thrust of his argument is decisively in the opposite direction. Just as Montesquieu consigns republican virtue to the remote past and bases his theory of modern politics upon psychological axioms not dissimilar to those of Hobbes or Hume, so does Madison (and the other authors of the American Constitution) reject civic virtue as a possible foundation for nonoppressive popular government. Madison and the other authors of the second American founding saw American society much as Montesquieu saw Great Britain—*a world animated by ceaseless self-interested motion, a restless striv-*

ing after power and profit. The moral axis of such a political universe is interest, not virtue" (1983, p. 63, italics added).

Alexander Hamilton also clearly expressed this emphasis on civic commercialism: "Political writers . . . have established it as a maxim, that, in continuing any system of government, and fixing the several checks and controls of the constitution, every *man ought to be supposed a knave; and to have no other end in all his actions but private interest. By this interest we must govern him; and by means of it, make him cooperate to public good notwithstanding his insatiable avarice and ambition.* Without this, we shall in vain boast of the advantages of any constitution; and shall find in the end that we have no security for our liberties and possessions except the good will of our rulers, that is, we should have not security at all" (1969, pp. 94–95, italics added).

While there are legitimate differences of opinion on what the founding fathers' philosophical and moral premises actually were, it is fair to conclude that most public administration theorists have overstated and distorted their meaning because we have chosen to ignore or politely dismiss the Manichean vision that dominated the founding fathers' thinking. What needs to be kept in mind is that today we are still captive, to a large degree, to the tension between civic commercialism and civic virtue. What matters, therefore, is the particular configuration of that tension in the body politic as well as the intellectual and normative implications of that configuration. It is for that reason that we need a public philosophy—one of civic virtue. In the final analysis, modern liberalism and the civic commercialism that it promotes provide us with no viable theory of citizenship and civic virtue that can be expected to arise (Barber, 1984; Horkheimer, 1947).

A Need for a Public Philosophy

If civic commercialism is an integral part of our political landscape, how do we, as the saying goes, get out of the belly of the whale? The answer, in part, is to develop a viable public philosophy that can guide our public actions and provide the normative foundations for them. Daniel Bell, for example, makes the following argument: "Any society, in the end, is a moral order . . . the problem inevitably, is the relation between self-interest and public interest, between personal impulses and community requirements . . . without a public philosophy, explicitly stated, we lack a fundamental condition whereby a modern polity can live by consensus and justice" (1978, p. 250).

While one can quibble with Bell's somewhat conservative tone, he does raise a critical point often overlooked in our discussions about administrative ethics: that government is no longer a community but rather "an arena in which there are no normative rules (other than bargaining) to define the common good" (Bell, 1978, p. 256). Moreover, this bargaining process only confuses and denigrates expectations about public institutions by corrupting democratic government by interest-group liberalism (Lowi, 1969). George Frederickson, echoing a similar view, has argued that "in the absence of a public philosophy, we consider the consequences of most human actions as strictly private, without anyone taking responsibility for public acts" (1989, p. 6).

What is needed, asserts William Sullivan, is a new public philosophy: *"The tradition of civic philosophy answers the question of how to respond to the challenge of competitive individualism with the vision of a political life that begins not with self-interest but with the moral culture of justice, dignity, and fellowship* . . . the civic conception euphorizes that such a moral order is only possible through a life that enables individuals to know themselves in regard to the *social interdependence* in which they live and to respond actively to, and share in, shaping that wider community. *That kind of moral understanding is the basis of civic virtue, and such a life is the civic meaning of politics"* (1986, p. 215, italics added).

Although Sullivan's argument may be dismissed as overly idyllic, he does pose a salient point that morally responsible behavior must also be linked to a morally public purpose. Thus administrative ethics, however tortured the word has become in practice, has as its purpose the clarification of our public role and purpose in revitalizing the body politic. As presumptuous as this may appear and as impractical as this seems to many, the ethical obligations of public administrators are part of renewing the meaning of citizenship in the system of democratic governance. A public philosophy for a renewed civic purpose must start with the meaning of the public: "Absent public awareness and spirit, absent the ability to translate individual concerns into larger common concerns, absent the people's ability to understand not just the particulars, *but the relationship of the whole, there is no capacity to public*. And with relations of the sort that we have in a country as diverse as ours, with issues as intertwined as they are, the task of 'publicking'—of understanding both consequences and potential in relationships, over time—is no small task.

"Educating for public life, educating the civic self, takes on new meaning when the public is recognized for what it really is. *Civic literacy, the capacity of people to think about the whole of things, of consequences and potential, becomes education of the most critical kind*" (Mathews, 1985, p. 124, italics added).

Our difficulty (or at least one of them) in developing a theoretical base for civic virtue is that we are still trapped in a utilitarian mind-set that converts ethical issues inevitably into issues of procedural reforms that must always conform to the broader values of *efficiency, expediency, economy, order,* and *predictability* (Frederickson, 1989). This is not to negate the importance of these goals. Rather, the central issue is: How can we have a viable ethics of civility without a moral vision of what can lead to a sense of community and human connectedness? Can we really come to terms with administrative ethics when we acquiesce to the view that government is nothing more than a bargaining arena? One astute scholar put it this way: "Adding to our prevailing style of communication the familiar emphasis on individualism, private interest, and private enterprise and the story of our education for democracy is almost told. We teach men to compete and bargain. Are we to be surprised, then, at the corruption of the tribunal into its marketplace parody?" (Tussman, 1960, p. 108).

Although some may accuse this claim of being overdrawn, it is interesting to note that while the market was supposed to be constrained by such restrictions as trust and custom, these restrictions have been undermined by the individualistic, rationalistic base of the market (Hirsch, 1976). Fred Hirsch, in extending Durkheim's critique of social bonds based on self-interest, asserts that modern liberalism has ironically eroded the market's traditional moral codes. It is precisely this potential corruption of the tribunal that prompts a need to reconstruct administrative ethics and to reexamine our view of the publicness of what we do and the public purpose we serve. We err grievously by thinking that civic virtue can be fostered in a political universe where self-interested action continues to carry moral weight. Is it no wonder that in public administration we have failed to spell out the public interest values that can address simultaneously the issues of efficiency and social justice? More concisely, why does administrative ethics represent a derivative rather than a primary focus of serious reflection, defined largely by the value orientations of *organization* rather than of *publicness* or *community* (Erie, 1978)? Let us now turn our attention to the different aspects of a public philosophy of civic virtue.

A Public Philosophy of Civic Virtue

A public philosophy, as conceived here, is a moral ecology based on public interdependence, public learning, and a public language. Briefly defined, *public interdependence* refers to a public discussion and public scrutiny of the externality of policy choices and their impact on various publics. This notion recognizes that the consequences of policy options are often hidden or have indirect costs and that desirable and undesirable consequences are difficult to separate and important effects of policy choices can go unnoticed (Ventriss and Luke, 1988). At this point, it is worth noting the salient contribution of Richard Flathman's (1966) thinking about what constitutes the public interest. Flathman asserts that the public interest is served when a policy's full impact is assessed on all affected persons and found to be desirable. The public interest, Flathman believes, is achieved only by observing the "universalizability principle," which requires the public agent to act on behalf of an entire class of persons directly affected by a policy. If Flathman is correct, this implies that there is a moral obligation to assess the impact of a policy's interdependence on the public. Only by this approach, Flathman declares, can we promote what he calls the "politics of public interest."

Thus, as policy action becomes increasingly intertwined in intersectoral activity, public administrators must account not only for the visible costs of policy action but also for the less visible costs borne by the organization and passed on to others who may not have any direct recourse. Based on this, public interdependence exhibits some of the following ethical characteristics (Ventriss and Luke, 1988, pp. 348–349):

- It assumes that public organizations exist in an environment rich with both subtle and direct interconnections, networks, and ripple effects.
- It focuses on social values and seeks critical awareness on the part of individual organizational members to identify unintended and indirect outcomes or other normative consequences on the environmental context or life span in which the organization exists.
- It focuses on past, present, and future policy choices for the purposes of human betterment rather than developing instrumental means to implement enacted policy. As such, it is value creating rather than value conserving.

Public learning, in contrast, is a substantive strategy to learning that tries to initiate a "maieutic approach" that can help guide what is called an axiological inquiry into public affairs. A maieutic approach, as applied by Socrates, is the attempt to uncover the underlying factors that tend to camouflage or obscure our knowledge of the true source of our political and economic problems. It is an approach, in other words, that mandates a normative inquiry that can create conditions for a public dialogue of the organizational ends themselves—conditions that are not necessarily bound to utilitarian considerations. An axiological inquiry, in contrast, refers to the acknowledgment that all political or organizational configurations of reality carry with them some aspects of value distortion and misrepresentation (Dewey, 1903). It is thus an integral part of substantive learning to investigate and act on those value distortions.

Without ignoring the difficulty of this approach, Robert Denhardt writes that "the connection between theory and practice can only occur through a process of personal learning—[because] only as individuals reflect on their experiences and generalize from

them will they develop theories of action" (1984, p. ix). Public
learning, moreover, denotes a reciprocal learning process between
the public and the administrator so that new knowledge can be
incorporated into the policy process without fundamental distortion. In this manner, public learning is more than a personal strategy to reestablish an administrative ethic; rather, it is a process of
linking the administrator's personal learning to citizen learning,
thus establishing a learning loop in building the capacity for future
debates in formulating policy issues. As David Korten (1980) has
argued, this presupposes a social knowledge transfer that exposes
administrators to the unique experiential knowledge of different
publics and the creation of an open forum for critical dialogue and
exchange of information critical to the community.

Finally, a *public language* is one that gives primacy to substantive political ends and societal interdependencies over the utility language of economics, a language that does not cloak its value
assumptions under the veil of scientific objectivity. While very little
attention has been given to how public language has become distorted, almost no attention has been focused on how political language shapes our conceptualization of social reality (Habermas,
1970). As Ludwig Wittgenstein (1958) reminds us, language is not
only a way of developing "discursive games," it is also a way of
developing a "form of life"—a form of life in which language becomes action in how to do certain things. Thus it could be argued
that the choice of language is a political act that defines how reality
is interpreted and experienced.

When we use such terms as *efficiency* and *economy* in government, public administrators are in the process of transforming these
terms (which are economic in origin, according to Dwight Waldo)
into actions that consciously or unconsciously inculcate economic
reasoning, with all its posited assumptions. It is a political language
that tries to economize the polity by a public philosophy predicated
on a utilitarian calculus (Wolin, 1981). In its crudest form, this language addresses substantive issues (for example, ethics, justice, and
equality) as having only market definitions. When defined in this
manner, public discourse itself becomes instrumental, whereby any
mention of the common good is reduced to a utilitarian sum of individual satisfactions. Sheldon Wolin is correct when he argues that

a public philosophy predicated on economics is, in fact, antipolitical power "because it contains no principle for transcending conflict to find common ground . . . [and] citizen and community become subversive words in the vocabulary of the new public philosophy" (1960, p. 36). A public language, in contrast, attempts to examine the value assumptions of policy decisions and explore the relationship of political means to political ends. It is a language that nurtures a non-distorted communication between the public and administrators that can clarify differing policy choices and address political conflicts (Habermas, 1984).

The central issue, however, confronting the viability of any public philosophy is how it can address the moral reasoning that views individuals as merely atomized and isolated in their motivations and identities. As Tocqueville (1956) recognized, the transformation of self-interest implies an educative process of participating in substantive public life—a process that can cultivate public virtues. This educative process implies that "the capacity, the maturity, and the learning process of the public must be inexorably linked with the activities of public administration to facilitate a political educative process between the public and the administrators. *The [ethical] theory we have been so desperately looking for may be only a process: an asymptotic exercise in deliberative public learning, a public learning that jointly links public administration and the public in furthering their capacity, maturity and knowledge*" (Ventriss, 1987, p. 37, italics added).

This focus on an educative process differs from modern liberalism in that the substantive value of public life is determined by the moral cultivation of responsible selves in relationship to others. Furthermore, this process implies what Louis Gawthrop (1984) refers to as an ethics of civility. This call for an ethics of civility is a dynamic relationship between public administrators and the public that is an exercise not in furthering statecraft but in promoting soulcraft among the citizenry. The ethics of a polity is therefore not a question of promoting a particular institutional mechanism to foster the routinized planning of virtue but the development of a particular frame of mind. It is a public philosophy that teaches us how, not what, to think about the public (Will, 1983). Of course, such a posture is prone to attack by those who claim that without a strong criterion of such normative categories as fairness and justice, this approach is unrealistic to the point of being illegitimate (Mackie, 1977; Williams, 1977). For example, it can be claimed that a public philosophy that calls for the sort of changes argued for here leads only to an intellectual cul de sac, or worse yet, a moral abstraction devoid of any practical import.

The seriousness of this charge must be directly addressed. First, a public philosophy of civic virtue is best regarded as minimal ethics (White, 1988). Minimal ethics refers not only to the public philosophy's restriction to the broader issues of public values and citizenship (as opposed to specific ethical codes) but also to the admission that a public philosophy of civic virtue cannot provide us with unambiguous guidelines to public action. A public philosophy can direct us only to a particular way of thinking about substantive procedures for addressing normative concerns. However, the importance of the approach advocated here is that it helps frame pertinent questions that can bear on the decision-making process. For example, it can direct our attention to the normative implications of policy interdependence, to the importance of establishing concrete relationships with the public that are not merely procedural in nature, and to a public language that can sort out misinformation and distortion of data that hinder public debate and public discussion. At its best, a public philosophy can promote the proper understanding of what public institutions aim to achieve and the civic culture necessary to achieve these substantive goals.

Admittedly, the development of any new public philosophy so at odds with modern liberalism is a tricky business in which to engage, given how entrenched liberalism has become. Such a public philosophy may not be as unrealistic as we think if we start to question modern liberalism's fundamental rationale: namely, the inherent moral equality of appetites. As we are beginning to understand, this moral laissez-faire only degrades civic virtue by making it an accidental by-product of a mechanized process whose only claim is its ability to keep in check the political passion in the policy process. Concomitantly, it undermines any notion of commonality and any desire to promote civic virtue. In the end, the regeneration of the moral foundations of our polity and the institutions, public, and leaders in which it embodies will mean making moral decisions in a new public philosophy that better reflects the better angels of our nature—if nothing else, a noble calling.

Summary

With apologies to the framers of the American Society for Public Administration's code of ethics, if we are ever to weld together ethics and politics, we need more than a general statement of ethical behavior. As important as this code of ethics is, a more salient step is needed: a reexamination of our present disposition of political character, which is based primarily on an instrumental theory of human nature. This instrumental view of human nature, when stripped to its bare essences, confines the purposes of governing to how successfully it orients politics to the individual's low but steady passions. Perhaps this is an overstatement, but the present bifurcation of our political moral character (so forcefully argued by Kammen) may be only a reflection of how we have come to the unsettling conclusion that the submersion of passion and the quest for private gain has become more important than the pursuit of civic virtue as a basis of political stability. Given this state of affairs, it is hardly surprising that the cultivation of civic virtue has become a mere pipe dream for most administrators and theorists, devoid of any practical substance. Thus, with little maneuvering room to pursue civic virtue, we are left with the troubling conclusion that "the public turns [into] the dust of mere interests [and administrators are] reduced to hoping that the wind will not rise" (Will, 1983, p. 149).

Without negating the valuable insights offered by moral philosophers, John Gardner (1963) has argued that we know to which values or ethical standards we have not been faithful. The major problems we face, notes Gardner, are a result not of some theoretical confusion (although he admits this may account for some of them) but rather of infidelity. Assuming the validity of Gardner's claim, this infidelity can be partially attributed to a political environment that sanctions a moral market in conformity to what has been referred to as an emulative ethic. This emulative ethic, states Gary Wills, is based on the rationale that "once today's market has spoken, however provisionally, one must go along with its decision, never arrogating oneself the right to defy it except through future market procedures, [for] to claim that one is right, over the decision of the majority, is a claim to infallibility, a wish to destroy the market" (1969, p. 317). The obvious danger of this notion is that any serious ethical reflection will be circumvented by a crude form of ethical pragmatism that judges the viability of a public action by how closely it conforms with the status quo.

The antidote to this serious problem may be just the simple reminder that "the principles of true politics are those of morality enlarged" (Will, 1983, p. 79). What awaits us, if we take this statement seriously, may be the rediscovery of what constitutes the substantive meaning of politics. As ambitious as this may sound, it is probably central to redefining our civic purpose in providing any viable normative foundation for public administration (Ramos, 1981).

In this analysis, an attempt has been made to outline the implications of a public philosophy based on mutual concern and social interdependence. While the arguments presented here have been normative and descriptive, more research is needed along the following lines. First, an analysis of the differences between a public philosophy of civic virtue and the theoretical approaches of such scholars as Glendon Schubert (1960), Frank Sorauf (1957), C. W. Cassinelli (1962), John Rawls (1971), Stephen Bailey (1962), Anthony Downs (1962), and Paul Appleby (1952) is needed. Secondly, a reexamination of the impact of economic assumptions on the policy decision-making process and the normative implications of such assumptions in formulating any notion of the public interest should be made. Finally, the role of a public philosophy in shaping public values in a highly differentiated society needs to be more carefully examined. These research questions, if fully explored, will hopefully give us a better understanding of the task that awaits us in exploring the frontiers of administrative ethics.

Notes

1. What exactly is civic republicanism? As noted by William Sullivan (1986), it is a philosophy of government that emphasizes the primacy of human interdependence and mutual trust among the citizenry. Unlike the nineteenth-century liberalism

of possessive individualism, which views persons as mere atoms unrelated by any system of interconnectedness, civic republicanism sees individuals as trying to realize their responsible selfhood in relationship to broader societal concerns—concerns that transcend utilitarian considerations. It is this moral cultivation of responsible selfhood, as part of a cooperative project, that makes civic republicanism so starkly different from modern liberalism.

2. An important assumption of this article needs posing: What is so wrong with moral dualism? Perhaps by nature we seek (and need) both instrumental and substantive values. Some may argue that as long as we keep these two value systems in balance, moral dualism represents no real dilemma for formulating an administrative ethic. The difficulty with this rationale is that it ignores how liberalism has skewed this balance by its antipublic premises. Modern liberalism, as a public philosophy, lacks a coherent public discourse adequate to the complexities facing society. It lacks this capacity because it has erected artificial barriers against human interdependence that make any discussion of the balance between instrumental and substantive values seem rather problematical.

References

Appleby, P. H. *Morality and Administration in Democratic Government*. Baton Rouge: Louisiana State University Press, 1952.

Arendt, H. *The Human Condition*. New York: Doubleday, 1958.

Bailey, S. K. "The Public Interest: Some Operational Dilemmas." In C. J. Friedrich (ed.), *NOMOS V: The Public Interest*. New York: Atherton Press, 1962.

Barber, B. *Strong Democracy*. Berkeley: University of California Press, 1984.

Beiner, R. *Political Judgment*. Chicago: University of Chicago Press, 1983.

Bell, D. *The Cultural Contradictions of Capitalism*. New York: Basic Books, 1978.

Bentham, J. *Introduction to the Principles of Morals and Legislation*. New York: Methuen, 1982.

Bowles, S., and Gintis, H. *Democracy and Capitalism*. New York: Basic Books, 1986.

Brodsky, J. "Isaiah Berlin at Eighty." *New York Review of Books,* 1989, *36,* 44–46.

Cassinelli, C. W. "The Public Interest in Political Ethics." In C. J. Friedrich (ed.), *NOMOS V: The Public Interest.* New York: Atherton Press, 1962, pp. 44–53.

Dahl, R. *A Preface to Economic Democracy*. Cambridge, Eng.: Polity Press, 1985.

Denhardt, R. *Theories of Public Organizations*. Pacific Grove, Calif.: Brooks/Cole, 1984.

Dewey, J. *Studies in Logical Theory*. Chicago: University of Chicago Press, 1903.

Dewey, J. *Individualism Old and New*. New York: Minton Balch, 1930.

Downs, A. "The Public Interest: Its Meaning in a Democracy." *Social Research,* 1962, *29,* 1–36.

Erie, S. "Historical Crisis of Pubic Administration." Unpublished manuscript, 1978.

Flathman, R. E. *The Public Interest: An Essay Concerning the Normative Discourse*. New York: Wiley, 1966.

Frederickson, G. H. "Finding the Public in Public Administration." *Working Papers in Public Administration*. Lawrence: University Press of Kansas, 1989.

Gardner, J. *Self-Renewal*. New York: Harper, 1963.

Gawthrop, L. G. *Public Sector Management, Systems, and Ethics*. Bloomington: Indiana University Press, 1984.

Habermas, J. "Toward a Theory of Communicative Competence." In H. Dreitzel (ed.), *Patterns of Communicative Behavior*. New York: Macmillan, 1970.

Habermas, J. *The Theory of Communicative Action*. Vol. 1. *Reason and the Rationalization of Society*. Boston: Beacon Press, 1984.

Hamilton, A. *The Papers of Alexander Hamilton*. Vol. 1. H. C. Syrett, ed. New York: Columbia University Press, 1969.

Hirsch, F. *Social Limits to Growth*. Cambridge, Mass.: Harvard University Press, 1976.

Horkheimer, M. *Eclipse of Reason*. New York: Oxford University Press, 1947.

Kammen, M. *People of Paradox*. New York: Vintage Books, 1973.

Korten, D. "Community Organization and Rural Development: A Learning Process Approach." *Public Administration Review*, 1980, *40*, 480–512.

Krouse, R. W. "Classical Images of Democracy in America: Madison and Tocqueville." In G. Duncan (ed.), *Democratic Theory and Practice*. Cambridge, Eng.: Cambridge University Press, 1983.

Lindbloom, C. E. *Politics and Markets*. New York: Basic Books, 1977.

Lowi, T. J. *The End of Liberalism*. New York: Norton, 1969.

MacIntyre, A. *After Virtue: A Study of Moral Theory*. Notre Dame, Ind.: University of Notre Dame Press, 1981.

Mackie, J. L. *Ethics: Inventing Right and Wrong*. Harmondsworth, Eng.: Penguin, 1977.

Macpherson, C. B. *The Political Theory of Possessive Individualism: Hobbes to Locke*. New York: Oxford University Press, 1964.

Mathews, D. "The Public in Practice and Theory." *Public Administration Review*, 1985, *44*, 121–126.

Nisbet, R. *The Quest for Community*. New York: Oxford University Press, 1953.

Ramos, A. G. *The New Science of Organizations*. Toronto: University of Toronto Press, 1981.

Rawls, J. *A Theory of Justice*. Cambridge, Mass.: Belknap Press, Harvard University Press, 1971.

Richardson, W. D., and Nigro, L. G. "Administrative Ethics and Founding Thought: Constitutional Correctives, Honor, and Education." *Public Administration Review*, 1987, *47*, 367–376.

Rohr, J. A. *Ethics for Bureaucrats: An Essay on Laws and Values*. New York: Marcel Dekker, 1978.

Schubert, G. A. *The Public Interest: A Critique of the Theory of a Political Concept*. New York: Free Press, 1960.

Sorauf, F. J. "The Public Interest Reconsidered." *Journal of Politics*, 1957, *19*, 616–639.

Sullivan, R. J. *Immanuel Kant's Moral Theory*. Cambridge, Eng.: Cambridge University Press, 1989.

Sullivan, W. M. *Reconstructing Public Philosophy*. Berkeley: University of California Press, 1986.

Tocqueville, A. *Democracy in America*. New York: Mentor, 1956.

Tussman, J. *Obligation and the Body Politic*. New York: Oxford University Press, 1960.

Ventriss, C. "Two Critical Issues of American Public Administration." *Administration and Society*, 1987, *19*, 25–47.

Ventriss, C., and Luke, J. "Organizational Learning and Public Policy: Towards a Substantive Perspective." *American Review of Public Administration*, Dec. 1988, *18* (4), 337–357.

Walzer, M. *Radical Principles: Reflections of an Unreconstructed Democrat*. New York: Basic Books, 1980.

Walzer, M. "Liberalism and the Art of Separation." *Political Theory*, 1984, *12*, 312–320.

White, S. K. *The Recent Work of Jurgen Habermas: Reason, Justice and Modernity*. Cambridge, Eng.: Cambridge University Press, 1988.

Will, G. F. *Statecraft as Soulcraft*. New York: Touchstone, 1983.

Williams, B. "Persons, Characters and Mortality." In A. O. Rorty (ed.), *The Identities of Persons*. Berkeley: University of California Press, 1977.

Wills, G. *Nixon Agonistes*. New York: Mentor, 1969.

Wittgenstein, L. *Philosophical Investigations*. New York: Macmillan, 1958.

Wolin, S. *Politics and Vision*. Boston: Little, Brown, 1960.

Wolin, S. "The New Public Philosophy," *Democracy*, Oct. 1981, *1* (4), 23–36.

6 Assessing Ethics Theories from a Democratic Viewpoint

Brent Wall

Moral Bankruptcy of Public Administration Ethics

Adminstrators frequently face frontiers of ethical ambiguity and contentiousness. Ethical problems in government have no clear resolution in part because public servants do not have an enduring public ethos or ethics to guide their deliberations (Liebman, 1973; Bollens and Schmandt, 1979; Feldman, 1981). There is no legitimated normative frame of reference for administrative action (Stewart, 1988, p. 68).

As a first step in the development of such a framework, this chapter presents a cognitive map that classifies and criticizes central works in public administration ethics since 1940. This effort is a heuristic device that simplifies a complex domain and highlights central differences and similarities among ethical theories. The framework operates as a root metaphor (Pepper, 1942) or as a generative idea (Langer, 1951) by ordering cognitive and affective experience and inviting reflection and spurring discussion. Truth claims are not made; rather, the existing theoretical domain is reinterpreted from a different vantage point (Bultman, 1958).

This chapter assesses public administration ethics theories from a democratic and moral viewpoint. It suggests that these theories and the way we have tended to frame ethical issues are not consistent with democratic and moral ideals, because the terms *democracy* and *morality* are linked by definition. Democracy, whatever else it may mean, is self-determination; it is the empowerment of others to make their own decisions; it is the absence of coercion. To advocate noncoerciveness is to advance other-regardingness, disinterestedness, or the moral point of view (Frankena, 1973; Baier,

1965). Self-interested bargaining or manipulation cannot result in democracy, since self-interest is inconsistent with the disinterested endeavor to let others make up their own minds. In short, democracy has to be a moral point of view. A "democratic" political regime in which people are coerced or self-interested may be many things, but it cannot be democratic or moral.

The literature reviewed dates from the Friedrich-Finer debate (Friedrich, 1940; Finer, 1941) over administrative discretion and the ethics of responsibility and accountability. To identify key works, the author consulted the social science citator, bibliographies (Bergerson, 1988; Bowman, Elliston, & Lockhart, 1984; Caiden and others, 1986; McCurdy, 1986), and recent contributions not yet indexed. Although there are earlier relevant writings (for example, Dimock, 1937; Gaus, 1936; Goodnow, 1900; White, 1939), this exchange was a key turning point in the normative self-conscious of the field. It was occasioned by the discipline's growing realization that the politics-administration dichotomy was neither an accurate description of nor a prescription for the conduct of administrative duties (Waldo, 1984).

This chapter classifies ethical theories from a philosophical and sociohistorical standpoint, assesses them from a democratic and moral standpoint, discusses key implications of each, and concludes by calling for the institutionalization of a new democratic ethics and ethos.

Typology of Ethical Theories

The cognitive map of ethical theories presented here includes their units of normative description (their premises) and their level of normative analysis (the type of legitimation of their ethical premises). It sketches how premises are philosophically validated and socially legitimized. This presentation also assumes a rough correspondence between the dominant philosophical ideas and the social institutions of an age (Sorokin, 1969).

To validate an answer to the question "What is the basis of ethical decisions?" requires a charting of a premise's ontological (whether they are based on an idealist or a realist philosophy) and epistemological assumptions (whether its claims are knowable by reference to objective facts or subjective states) (Burrell and Morgan, 1979). As used here, the term *ontology* refers to the nature of existence—whether, for example, ideas or empirical facts are "real"—while the term *epistemology* refers to how knowledge claims or truth is justified. To determine the legitimacy of an answer to the question "What kind of politics warrants these bases?" necessitates an investigation into the extent to which these values are sanctioned by traditional, modern, or postmodern cultural contexts (Habermas, 1984).

A mapping of the units of normative description suggests that there are four types of validity or truth claims and four sources of legitimation (see Figure 1). The types are: traditional ethics based on objectively validated ideals and legitimated by aristocratic traditions, modernist theories supported by empirical philosophies and legitimated by organizational elites, postmodern ethics that involve the exchange of opinions legitimated by consensual agreements, and axial (that is, other-regarding) ethics based on subjective ideals and legitimated by the polity because it is based on an other-regarding ethos. Based on this categorization, most theories fall into a modernist ethics, a moderate number in the traditional class, one in the postmodern, and none in the axial category. When authors straddled categories, I placed them in the class that seemed to best capture the essence of their position.

By exploring the nature of the philosophical premises and linking them to their potential sources of legitimation, the typology uncovers similarities and differences that tend to be glossed over in other taxonomies [for other structural essays see Willbern (1988), Pops (1988), Cahill and Overman (1988), and Huddleston (1981)]. These reviews classify ethical theories in widely divergent ways. By contrast, this venture, by adapting the philosophical and sociological approach employed by Burrell and Morgan (1979), results in both a critique of these classification schemes and a dissimilar typologization of ethical viewpoints. By knowing the validating and legitimating dimensions of an ethical viewpoint, academicians and practitioners can be sensitized to the type of truth claim being forwarded and what group or institution supports the claim. The schema is normative because it provides, through its axial frame of reference, a way to assess ethical theories from a democratic and moral point of view.

Traditional Theory. A number of authors base their theories on an objective epistemology, an idealist ontology, and traditional (historically sanctioned) social organizations, or a traditional ethic. According to these ethicists, there exist, independent of the deliberations of humankind, substantive ethical claims that are objectively knowable and are claimed to exist "out there" as in natural law philosophies. The central legitimating institution is tradition, in which aristocrats discover and institutionalize "objectively true" values. The dominant form of politics is "reactionary" in the sense that many modern advocates of traditionalism pine, like Edmund Burke and George Will (1984), for a return to the values of the past, which have an objective status. The use of the terms *aristocrat* and *reactionary* is not meant to imply that these authors necessarily employ aristocratical or reactionary views, such as the founding fathers' of slavery, to support their contentions; rather, it suggests that they use the epistemological habits of traditionalists when they claim that truth is discoverable. From the perspective of the modernist's cynicism that values are what institutional elites declare them to be or from the postmodernist's view that values are the outcome of bargaining, those who believe that there are true values are antiquarians; they vouch for the mind life—the epistemological bias—of eighteenth-century aristocrats and reactionaries who employed this conceit to stave off the threatening advances of mass democracy and its "unfortunate" epistemology.

To combat the social disorganization of modern times, some of these thinkers wish for a return to the ethos of classical republicanism. Perhaps the most dramatic example is Nigro and Richardson (1987), who advocate a return to the constitutional regime values of the 1700s: individualism, acquisitiveness, civility, moderation, reputation, and courage. Similarly, McSwain (1985) claims that our liberal heritage does not adequately ground our notions of citizenship and public service. She argues for a rediscovery of classical, communitarian citizenship that derives from "a social rather than an individual identity of the good life" (1985, p. 136). Lane also asserts that "the responsiveness of public administration is fundamentally to the totality of American regime values," for the "true normative base of American public administration . . . is the linkage to the civic virtue . . . of classical republicanism," which balances individual and communal values (1988, p. 41). Finally, Lilla (1981) believes that public administration must recapture the original ethos of the democracy as contrasted to its current reliance on ethical casuistry.

Works validated on such absolutist grounds include Hart's later efforts, where he insists that the "most urgent need in contemporary America is for a renaissance of the Founding values" (1989, p. 101). He asks his readers to assume that the values of individual rights, among others, are the ideals of the founders. Scott and Hart urge that the corrective to the organizational imperative is an "ethical individualism, based upon the Founding Values," and they rest this claim "upon the moral validity of the Founding Values, which bespeak a transcendent moral truth" (1989, p. 162). Denhardt believes, further, that administrative ethics are based on core social values that can be discovered. These values abide in a "lasting moral order . . . which can be understood and followed by administrators in making ethical decisions" (1988, p. 72). Similarly, Golembiewski (1973, p. 64) contends that a moral approach to organizing should be guided by Judeo-Christian values.

Dwivedi states that "all government acts . . . must be measured against some higher law" (1988, p. 317). He argues for the development of an "administrative theology" as the basis for the conduct of public service. Frederickson and Hart (1985) summarize this approach in their advocacy of benevolence and patriotrism when they state that "*all* public administration must rest upon, and be guided by, the moral truths embodied in the enabling documents of our national foundation" (1985, p. 548). They continue, "The regime values *are the absolute values*" (emphasis added, p. 550).

In summary, traditional theorists believe that the foundation of ethical action is made up of true objective ideals that can be used to inform ethical decision making. Two problems with this approach stand out. First, a traditionalist ethic cannot be democratic because there is no reasoned dialogue among peers to determine the nature and scope of regime values; in a democracy, values are enactments, not discoveries. The legitimating structure of traditional theories is, in a word, authoritarian. Second, every attempt to establish "true values" by philsophical argument has failed. From Plato to the present, there is no "accepted" philosophical system. Because philosophy underdetermines truth, people, for extraphilosophical reasons such as "taste" and "feel," cannot rationally agree on any single approach. There is no Archimedean perspective that can be used to adjudicate contending claims. To anchor public administration to this sunken enterprise is to invite endless disputation.

Modernist Theory. The approaches revealed in a modernist culture are supported by an objective epistemology and a realist ontology and by large institutions and organizations (Habermas, 1984). Ethical claims are empirically knowable and are said to exist as fact in the world. Organizations managed by elite classes are the primary legitimating institutions; they socialize their members to reproduce values that preserve and promote organizational ends (Scott and Hart, 1980; Perrow, 1986). The primary form of politics is "conservative" in the sense that elite managers emphasize the status quo and the imperatives of their organizations. These institutions legitimate their value systems through payments—in cash or in kind—to individuals and groups who have traded their rights to self-determination for the benefits (mostly material) that large bureaucracies can bestow (Scott and Hart, 1979; Chackerian and Abcarian, 1984; Perrow, 1986).

Works written from a modernist perspective fall into four subclasses: individual, professional, bureaucratic, and democratic. The individual subtype holds that a person makes judgments according to self-referential, not social, standards. When faced with conflicting values, people are exhorted to look into themselves, into their consciences, to find a basis for decision. Individualist ethics are artifacts of modernity because individuals, as shaped by their organizational environments, and not tradition, ground ethical beliefs (Foucault, 1979; Williams, 1985; Rorty, 1979).

Authors who argue for individualist approaches to public administration ethics include Leys (1952), who maintained that administrators should not rely on custom. Rather, they should use philosophical ethics to bring up "deliberative questions" that will help them think through ethical problems. To Leys, ethics is the "study of standards for decision making" (1952, p. 4). In Harmon's earlier works (1971, p. 179), he argued that individual values are required in the development and institutionalization of a concept of personal responsibility. The existential individual could be the countervailing power to the overriding power of bureaucratic enterprises. Debra Stewart also believes that when value systems collide, "managers are guided by their own ethical systems" (1988, p. 71). Last, Fleishman and Payne assert that "because moral reasoning is fundamentally about the conscious choices of individuals . . . our emphasis . . . is largely on individual choice," since "a substantial portion of the important choices [in government] are made by individuals acting consciously" (1980, p. 16). They conclude that these judgments "among conflicting values ought to be made according to a theory of democracy [that] ought to reflect the will of the people" (1980, p. 34).

One central problem with ethical individualism lies in its making the uncritical assumption that persons can discover moral truth, pure and unsullied, in their consciences. It does not appear to give adequate weight to the forces of political or moral socialization that form the structure and content of awareness (Lukes, 1974). French notes that if we abandon the view that ethical decision making is a deductive and linear enterprise, then "we may accept the fact that most sound moral reasoning proceeds on the basis of principles and concepts that are a part of a common socio-historical endowment" (1983, p. 33). These authors thus confront a large burden of proof: that moral consciousness is beyond social influence. A second problem is rooted in its avoidance of democratic process. The individual who looks into his conscience, consorts with normative "laws," or is guided by no norms whatsoever manifests an undemocratic attitude. These authors confuse the locus of decision making (the individual) with its content (societal norms). These forms of inquiry are monologues with the self; democracy is dialogue in the community (Bellah, 1987). In democracy, individual ethics must stand the test of group decision making (Habermas, 1984).

The professional subtype holds that when norms conflict, professional standards can be used to decide what to do. An analysis of the normative premises of relevant works suggests that most of these authors justify professional interests by linking them to democratic values. Friedrich (1940), for example, believed that the fellowship of the professions could provide a check on abusive bureaucratic power. He tied the final justification for professional decision making, however, to the notion that professional groups exercise power in the name of the citizenry. Bayles, for instance, states that "the norms for professional roles are justified by their promoting and preserving the justifiable values of liberal society" (1981, p. 24).

Willbern argues that professionals "try to give the people what they would want if they had full information"; accordingly, "democracy may be interpreted not as government by the people but as with the consent of the people, with professionals . . . making most of the decisions" (1988, p. 17). Cooper, following MacIntyre's (1984) discussion of goods internal to a practice or those norms that practitioners agree define the excellence of a practice, holds that these are attained where the value is shared by the community of practice and the larger community as well. The ethical norms of public administration are grounded in these internal goods, and these are justified because "they provide goods which a democratic citizenry has determined to be . . . in its collective interest" (Cooper, 1987, p. 322). Scott and Hart contend that the power of the organizational imperative can be counteracted by professionals who work for reform. The push for the institutionalization of the individual imperative "will have to be supplied by the professions" (1979, p. 213).

In these works, the professional viewpoint tends to decay into a democratic approach because the authors (and others such as Sherwood, 1975, and Mosher, 1982) realize that professional power can be autocratic and self-serving (Foucault, 1979).

In contrast, the bureaucratic subtype was first represented by Finer (1941), who advocated that administrators had no business striking out on their own to make policy. Their duty was to obey their political superiors. Similarly, Rohr (1978) admits that administrative discretion exists, but constitutional regime values, as interpreted by court decisions and as dynamically reproduced in democratic society, should be the guiding principles for administrators. These values are "principles that have been held by several generations of the overwhelming majority of the American people" (1978, p. 65), and they "are normative because they are regime values" (1978, p. 67). Rohr thus anchors his bureaucratic theory to the values of the democratic context when he ties court cases to the Constitution and thence to the regime values subscribed to by the American people. Burke also contends that at times administrators must go beyond simple adherence to bureaucratic rules. Administrators must see how a decision can be grounded in the rules of the governmental enterprise as a whole, which he defines as "the practice of democratic politics" (1985, p. 42), because "good . . . reasons can be marshalled on behalf of a democratic concept of responsibility" (1985, p. 229).

In these examples, the bureaucratic ethic tends to merge into a democratic ethics. There are a number of problems with this view. First, as in the professional approach, there is scant critique of the regime values. An uncritical approval of democratic values is too often an unselfconscious acquiescence to the values that organizations have socialized us to believe. Regime values are meaningless unless they are interpreted. What these values are thought to mean in a culture where the privileged position of business dominates, as Lindblom says, is not thoroughly critiqued in the works reviewed. Without such a criticism, we do not know if we are affirming a democratic consensus or merely reproducing the values that we have been socialized to accept. Moreover, the acceptance of regime values without debating their appropriateness is not a democratic, or deliberative, attitude. Second, systems that claim to be based on regime values tend to ignore regime power (Foucault, 1979); individualism, freedom, and acquisitiveness are meaningless unless they are interpreted. In our times, large institutions constitute the power domain that construes these terms to fit their purposes. For example, an individual is one who consumes. In Foucault's (1979) view, all references to regime values should be accompanied by an analysis of regime power.

The last, and largest, subtype is the democratic ethics. In this view, the ultimate warrant for an administrative action is made by referencing the values held by the people. In most treatments, these values or preferences are objectified in markets with purchases and in hierarchies with votes.

Hart and Henry, in their advancement of Rawlsian justice, appear to subscribe to a democratic ethics. Hart holds that "a theory of social equity must be derived from a carefully explicated ethical paradigm" such as Rawls's theory of justice (1974, p. 4). Henry states that "what is needed . . . is a simple and operational conceptualization of the public interest" (1980, p. 40), which he says is set forth in Rawls's theory of justice. Although Frederickson (1971) does not address its grounding, his call to add equity to the standing public administration values of efficiency and economy is probably justified by reference to the values of the polity.

Redford (1969) urges the development of a liberal democracy in which the Constitution is seen as a process that defines participation in the affairs of the state. Appleby (1959) also supports institutional arrangements as a check on bureaucratic power: moral decision making should conform to institutional devices, which are themselves accountable to the public will. Bailey believes that individual qualities conjoint with institutional devices are both justified by a "working definition of the public interest" (1965, p. 243). Finally, Wakefield argues for the importance of individual decision making in the public sector but concludes that individual values result from internalized value structures that are "grounded in Western political thought and widely held American values" (1976, p. 664).

In most cases, then, the subdivisions of modernist theories are reducible to the democratic type because many either directly or indirectly ground their views in the will of the people, the public interest, the regime values of the polity, or similar notions. The fundamental problem with modernist theories in general, and of the democratic subtype in particular, is their lack of critique—that is, to make reference to regime values or to the public interest and the like and to advocate them is, in many cases, to mirror organizational values (Scott and Hart, 1979). Without a critical deliberation of the sources and premises of these "democratic" values, it is inaccurate at best and deceptive at worst to call them democratic.

Postmodern Theory. Postmodern theories are based on a subjective epistemology and a realist ontology legitimated by consensual agreements or on what Habermas (1984) calls noncoercive discourse. Ethical assertions are knowable propositions that are expressions of subjective states (Oppenheim, 1968), and their legitimacy is a function of interactive and critical discourse in which coercion is minimized because it is governed by consensually determined speech acts. In this postmodern perspective, individuals and groups represent their own interests, and they are socialized to reproduce and enact values that support decisions free from manipulation (Habermas, 1984). The form of politics is "liberal" in that communities of participants—not organizational elites—establish and institutionalize a deliberative or democratic ethos.

The public administration theory that falls in this viewpoint is represented by Harmon's later work. Writing in 1989, he states that "the good . . . is . . . a matter of the character of social relations through which ends or purposes are revealed" (p. 149). In this approach, power is a capacity to agree to some group action that is uncoerced, one that operates through persuasion and "good reason-giving" activities. It is a horizontal, not a vertical, model that emphasizes transactions among equals.

This critical-democratic method promises a philosophical validity and a sociological legitimacy based on communicative dialogue. Its shortcomings, however, are many. First, it may become coopted by elites who will seek to manipulate dialogical outcomes in their favor (Dumm, 1988; White, 1988). Second, it is a relativism: enormities such as the Holocaust could result from interested dialogue; postmodernism runs the risk of turning into a nihilism. Third, interested dialogue lacks moral worth because it is interested. Self-interest is the antithesis of morality. Fourth, as Foucault contends, modern regimes mask themselves by producing discourses; their "success is proportional to [their] ability to hide [their] own mechanisms" (1980, p. 86). In short, the relativism and the contentiousness of the postmodern is so unstable that it may regress to an easier authoritarianism. The thirst for order and knowledge, for an Archimedean point that anchors the oscillations of Foucault's pendulum, is the intractable problem of postmodernism.

Axial Theory. The axial (from the Greek *axioma*, meaning worthy) class is based on a subjective epistemology or an insight into nondiscursive "truth" (Quinn, 1988) and an idealist ontology that receives its support from the people. According to this view, citizens would confer legitimacy on leaders who practice an ethos in which motives and actions are grounded in other-regarding behavior. None of the ethics theories surveyed advocate this approach because, in our times, it is an ideal and limiting type: it sets conceptual and ideal boundaries but describes no real-world situation. In axial theory, ethical claims are substantive and subjectively knowable, and their legitimacy is based on the espousal and practice of an other-regarding ethos. The politics of the axial is radical in that it questions the legitimacy and conclusions of democratic dialogue because these are relative and self-interested. In an axial polis, there would be no self-serving politicians or administrators or self-serving dialogues; rather, there would be statespeople who would live "for and not off of" politics (Weber, 1958), who would live for the and not off of the citizenry.

An axial ethos is moral and democratic because it is based on disinterestedness, other-regardingness, and self-determination. It is an idealism in that it supports the ideals of democracy and morality, which cannot be shown to be objectively true (discovered "out there"); rather, they are intersubjectively valid (noncoercive enactments among autonomous individuals). That is, they are not values that we discover, nor do we bargain over them, nor are they established by elites. Rather, they are values that we validate in a mythopoetic enactment (Goffman, 1959). It is a mythopoesis (a myth-making activity) because it does not make discursive truth claims. The propositions and enactments of the axial are corrigible. Quinn, for example, believes that master managers operate at a "metalevel . . . that takes [them] to a transformational logic" (1988, p. 165). This level is an enactment because an "unconscious, fluid, and effortless *performance* begins to emerge" (emphasis added, p. 9).

Axial judgments are parabolic and metaphoric: truth is not proven; it is made by good thoughts and deeds (Quinn, 1988). These assertions cannot be proven because they have only performative validity (Goffman, 1959): that is, the truth is in the *dromenon* (deed) and not in the *logos* (word). A performative philosophy is a dromenology: an inquiry into the moral efficacy of deeds and not into the truth claims of utterances. These axial precepts are the insights of the masters of management vindicated by appreciative onlookers.

Masters work at the level of no rules (Dreyfus and Dreyfus, 1986). These insights are the result of a philosophy without mirrors (Rorty, 1979), because they are not the result of philosophical reflection. They are, on the contrary, the outcomes of a certain mind life that lives a life of service. People are not shown, or proven to, that democracy and morality are good; rather, they are invited to see for themselves.

One strength of this view—the promise of a substantive ethics—is also its great weakness: the intersubjective validation of substantial truth is a philosophical graveyard. The primary advantage of an axial perspective is its ethicality, for it is the only vantage point that represents the "moral point of view [which] is *disinterested*, not interested" (Frankena, 1973, p. 18). Kurt Baier likewise writes that "the very *raison d'etre* of morality is to yield to reasons which overrule the reasons of self-interest" (1965, p. 155). In short, the moral point of view is other regarding. Neither traditional theory, with its authoritarianism, nor modern theory, with its elite socialization, nor the postmodern, with its interested bargaining, is a moral point of view, because none of them is a disinterested perspective.

An axial ethics thus posits the self-identity of two precepts for assessing ethical theories: first, democracy or self-determination in an emancipative culture and, second, disinterestedness or the advocacy of other-regardingness. Democracy, to be such, must be moral.

Figure 1 summarizes the different types of public administrative ethics. The surface diversity of the premises of public administration ethical theories masks an underlying predominance of modern theories, with their emphasis on objectively real values vindicated in and sanctioned by an organizational frame of reference.

Discussion

This mapping of public administration ethics theories can give conceptual coherence to (a) the teaching of public administration ethics, (b) the framing of ethical issues by practitioners, and (c) the form of politics practiced in each ethical type. A traditionalist scenario involves the teaching and socialization of students and practitioners

**Figure 1. A Typology of Public Administration Ethical Theories
and Their Adherents.**

```
                            Idealism
         Axial                  │              Traditional

     None                       │         Late Hart, Denhardt,
                                │         Frederickson and Hart,
                                │         Nigro and Richardson,
                                │         Scott and Hart (1989),
                                │         Golembiewski

Subjectivism ───────────────────┼─────────────────────── Objectivism

     Late Harmon                │         Individual: Leys, early
                                │         Harmon, Fleishman and Payne
                                │
                                │         Professional: Bayles, Scott
                                │         and Hart (1979), Friedrich,
                                │         Cooper, Willbern
                                │
                                │         Bureaucratic: Finer, Rohr,
                                │         Burke
                                │
                                │         Democratic: Early Hart,
                                │         Henry, Redford, Appleby,
                                │         Bailey, Wakefield

         Postmodern            │              Modern
                            Realism
```

to the fundamental regime values of the republic—Plato's and ours.
Professors would have validated lists of ethical principles to teach,
and practitioners would have normative criteria for use in policy
analysis and in the solution of the ethical problems in the workplace. The politics of the traditionalists would return us to aristo-
cracy, to the view that those who manage the state according to the
ways of our fathers are uniquely qualified to practice the art of
statecraft and to mold the populace in the image of these founding
values.

    Modernist theory entails the teaching of students and prac-
titioners about preference determination. The professoriate would
teach students how to measure the public's will. Few would stress
the societal or organizational locus of these preferences; rather, the
efficacy and autonomy of individual decision making would be
stressed. Practitioners facing ethical dilemmas would need to ascer-

tain the will of the people that, once known, they could use to resolve ethical problems. A modernist scenario stresses more of the same, more of the current ethos: pluralism, incrementalism, individualism. It is the politics of the status quo and of the elite management of demand and of consciousness; it deflects attention away from the sources that structure the democratic will: large organizations (Scott and Hart, 1979). In doing so it perpetuates the idea that we live in a democracy in which individuals are autonomous decision makers.

A postmodern or critical scenario would involve the teaching and practice of the processes of noncoercive ethical decision making. It is based on a procedural, not a substantive, rationality. In academe, students would be taught how to critically assess, discuss, and argue their ethical viewpoints (Harmon, 1989). Practitioners would be required to critically assess the precepts germane to an ethical problem and act on those interactively and noncoercively established by relevant reference groups. Since there are no critical democracies, these problems can be approached only with a counterfactual test: What would a critical democratic outcome be if ethical problems were approached from a noncoercive and consensual viewpoint? The politics of the postmodern would minimize the use of organizational pressure to influence ethical outcomes. One man, one vote, no matter the power of the participant, would be the byword. Ideally, preference revelations would be autonomous expressions and not the reflection of gratuitous organizational socialization.

An axial scenario incorporates the interactive approach of the critical approach and converts it to a moral point of view. In pedagogy, students would be taught to know themselves, to critically assess their views, and to interact with their fellow humans. They would be taught how to become masters of management (Quinn, 1988) and moral exemplars. Above all, they would be taught to serve: to act, once their minimal needs are met, for the sake of others. In like manner, administrators would solve ethical problems by giving primary weight to an other-regarding orientation. The question would not be "What's in it for me or for my bureau?" but "What, given the conclusions of critical discourse and the insights of mastery, should be done for the sake of the party to be served?" The politics of the axial are radical for the curious reason that they advocate positive self-effacement and a debunking of the accepted normative bases of public administration, politics, and economics: self-interestedness in almost all of its forms is condemned, and in this condemnation these three social sciences, as practiced, are largely devoid of moral worth.

Toward a New Democratic Ethos

This chapter has presented a heuristic map and a polemic that assess the domain of public administration ethics theories. It concludes that none of these theories supports a democratic perspective and the moral point of view. Most recode the needs of organizational power regimes in myths that mask their coerciveness (Foucault, 1980). Thus these theories, while claiming to be democratic and moral, are neither. They are subtly coercive myths.

The denial of the moral point of view and autonomy may represent more than the capture of the public administration by the dominant myths of the age; it may also represent a dire loss to the field of options in terms of which it could better conceptualize its nature. If theory is driven by value-laden practice (Skinner, 1978), then the future paradigm of the field may lie in its normative and not its positive dimensions. Public administrative praxis, along with democratic and moral criteria, could be used to develop a model of a normative (good) and emancipative (free) political and social theory that has the potential of subsuming both the "moralities" of political science and economics under its praxeological frame of reference. The performative art of management may constitute the key to a normatively grounded theory of public administration.

In traditional ethics, aristocrats discover and impose their ethical truth; in modern ethics, organizations condition citizens to reproduce those ethical principles that support their needs; and in postmodern ethics, self-interested discourse establishes a consensual ethic. While the latter, insofar as it is not manipulated by organizational interests, is democratic, it is not a moral point of view. Only the axial standpoint, with its substantive ethics of service, represents democracy and the moral perspective. However, it is today an ideal type that can be used only to gauge the remaining vantage points. In sum, the traditional may be moral, but it is not democratic; the modern is neither moral nor democratic; and the postmodern, while democratic, is not moral. Only the axial is both moral and democratic.

This polemic makes a host of controversial claims about the present status of public administration ethics theories. To determine the extent to which these assertions represent supportable views, much additional work is required. First, analyses of additional ethical works (for example, Lasswell and Cleveland, 1962; Glenn, 1984; Gutman and Thompson, 1986) need to be conducted to see whether they would confirm the schema postulated here. Second, research could empirically test the hypothesized relationship among legitimation factors (the independent variables), premises (the intervening variables), and practitioner values and behavior (the dependent variables). Third, the claims set forth above should be further explored to see the extent to which they would continue to provide "good reasons" (Baier, 1965) for the contention that public administration ethics theories are sociohistorical artifacts of dubious parentage that are neither democratic nor moral.

The most that can be hoped for in the foreseeable future is the emergence of a postmodern ethics. While the substantive approach of a disinterested and autonomous ethics is morally superior to critical theory, we have many travails to endure before we are ready for such an ethos. If the conclusions of this chapter are sound, existing public administration ethical theories enslave us, unwittingly, to the whims of self-interest and to the caprices of interest group and organizational need rather than emancipating us from these burdens. For these reasons, it would be no small accomplishment if public servants could assist in the laborious process of instituting a new frontier in which the light of a democratic ethics and its supporting ethos would supplant the dark contentiousness that today swirls around the weary administrator.

Bibliography

Appleby, P. H. *Morality and Administration in Democratic Government*. Baton Rouge: Louisiana State University Press, 1959.

Baier, K. *The Moral Point of View: A Rational Basis for Ethics.* New York: Random House, 1965.

Bailey, S. K. "Ethics and the Public Service." *Public Administration Review,* Dec. 1965, *24,* 234–243.

Bayles, M. D. *Professional Ethics.* Belmont, Calif.: Wadsworth, 1981.

Bellah, N. "The Quest of the Self: Individualism, Morality, and Politics." In P. Rabinow and W. M. Sullivan (eds.), *Interpretive Social Science: A Second Look.* Berkeley: University of California Press, 1987.

Bergerson, P. J. *Ethics and Public Policy: An Annotated Bibliography.* New York: Garland, 1988.

Bollens, J. C., and Schmandt, H. J. *Political Corruption: Power, Money, and Sex.* Pacific Palisades, Calif.: Palisades, 1979.

Bowman, J. S., Elliston, F. A., and Lockhart, P. *Professional Dissent: An Annotated Bibliography and Resource Guide.* New York: Garland, 1984.

Bultman, R. *Jesus Christ and Mythology.* New York: Scribner's, 1958.

Burke, J. P. *Bureaucratic Responsibility.* Baltimore, Md.: Johns Hopkins University Press, 1985.

Burrell, G., and Morgan, G. *Sociological Paradigms and Organizational Analysis.* Portsmouth, N.H.: Heinemann, 1979.

Cahill, A. G., and Overman, S. "Contemporary Perspectives on Ethics and Values in Public Affairs." In J. S. Bowman and F. A. Elliston (eds.), *Ethics, Government, and Public Policy: A Reference Guide.* Westport, Conn.: Greenwood Press, 1988.

Caiden, G. E., and others. *American Public Administration: A Bibliographic Guide to the Literature.* New York: Garland, 1986.

Chackerian, R., and Abcarian, G. *Bureaucratic Power in Society.* Chicago: Nelson-Hall, 1984.

Cooper, T. L. *The Responsible Administrator: An Approach to Ethics for the Administrative Role.* (2d ed.) Millwood, N.Y.: Associated Faculty Press, 1986.

Cooper, T. L. "Hierarchy, Virtue, and the Practice of Public Administration: A Perspective for Normative Ethics." *Public Administration Review,* July/Aug. 1987, *47,* 320–328.

Denhardt, K. G. *The Ethics of Public Service: Resolving Moral*

Dilemmas in Public Organizations. Westport, Conn.: Greenwood Press, 1988.

Dimock, M. E. *Modern Politics and Administration.* New York:
American Book, 1937.

Dreyfus, H. L., and Dreyfus, S. E. "From Socrates to Expert Sys-
tems: The Limits of Calculative Rationality." In C. Mitcham and
A. Huning (eds.), *Philosophy and Technology II.* Dordrecht,
Holland: D. Reidel, 1986.

Dreyfus, H. L., and Rabinow, P. *Michel Foucault: Beyond Struc-
turalism and Hermeneutics.* (2nd ed.) Chicago: University of
Chicago Press, 1983.

Dumm, T. L. "The Trial of Postmodernism II: The Politics of Post-
Modern Aesthetics, Habermas Contra Foucault." *Political Theory,* May 1988, *16,* 209-228.

Dwivedi, O. P. "Conclusion: A Comparative Analysis of Ethics,
Public Policy, and the Public Service." In J. S. Bowman and
F. A. Elliston (eds.), *Ethics, Government, and Public Policy: A
Reference Guide.* Westport, Conn.: Greenwood Press, 1988.

Feldman, D. L. *Reforming Government.* New York: Morrow, 1981.

Finer, H. "Administrative Responsibility in Democratic Government." *Public Administration Review,* 1941, *1,* 335-350.

Fleishman, J. L., and Payne, B. L. *The Teaching of Ethics.* Vol. 8:
Ethical Dilemmas and the Education of Policymakers. Hastings-
on-Hudson, N.Y.: Institute of Society, Ethics and the Life Sciences, Hastings Center, 1980.

Foucault, M. *The Order of Things: An Archeology of the Human
Sciences.* New York: Vintage Books, 1973.

Foucault, M. *Discipline and Punish: The Birth of the Prison.* (A.
Sheridan, trans.). New York: Vantage Press, Random House,
1979.

Foucault, M. *The History of Sexuality.* Vol. 1: *An Introduction.*
(Robert Hurley, trans.). New York: Vantage Press, Random
House, 1980.

Frankena, W. K. *Ethics.* Englewood Cliffs, N.J.: Prentice-Hall,
1973.

Frederickson, H. G. "Toward a New Public Administration." In F.
Marini (ed.), *Toward a New Public Administration.* Scranton,
Pa.: Chandler, 1971.

Frederickson, H. G., and Hart, D. K. "The Public Service and the Patriotism of Benevolence." *Public Administration Review*, Sept./Oct. 1985, *45*, 547–553.

French, P. *Ethics in Government.* Englewood Cliffs, N.J.: Prentice-Hall, 1983.

Friedrich, C. J. "Public Policy and the Nature of Administrative Responsibility." In E. S. Mason and C. T. Friedrich (eds.), *Public Policy, 1940.* Cambridge, Mass.: Harvard University Press, 1940.

Gaus, J. "The Responsibility of Public Administration." In J. M. Gaus, L. D. White, and M. Dinock (eds.), *Frontiers of Public Administration.* Chicago: University of Chicago Press, 1936.

Gerth, H. H., and Mills, C. W. (eds.). *From Max Weber: Essays in Sociology.* New York: Oxford University Press, 1958.

Glenn, J. R., Jr. *Ethics and Politics.* Chicago: Nelson-Hall, 1984.

Goffman, I. *The Presentation of Self in Everyday Life.* New York: Doubleday, 1959.

Golembiewski, R. "Organization as a Moral Problem." *Public Administration Review*, Jan./Feb. 1973, *33*, 63–74.

Goodnow, F. J. *Politics and Administration.* New York: Macmillan, 1900.

Gutman, A., and Thompson, D. F. *Ethics in Decision Making.* New York: Wiley, 1986.

Habermas, J. *The Theory of Communicative Action.* Vol. 1: *Reason and the Rationalization of Society.* (T. McCarthy, trans.). Boston: Beacon Press, 1984.

Habermas, J. "Modernity—An Incomplete Project." In P. Rabinow and W. M. Sullivan (eds.), *Interpretive Social Science: A Second Look.* Berkeley: University of California Press, 1987.

Harmon, M. M. "Normative Theory and Public Administration: Some Suggestions for a Redefinition of Administrative Responsibility." In F. Marini (ed.), *Toward a New Public: The Minnowbrook Perspective.* Scranton, Pa.: Chandler, 1971.

Harmon, M. M. " 'Decision' and 'Action' as Contrasting Perspectives in Organizational Theory." *Public Administration Review*, Mar./Apr. 1989, *49*, 144–150.

Hart, D. K. "Social Equity, Justice, and the Equitable Administration." *Public Administration Review*, Jan./Feb. 1974, *34*, 3–11.

Hart, D. K. "The Virtuous Citizen, the Honorable Bureaucrat, and

Public Administration." *Public Administration Review*, Mar. 1984, *44*, 116–117.

Hart, D. K. " A Partnership in Virtue Among All Citizens: The Public Service and Civic Humanism." *Public Administration Review*, Mar./Apr. 1989, *49*, 101–106.

Henry, N. "Toward a Bureaucratic Ethic." In *Public Administration and Public Affairs*. (2nd ed.) Englewood Cliffs, N.J.: Prentice-Hall, 1980.

Huddleston, W. "Comparative Perspectives on Administrative Ethics—Some Implications for American Public Administration." *Public Personnel Management*, 1981, *10*, 67–76.

Lane, L. "Individualism, Civic Virtue, and Public Administration: The Implications of American Habits of the Heart." *Administration and Society*, May 1988, *20*, 30–45.

Langer, S. K. *Philosophy in a New Key*. New York: New American Library, 1951.

Lasswell, H., and Cleveland, H. *The Ethics of Power: The Interplay of Religion, Philosophy, and Politics*. New York: Harper, 1962.

Leys, W.A.R. *Ethics for Political Decisions: The Art of Asking Deliberative Questions*. Englewood Cliffs, N.J.: Prentice-Hall, 1952.

Liebman, J. K. *How Government Breaks the Law*. New York: Penguin, 1973.

Lilla, M. T. "Ethos, 'Ethics,' and the Public Service." *The Public Interest*, Spring 1981, *63*, 3–17.

Lukes, S. *Power: A Radical View*. London: Macmillan, 1974.

McCurdy, H. E. *Public Administration: A Bibliographic Guide to Literature*. New York: Marcel Dekker, 1986.

MacIntyre, A. *After Virtue*. (2nd ed.) Notre Dame, Ind.: University of Notre Dame Press, 1984.

McSwain, C. J. "Administrators and Citizenship: The Liberalist Legacy of the Constitution." *Administration and Society*, Aug. 1985, *17*, 131–148.

Mosher, F. C. *Democracy in the Public Service*. (2nd ed.) New York: Oxford University Press, 1982.

Nigro, L., and Richardson, W. D. "Public Administration and the Foundation of the American Republic." In R. Denhardt and

E. T. Jennings (eds.), *The Revitalization of the Public Service*. Columbia, Mo.: Department of Public Administration, 1987.

Oppenheim, F. E. *Moral Principles in Political Philosophy*. New York: Random House, 1968.

Pepper, S. *World Hypothesis*. Berkeley: University of California Press, 1942.

Perrow, C. *Complex Organizations: A Critical Essay*. New York: Random House, 1986.

Pops, G. M. "Ethics in Government: A Framework for Analysis." In J. S. Bowman and F. A. Elliston (eds.), *Ethics, Government, and Public Policy: A Reference Guide*. Westport, Conn.: Greenwood Press, 1988.

Quinn, R. E. *Beyond Rational Management: Mastering the Paradoxes and Competing Demands of High Performance*. San Francisco: Jossey-Bass, 1988.

Rabinow, P., and Sullivan, W. M. (eds.). *Interpretive Social Science: A Second Look*. Berkeley: University of California Press, 1987.

Redford, E. S. *Democracy in the Administrative State*. New York: Oxford University Press, 1969.

Rohr, J. *Ethics for Bureaucrats: An Essay on Law and Values*. New York: Marcel Dekker, 1978.

Rorty, R. *Philosophy and the Mirror of Nature*. Princeton, N.J.: Princeton University Press, 1979.

Scott, W. G., and Hart, D. K. *Organizational America*. Boston: Houghton Mifflin, 1979.

Scott, W. G., and Hart, D. K. *Organizational Values in America*. New Brunswick, N.J.: Transaction, 1989.

Sherwood, F. P. "Professional Ethics." *Public Management*, June 1975, *57*, 13-14.

Skinner, Q. *The Foundation of Modern Political Thought*. Vol. 1. Cambridge, Eng.: Cambridge University Press, 1978.

Sorokin, P. *Society, Culture and Personality*. New York: Cooper Square, 1969.

Stewart, D. "An Ethical Framework for Human Resource Decision Making." In E. K. Kellar (ed.), *Ethical Insight and Ethical Action: Perspectives for the Local Government Manager*. Washington, D.C.: International City Managers' Association, 1988.

Wakefield, S. "Ethics and the Public Service: A Case for Individual

Responsibility." *Public Administration Review,* Nov./Dec. 1976, *36,* 661–666.

Waldo, D. *The Administrative State.* (2nd ed.) New York: Holmes & Meier, 1984.

Weber, M. "Politics as a Vocation." In H. H. Gerth and C. W. Mills (eds.), *From Max Weber: Essays in Sociology.* New York: Oxford University Press, 1958.

White, L. D. *Introduction to the Study of Public Administration.* New York: Macmillan, 1939.

White, S. K. "The Trial of Postmodernism I: Poststructuralism and Political Reflection." *Political Theory,* May 1988, *16,* 186–208.

Willbern, Y. "Types and Levels of Public Morality." In E. K. Kellar (ed.), *Ethical Insight and Ethical Action: Perspectives for the Local Government Manager.* Washington, D.C.: International City Managers' Association, 1988.

Will, G. F. *Statecraft as Soulcraft.* New York: Random House, 1984.

Williams, B. *Ethics and the Limits of Philosophy.* London: Fontana Books/Collins, 1985.

7   New Leadership Requirements

for Public Administrators:

From Managerial to Policy Ethics

Jeffrey S. Luke

The recent rapid development of global and local interdependencies has created a web of intersocietal and interorganizational connections that now encircles the planet. A political, economic, or technological development in one part of the world often has a direct or immediate impact on other parts of the world. These interconnections and interdependencies did not develop incrementally over successive generations in some linear, additive fashion. Rather, their emergence is more analogous to the process of crystalization (Rosenau, 1980), of interrelated networks forming at an accelerating pace linking historically separate and autonomous agencies, organizations, institutions, and societies. This accelerated development is similar to what evolutionary biologists call "anagenesis," a sudden, qualitative shift in evolutionary development. As a result of this anagenesis, public administrators now live in an intergovernmental and intersectoral network existing in specific natural resource boundaries, changing the historical nature of public policy and administration in fundamental ways at the local, state, and federal levels. Nothing so interdependent has existed in American history.

One key area that has avoided consideration of interdependencies is contemporary discussions of governmental ethics. This is unfortunate, because managing interconnectedness—humanely and ethically—may be the greatest challenge to public administrators in the 1990s. The ripple effects of policy choices made by administrators and elected officials—whether local, state, or federal—now have expanded consequences in terms of both time and geography. The crystalization of global interdependencies and the novel dimensions and long-term consequences of public action raise moral and ethical issues that contemporary governmental ethics ignores. Interconnectedness moves policy ethics into the center of ethical discourse, and an expanded sense of responsibility and foresight is the starting point of policy ethics. Further, policy ethics is the unique responsibility of chief elected and appointed public executives because they have authority and responsibility that span longer time horizons than those of middle-level administrators and managers. Governmental ethics, currently preoccupied with concerns for individual behavior, must now include an ethical theory of policy choices. This shift, or expansion, from behavioral ethics to policy ethics is a new ethical frontier.

Scandals, Scoundrels, and Saints: Contemporary Governmental Ethics

The central concern of governmental ethics and the central ethical concern for career civil servants has been the responsible use of an individual's administrative discretion (Rohr, 1990). As a result, discussions of governmental ethics most often focus on the norms and standards of conduct in public and organizational life. Since the public's trust is an essential element in effectively leading and "managing in the public interest," the personal conduct of public managers and the perceptions of personal conduct are continuously being scrutinized. The media tend to focus on misbehavior, impropriety, influence peddling, waste, and fraud. At the federal, state, and local levels, common concerns are conflicts of interest, disclosure requirements, purchasing and personnel regulations, abuse of authority, and postemployment restrictions. This results in rules and procedures that attempt to guide administrative behavior by governing individual discretion and protecting against personal abuses of authority.

Governing individual administrative behavior, as well as forcing administrators to pay attention to the appearance of personal conduct, is accomplished through professional codes, ordinances, regulations, administrative rules, and statutes. The goal is to eliminate or prevent government scandals, restrain or jail political scoundrels, and create virtuous public leaders, or saints. Moral virtues, including integrity (honesty, truthfulness, courage), loyalty (consideration of citizens and constituents, strength of mind, responsible representation), and judgment (commitment to the common good, respect for law), are at the center of this discussion.

More recent suggestions by younger public administration scholars encourage us to expand our ethics discussion to include an administrator's obligation to a democratic ethos (Burke, 1989) or democratic ideals (Denhardt, 1989). Such institutional virtues are required to balance the tension between bureaucratic values (efficiency, expediency, neutrality) with political or democratic values (justice, equity, and the virtues of democracy). These newer discussions of governmental ethics are very important extensions in the moral development of public administration as a profession; however, it appears that they, too, focus on individual behavior, albeit in newer terms such as administrative responsibility, virtuous administrative judgment, and administrative ethics in a politicized environment.

This focus on personal conduct or administrative behavior, however, is insufficient to guarantee a virtuous "polity," an ethical public policy, or a moral organizational outcome. Current discussions in governmental ethics are prematurely fastened on issues of administration, to the exclusion of higher-level concerns inherent in the executive responsibilities of public organizations. Effective governmental leaders and executives must focus on longer-term collective outcomes, not just an individual's administrative obligations. *At the executive level, the ethics of policy choices and organizational outcomes become paramount.* This is occurring for at least two reasons. First, the role of the leader is to look farther into the future (five to twenty years) rather than the shorter time horizons of administrators, middle managers, and first-line supervisors. Second, the environmental context of public administration is now more interdependent and interconnected than in any time during this country's history. Together, these two factors require the public executive to look outward more and inward less.

Leadership: The Higher You Go, the Farther
and Wider You Must Gaze

There is considerable evidence, both anecdotal and empirical, that executive-level administrators require longer time horizons to be effective. Ground-breaking empirical research by Elliot Jaques on the concept of "time span" (1976) shows that at different organizational levels, different analytical and conceptual time spans are required. Observers of leaders and leadership processes, such as John Gardner, Warren Bennis, and Richard Neustadt, have reached similar conclusions with less empirically based approaches.

An administrator's time span is measured by the maximum target-completion time of the longest tasks assigned in the particular organizational role. The higher one is in an organization, the longer the requisite time span. The scale of one's ability to work into the future, the cognitive capacity to sustain increasingly complex discretionary processes over long time spans, is one's *time horizon* (Jaques, 1989). Jaques, through extensive survey research, has identified distinct strata in formal organizations that clearly show that the higher-level administrative/executive roles have longer time span requirements and time horizons than those of middle-level managers and administrators. As the administrator's time horizon increases, his or her feeling of weight of responsibility increases; the greater the outreach in time, the farther into the future that administrators not only plan but also carry those plans through to accomplishment (Jaques, 1976).

John Gardner (1986, p. 8) emphasizes that there are important long-term, vision-oriented aspects in which leaders and executive managers distinguish themselves from the general run of managers and administrators:

- They think longer term—beyond the day's crises, beyond the quarterly report, beyond the horizon.
- They look beyond the unit they are heading and grasp its relationship to larger realities—the larger organization of which they are a part, conditions external to the organization, global trends.

- They reach and influence constituents beyond their jurisdictions, beyond boundaries. In an organization, leaders overflow bureaucratic boundaries—often a distinct advantage in a world too complex and tumultuous to be handled "through channels." Their capacity to rise above jurisdictions may enable them to bind together the fragmented constituencies that must work together to solve a problem.
- They put heavy emphasis on the intangibles of vision, values, and motivation.
- They have the political skill to cope with the conflicting requirements of multiple constituencies.

Similarly, Bennis (1983) found in his interviews of successful corporate executives that they characteristically *created and communicated a compelling long-term vision.* Such a visioning process requires what Jaques (1989) calls cognitive capacities with large time horizons and what Neustadt and May (1986) call "thinking in time streams."

In analyzing how decision makers—in particular, political and military leaders—use history and time in their mental calculations, Neustadt and May found that effective leaders think about time as a stream. "Effective leaders see and think in *time-streams;* looking not only to the coming year but well beyond, and with a clear sense of the long past from which those futures would come" (1986, p. 248). They note that "the essence of thinking in time-streams is imagining the future as it may be when it becomes the past" (pp. 253-254).

Thinking in time streams is a special style of approaching choices requiring an expanded time horizon. Thinking in a time stream can involve visualizing a desired future and constructing a mental map of how to arrive at that future state, and it involves identifying a future that can be undesirable and making plans to avoid it. It requires from the policy leader and public manager a capacity and willingness to readily connect discrete phenomena over time and to repeatedly check those connections (Neustadt and May, 1986).

Managing Interconnectedness

Public administration is being transformed by an increasingly interconnected, globalized environment. Transnational, regional, and local interdependencies are connecting the political and economic fortunes of city, county, state, and national governments more closely than ever before. As a result, a major function of public executives—both elected officials and appointed managers—is to manage this increasing interdependence (Luke and Caiden, 1989).

As the definition implies, interdependencies involve "mutual dependence," where actions of one individual or agency influence or constrain actions of another. *Interdependencies*—high-cost, very important mutual dependencies—can further be distinguished from *interconnectedness*—low-cost, relatively unimportant mutual dependencies (Keohane and Nye, 1977). Although these have evolved since the 1950s, fundamental interdependencies and interconnections have recently occurred in three particular areas:

• *Worldwide communications and transportation and a global infostructure.* Technology has dramatically lessened geographical and social distance; the world is becoming smaller and smaller, making the interaction of international, national, and local public policies more pervasive and intense (Rosenau, 1980). Recent advances in transportation, information processing, and satellite communications now link countries together such that actions in one country can have both immediate and delayed effects on American states and communities (Luke and Caiden, 1989).

• *A global economy and the internationalization of trade, finance, and technology transfer.* This new global infostructure has ushered in an intricate global economy beyond the historical patterns of international trade. Capital markets, historically insulated in national boundaries, have now been integrated into a global financial web. Financial events in one part of the globe, Wall Street, for example, can have nearly instantaneous impacts around the world.

• *Natural resource constraints and interdependencies in the biosphere.* Environmental issues of the 1990s, unlike those of the 1970s, are essentially global issues, with significant ecological and

biological ripple effects. There is an expanding awareness of interdependence among natural resources, particularly the interconnectedness of natural life support systems on the planet and the
need to protect key biosphere subsystems such as the ozone layer,
the ancient forests, and biological diversity. The concept of "ecosystems" captures the essense of this interdependence among various levels of our biological and environmental systems. Cities and
states are recognizing these interconnections and are identifying appropriate strategic responses. The state of Oregon, for example, has
analyzed the possible impacts of global warming and has developed
a set of departmental actions to prevent and mitigate its effects (State
of Oregon, 1990).

*Expanding the Ethical Frontier: Space, Function, and
Time.* The global infostructure, the international economic fabric,
and the biological ecosystems create a web of overlapping interconnections and reduce separateness. Conceptually, there are three
types of interconnectedness. First, the interdependencies cross jurisdictional boundaries and create *geographic interconnections.* Significant policy choices and actions taken in one part of the globe
will often have consequences in other parts. As a result, the costs
and benefits of organizational action are not distributed evenly over
geographic space. The Council of State Planning and Policy Agencies noted that "turning Brazilian jungles into orange groves may
be good news for the food processor in Sao Paulo, the Dutch company that owns the tank ships, the juice distributor in Newark, the
Toyko banker who financed the project, and those of us who like
cheap OJ; but it is bad news for the Brazilian Indians, Florida
orange growers, and environmentalists" (1989, p. 6).

Functional interdependence, a second type, now exists between policy-making, administration, and judicial activity resulting in a noticeable blurring between the historical separation of
government functions. As a result, it is very difficult, if not impossible, to separate administration from politics; public administrators do make and influence public policy. Policy ethics become a
central concern for public managers and executives. In addition, the
joining of the polity and the economy expands the sphere of intergovernmental relations horizontally into the private sector at the

national, state, and local levels, creating issues of "intersectoral" relations. The intersectoral ethics of public-private partnerships thus emerges as another source of concern to public administrators due to the functional interdependence between the public, private, and nonprofit sectors. A concern for public administrators arising from functional interdependence is the increasing complexity of the policy issues themselves. There exists a complex web of interdependencies in key political issues such as crime, affordable housing, and economic development.

A third type of interconnectedness, and perhaps more difficult to grasp, is that generations of humans are now interdependent. There is a *temporal interconnectedness* that ties together past, present, and future generations. Decisions made by earlier generations directly shape the policy issues we face today, and policy choices made today can have significant influences on the quality of life and the capacity for self-governance of future generations. This adds a time horizon to the calculus of public policy-making.

Looking Outward More, Inward Less: The New Challenge for Governmental Ethics. An expanded notion of governmental ethics is now required. This new, interconnected context, coupled with the executive's responsibility to expand her or his time horizon, forces the expansion of the ethics frontier in two ways. First, the requisite time horizon for public sector executives is longer than that required at middle and lower levels. Current ethical efforts at guiding the personal short-term conduct of public officials may be more appropriate for administrators and middle-level managers. Public leaders, however, must *lengthen* their ethical considerations to take in more of the future, expanding ethical responsibility beyond the immediate act itself to its eventual impacts. Second, interconnectedness forces a *widening* to include what used to be regarded as externalities. With public action increasingly intertwined in intergovernmental and intersectoral activity, public administrators not only must account for immediate consequences and visible costs of policy choices but also must consider the less-visible consequences and costs borne by the organization and passed on to others who may not have any direct recourse (Stone, 1985).

As Jonas observes, "Public policy has never had to deal before with issues of such inclusiveness and such lengths of anticipation" (1984, p. 9). The focus of ethics, particularly for executives leading governmental agencies, must be expanded to now incorporate the *ethics of policy choices*. This expansion requires a new ethics of foresight and responsibility beyond the narrow constraints of intraorganizational accountability, personal codes of conduct, and administrators functioning as independent discretionary actors.

From Behavioral Ethics to Policy Ethics

Current discussions and legislative actions regarding governmental ethics are peroccupied with behavioral ethics of personal conduct and typically center around such issues as standards of individual conduct, accountability for administrative discretion, professional codes of conduct, and conflict of interest. Much of this results from the fact that public administrators work in a "glass house." The common concern for existing in a glass house is the perennial tension between self-interest and public interest.

However, public administrators have different responsibilities and ethical obligations, depending on their particular levels and roles in their organization. Burke (1989) suggests that the ethical obligations differ for street-level bureaucrats, administrative managers, and agency heads. Policy leaders, in particular, have an expanded set of ethical obligations because of their larger time horizons and because of the recent crystalization of a highly interconnected, interdependent environmental context in which policies are formulated and implemented. Policy leaders—elected and appointed—must consider ethical implications of policy choices. In their regard for the quality of life and well-being of society, policy leaders must pay attention to the long-term consequences and externalities of their policy decisions. As a result, ethics in public administration involves not merely the avoidance of dishonorable behavior or the virtuous behavior of an individual manager. It also involves new ethical principles of action that can guide leaders in making policy choices in an interconnected global society.

Unfortunately, foresight and the consideration of long-term ethical issues of policy choices are often very difficult. William Ruckleshaus (1989, p. 166) warns that it is hard for people to change their policies "in order to avert threats that will otherwise affect a world most of them will not be alive to see." Thinking about future consequences of policy choices is not easy. There are considerable cognitive barriers that circumscribe thinking about long-term consequences of public policies. Simon (1983) clearly articulates limits to rationality and limits in individual capacity for knowledge. Many other administrative theorists, relying on a variety of psychological findings, agree that we have inherent barriers to abstracting into the future. Jaques (1976) emphasizes that one's capability for gazing into the future is constrained by inherent limits in capacity for higher levels of abstraction. Those who require more concrete types of abstraction find it terribly difficult to look past present issues or actual problems that are close at hand, whereas individuals capable of higher levels of abstraction find it considerably easier to stretch their thinking into a longer-term perspective. Cochran (1980) adds that one's orientation toward the future is limited by what one already knows, and that with normal perceptual filters and the built-in constraints of our language, the definition of problems and the interpretations of their causes are very tenuous. The result is usually a constrictive orientation toward the future.

In addition to these cognitive difficulties, the interconnected environmental context further inhibits our efforts at forecasting. An interconnected environment makes it nearly impossible to ascertain cause-and-effect relationships and, thus, accurately project very far into the future. Extrapolations from future trends can be misleading or inaccurate, and forecasts are subject to an increasing multitude of errors the farther projections are extended. These cognitive and contextual barriers create a unique dilemma for contemporary public administration: the potential for public policy—once constrained by limits of geography, function, and time—to affect the future is immense, while the capacity to foresee the results and outcomes of government action is not.

Perhaps more problematical for articulating guiding principles for a policy ethics is that traditional ethical theory has largely ignored the notion of long-range responsibility. Interconnectedness has opened up a new area of ethical relevance for which there exist no standards, principles, or canons in traditional ethics. Traditional ethics is historically based on four assumptions (Jonas, 1984, pp. 4–6):

1. Ethical significance belonged to the direct dealings of "man with man."
2. In dealing with the nonhuman world, action was ethically neutral.
3. Ethics was of the here and now: the good and evil about which individual action was concerned lay close to the act, in either the praxis itself or its immediate reach; the long run of consequences was left to chance, fate, or providence.
4. Since its major concern was the immediacy of the day-to-day sphere of human interaction, ethics reckoned only with "noncumulative behavior."

Guiding Principles

Given the cognitive and contextual difficulties in foresight and the lack of a theory of responsibility in traditional ethics, where can we seek appropriate guiding principles of policy ethics? Two areas of public policy that have begun to articulate such guidelines are bioethics and environmental ethics.

Bioethics. This term, initially coined by Potter in his ground-breaking *Bioethics: Bridge to the Future* (1971), expanded the older concept of medical ethics to better address emerging ethical dilemmas precipitating from developments in genetic engineering, in vitro fertilization, and organ transplants. Contemporary bioethics is concerned with the ethics of health issues that have arisen due to the accelerating advances in biological discoveries and medical technology.

Bioethics is an excellent example of the issues of policy ethics in an arena characterized by extreme functional interdependence. Health policy is full of intersectoral and intergovernmental dependencies and involves an array of private sector stakeholders (for example, insurance companies, hospitals, and pharmaceutical firms), an extended governmental network of stakeholders (for example, counties, states, and federal agencies), as well as the legal system (for example, the courts, lawyers, and legal ethicists) and nonprofit advocate groups and associations (for example, the Association for Retarded Citizens). Bioethics fundamentally emerges from the interdependence of medicine, law, technology, philosophy, and politics. Stuhr (1989, p. 78), in a review of bioethical issues in public policy, identified the basic bioethical issues confronting policymakers today:

- The allocation of scarce resources: How much individual, group, and social wealth should be spent on health care generally and health programs in particular, and how, in turn, should scarce medical resources and facilities be used?
- The regulation of health care: To what extent, for what ends, and by whom should the delivery of health care be legislated, regulated, or otherwise controlled?
- The limits of experimentation and research: What limits, if any, should be placed on biological research, and how can such limits best be implemented?
- Responsibility for medically dependent persons: What obligations do individuals and society have for physically and psychically impaired persons, and how can these obligations (moral, legal, financial) be met?
- The discovery and definition of the beginning and end of human life: When does life begin and end, and are there relevant differences between the biological notion of a human life and the moral notion of a person's life?
- The sanctity and possible destruction or creation of life forms: Under what conditions, if any, should life forms or characteristics of those forms be destroyed, created, or otherwise manipulated?

Although Potter (1971) initially argued for a bioethics based on a realistic understanding of *ecology* in the broadest sense—focusing on a healthy biotic community as well as the survival and health of the individual—current bioethical discussions have taken a much narrower medical scope. It is in Stuhr's last concern, the sanctity and survival of life forms, that bioethics begins to consider issues of ecological or environmental ethics.

Environmental Ethics. The field of environmental ethics emerged almost simultaneously with bioethics. However, environmental ethics and bioethics involve different intellectual traditions, operate through different professional and academic outlets, and address different concerns—for example, short-term versus long-term considerations, individual survival and well-being versus community well-being, and ensuring human survival versus protecting the environment in which life is nurtured and sustained (Meine, 1989). More recently, Potter (1988) recognizes these two distinct "branches" of bioethics and attempts to develop a unified point of view he calls global bioethics. Nevertheless, in the last decade, a body of literature has emerged in environmental ethics that has begun to articulate underlying principles that may provide more insight for the frontier in policy ethics, especially those involving geographic and temporal interdependencies. These principles go beyond the traditional concerns of bioethics as well as what public administrators might consider as the "environmental movement" and examine Western moral traditions and ethical obligations from a historical and philosophical perspective.

Underlying environmental ethics are two assumptions:

1. Scientific discoveries have created new opportunities and perils, resulting in potentially serious consequences (intended and unintended) from individual and organizational actions in an interconnected world (Jonas, 1984).
2. The ripple effects of choices on future people, as well as other species, require policymakers to be more explicit about public sector responsibilities in their regard (Attfield, 1983).

As a result, the articulation of an "environmental ethics" has been considered critical. Although some suggest that John Passmore's *Man's Responsibility for Nature* (1974) has provided a recognized authoritative treatment, there are several divergent schools of thought today, ranging from "radical biotic egalitarianism"—which argues that there is no more value in human than in nonhuman lives and that all animals are of equal significance, whatever their species—to the "ecology movement"—which is more narrowly preoccupied with the problems of pollution and natural resource depletion as they currently affect the developed world (Attfield, 1983). In between these two extremes is the "land ethics" suggested by Aldo Leopold as the next stage in the development of ethics; the first stage of ethics dealt with relations between individuals, and the second dealt with the relation of the individual to society. The land ethics—the third stage—expands the definition of society to include all members of the "biotic" community—soils, waters, plants, animals, or collectively "the land." From this perspective, there is an obligation to earth's biosphere because of its intrinsic value; "a thing is right when it tends to promote the integrity, stability, and beauty of the biotic community. It is wrong when it tends otherwise" (Leopold, 1949, p. 224). Regardless of the diversity of sentiment, all schools of thought in environmental ethics agree that we need an ethics that heightens our awareness of obligations to diversity and posterity and that our moral horizons have to be broadened to assume an expanded set of responsibilities (Attfield, 1983; Rolston, 1988, Callicott, 1989).

Preliminary Guidelines for Policy Ethics

To explore policy ethics, one does not necessarily have to engage in a debate between utilitarianism, deontology, and the ethics of virtue. Although it may be difficult to agree on some transcendent objective, preliminary values that could suggest certain ethical parameters in policy choices can be articulated. These preliminary guidelines can be based on either instrumental values (Speth, 1989) or intrinsic values (Leopold, 1949; Attfield, 1983; Callicott, 1989) and imply obligations that are recognizable extensions of currently accepted public administration values, merely by expanding the range of policy consequences being considered.

Interdependence and interconnectedness do not imply an immediate moral reponsibility or obligation; mutual dependence in the polity, economy, or biosphere does not automatically create a moral relationship. Therefore, there is no a priori moral or ethical obligation among interdependent actors or agencies. However, the crystalization of interdependence between the economy, the polity, and the biosphere now strengthens the instrumental value of their interrelationships and amplifies the fact that it is in the human interest, for example, to preserve and enhance the natural resource systems on earth. Ozone depletion (caused by the industrial use of chlorofluorocarbons), acid rain (caused by the burning of fossil fuels such as coal), and deforestation (in developed and developing countries) result in long-term decline in economic and biological resources. One does not have to argue that the biosphere has some intrinsic (aesthetic or natural) value (although there is increasing sentiment in this direction); it has a recognizable instrumental value for current and future generations. It is thus in our human self-interest to constrain activities aimed at short-term gain that may undermine the economic well-being of future generations or threaten the biological life-support systems of the planet.

Duties to the Future. The central philosophical question, one that must be addressed before identifying appropriate guidelines or principles, is "What practical obligations or moral responsibility do public administrators have toward the posterity of future generations?" Moral philosophers differ on the issue of our duties to future generations; they take four different positions (Partridge, 1981):

- those who argue that the same consideration should be given to the rights and interests of future people as to those of contemporary people
- those who argue that there is a moral obligation to only the immediate future, the next generation
- those who acknowledge obligations to the future but do not take them seriously or assign them less weight
- those who deny any moral obligations beyond the current living generations.

Jonas (1984) provides a sound philosophical foundation for the position that there is a moral duty for later generations and argues that public leaders in particular have a moral responsibility for distant contingencies. Political action, he asserts, "has a longer time span of effect and responsibility than private action" (1984, p. 15). The fiduciary responsibility of public administration fundamentally asserts that public administrators are "bound by an obligation to the public of that jurisdiction" (Cooper, 1982, p. 35). The recent crystalization of interconnectedness and the existence of generational interdependence now suggest that public administrators have a fiduciary obligation to the future inhabitants of their jurisdiction as well as to their current citizenry. Jonas (1984) provides two general parameters for such a new ethics of responsibility: (1) ensuring that humankind exists in the future and (2) a duty toward the condition, the quality of life of future generations.

Two more specific principles can be identified for the new frontier of policy ethics: stewardship and intergenerational equity.

Stewardship. There currently exists a fundamental commitment to protect and enhance the public's resources through good management; this ethics of "stewardship" is a major part of our current moral thought and public administration tradition. The obligation of stewardship emerges from the ancient and continuing Jewish and Christian traditions and is often considered an obligation in public administration. On one hand, some argue that the notion of stewardship involves the belief that one person, or one species, dominates over some property. Environmentally, this conception of stewardship assumes that earth is "man's dominion." On the other hand, Black (1970) disputes this interpretation and suggests that stewardship is the responsible exercise of a specific trust, not despotism. Stewards are essentially managers who are trustees or guardians acting on behalf of owners. This fits well with the current definition of fiduciary relationships: an administrator or agency acts on behalf of a citizen, or citizens, because they lack the time, expertise, or capacity to undertake the action themselves.

Intergenerational Equity. Temporal interconnectedness— generational interdependence—requires that some obligation exists to future generations as well as to the present generation. In an interconnected and technological world, it is increasingly in the power of those living today to seriously affect the instrumental interests and quality of life of those who will exist in the future. As a result, we must consider intergenerational ethics in the policy choices we make today. Three different examples help illuminate.

One emerging issue revolving around intergenerational equity is aging policy (Neugarten and Neugarten, 1989). One perspective contends that in our aging society, we are being unfair to younger generations because we are allocating disproportionate resources and advantages for older people. From this vantage point, the elderly are receiving more than their fair share of social welfare expenditures to the detriment of children and are placing an intolerable burden on future generations (Longman, 1987). This policy inequity, or preception of inequity, produces intergenerational conflict over the division of scarce public and private resources (Kingson, Hirshorn, and Corman, 1986). One outcome of this debate is the realization that generational interdependence requires a longer-term view toward the distribution of the costs and benefits of public policies for children and the elderly.

Another more dramatic example is the production, transportation, and storage of toxic and hazardous wastes. The production of hazardous waste creates significant issues of intergenerational equity. Hazardous wastes—from biological hospital waste and untreated industrial waste to cancer-causing compounds containing deadly lead and mercury—pose both immediate threats and health risks to future generations. The waste problem is not a slight one; nuclear waste disposal, in particular, poses the most poignant intergenerational threat. Each nuclear reactor produces an average of annual waste containing one thousand times the radioactivity of the Hiroshima bomb (Roberts, 1976). Safe storage periods vary from one thousand years (for fission products) to one-half million years for plutonium by-products (Weinberg, 1972). Is it ethical, for reasons of intergenerational inequity, to produce nuclear waste around the globe that will be radioactive over thousands of years when there is no known way to safely package and store it? With nuclear waste, it would appear that we have obligations to at least thirty thousand future generations (Routley and Routley, 1978).

A third, more economically driven issue is the provision of government tax incentives to attract industrial firms. State and local governments responded to the economic shifts of the 1980s by offering tax deductions and subsidies to attract firms to generate new jobs. Enterprise zones and tax increment finance districts are the two most popular, in addition to the individually negotiated tax package for a "prospect" (Luke, Ventriss, Reed, and Reed, 1988).

Although having immediate impacts, long-term consequences are often ignored, in particular the fiscal impacts that directly reduce future revenue-generation capacity. Research shows that such tax breaks reduce the fiscal capacity and tax revenue of a government jurisdiction over a period of twenty to thirty years. This deprives future generations of generating sufficient revenues to provide essential public services. As infrastructure and education become more important and increasingly more difficult to finance, these long-term fiscal drains can create serious intergenerational inequities and emerge as an important ethical policy concern.

Conclusion

The crystalization of interconnectedness has created a context where public administrators and policy leaders must look outward more and inward less (Luke, 1991). This suggests a new frontier for governmental ethics, a shift from behavioral ethics to policy ethics (see Table 1).

Table 1. From Behavioral to Policy Ethics.

Behavioral Ethics ⟶	*Policy Ethics*
Personal conduct and individual behavior	Agency outcomes and collective behavior
Standards of behavior, codes of conduct	Impacts of policies and programs
Web of administrative and political complexity	Web of environmental interdependencies and interconnectedness
Tension between self-interest and local public interest	Tension between multiple definitions of public interest (crossing geographical boundaries and generations)
Restrictive measures, forcing administrators to pay attention to appearance of personal conduct	Restrictive measures and expansive thinking to embody considerable constraints for interests of contemporary and future people
Educating public administrators to make personal choices in honest, ethical, and accountable ways in public interest	Educating public leaders to make policy choices that consider expanding ripple effects and longer-term consequences of policy and programmatic outcomes

Policy ethics involves an ethics of foresight and responsibility as well as increased awareness of geographical, functional, and temporal interdependence. Before policy leaders can act responsibly, however, they must acknowledge and recognize a larger set of responsibilities now required in today's interconnected context. We must be more conscious and constrained in making policy choices, whether concerning the federal budget deficit, cleanup and storage of toxic waste, or the provision of tax breaks to relocating industries. Specific ethical parameters, such as stewardship and intergenerational equity, can guide our activities toward human well-being, not just in the immediate future for ourselves but also in the interest of future generations.

The Administrator's Task. Appointed public managers and executives must take the lead role in considering policy ethics, taking into account the interests of future people, extending and broadening the range of ethical obligations beyond those conventionally acknowledged. Elected public leaders too often have short time frames (for example, their terms of office). Current political interest and media attention on conflicts of interest and other behavioral ethics are too narrowly focused for public executives who characteristically deal with longer time horizons. Ethical responsibility in the public sector grows with foresight.

For public executives this suggests a second, unique role in ethics. Barnard ([1936] 1968) noted that in addition to the normal responsibilities inherent in behavioral ethics, executives have a responsibility for establishing moral codes for those whom they supervise and manage. The executive's responsibility for setting an ethical example is unique to her or his higher level of authority. Policy ethics is a second area that further distinguishes the executive's moral responsibility from the behavioral ethical obligations of middle- or lower-level managers.

This suggests a fundamental expansion of the role of the public executive in the American democratic polity. Not only is expanded responsibility required with the executive's commensurate broader time horizon, but also the administrator's traditional "ethics of neutrality" (Rohr, 1990) must be transformed to an "ethics of responsibility." This suggests a much broader interpretation of the public administrator's duty or obligation.

Decision Criteria. Shifting from behavioral ethics is no easy task. Making ethical policy choices can be difficult in an interconnected web because information may be inadequate and understanding of causes and effects is limited. However, this uncertainty, unpredictability, and impossibility of long-term calculation do not eliminate or reduce the public executive's responsibilities, nor do they imply that the distant future should "take care of itself." Public administrators and executives have a responsibility to assess the probability (not necessarily the certainty) of policy choices causing harm or damage (Jonas, 1984).

Three decision-making criteria can be suggested to guide the executive's policy calculations: irreversibility, aggregate magnitude, and sustainability. First, are the potential outcomes or impacts *irreversible?* As new information is revealed in the future, can any damaging or forceful effects be effectively reversed? Second, how large is the *aggregate magnitude* or impact of the policy action? The larger the impact, the more deliberate the policy discussion should be. Third, does the policy choice lead to *sustainability?* Does the policy satisfy current resource and economic needs without diminishing equivalent opportunities for future generations?

Educational Tasks. Lastly, ethics education and the broadening of vision both have a key role to play. However, education for policy ethics is different than that provided for behavioral ethics. As Derek Bok noted, "The study of literature can awaken one's conscience by making more vivid the predicament of others. Traditional courses in ethics can provide a philosophical foundation for thinking precisely about moral issues. Studying the social sciences can help students *to understand the causes and effects of various policies and practices* and thus appreciate their moral significance more precisely" (emphasis added, 1988, p. 4).

Ethical education alone will not suffice for policy leaders in today's interconnected world. First, we need to rekindle an innate sense, now forgotten by many, of the interconnectedness of each other's well-being. Adam Smith (1975, p. 195) argued over two hundred years ago in *The Theory of Moral Sentiments* that "[man] is sensible that his own interest is connected with the prosperity of society, and that the happiness, perhaps the preservation of his existence, depends upon its preservation." This same notion emerged with de Tocqueville ([1835, 1840] 1945) when he suggested the expanded concept of "self-interest well understood." Native American beliefs amplify this point (see especially Booth and Jacobs, 1990). Chief Seattle stated to the U.S. Congress, in 1854, "This we know: the earth does not belong to us; we belong to the earth. All things are connected like blood which unites one family. Whatever befalls the earth befalls the children of the earth. Humanity did not weave the web of life; we are merely strands in it. Whatever we do to the web we do to ourselves."

Second, our vision needs to be broadened to include an ethical perspective that goes beyond the immediate and captures time horizons of ten to fifty years, and even longer, into the future. Public administrators need to expand their perspective, to perceive themselves (and their generation) as part of an ongoing historical process. This requires a different type of education, one that prods us to observe long-term, large-scale changes in the physical, social, and political environments—developing the capacity to detect threats and opportunities that materialize not just daily or yearly but over decades. These two new elements in ethical education—rekindling the sense of interconnectedness and developing a longer time horizon—can help policy leaders and public executives live an ethically active life. As Hartman (1932, p. 311) suggests, "All ethically active life is prospective, a living in the future and for the future."

References

Attfield, R. *The Ethics of Environmental Concern.* New York: Columbia University Press, 1983.

Barnard, C. *Functions of an Executive.* Cambridge, Mass.: Harvard University Press, 1968. (Originally published 1936.)

Bennis, W. "The Artform of Leadership." In S. Srivastva and Associates, *The Executive Mind: The Search for High Human Values in Organizational Life.* San Francisco: Jossey-Bass, 1983.

Black, J. *Man's Dominion.* Edinburgh, Scotland: Edinburgh University Press, 1970.

Blackstone, W. "The Search for an Environmental Ethic." In T. Regan (ed.), *Matters of Life and Death.* Philadelphia: Temple University Press, 1980.

Bok, D. "Ethics, the University, and Society." *Harvard Magazine,* May/June 1988, pp. 2–4.

Booth, A., and Jacobs, H. "Ties That Bind: Native American Beliefs as a Foundation for Environmental Consciousness." *Environmental Ethics,* Spring 1990, *12,* 27–44.

Burke, J. "Reconciling Public Administration and Democracy: The Role of the Responsible Administrator." *Public Administration Review,* Mar./Apr. 1989, *49* (2), 180–185.

Callicott, B. *In Defense of the Land Ethic.* Albany, N.Y.: State University of New York Press, 1989.

Cochran, N. "Society as Emergent and More than Rational." *Policy Sciences,* 1980, *12* (2), 453–467.

Cooper, T. L. *The Responsible Administrator.* Port Washington, N.Y.: Kennikat Press, 1982.

Council of State Policy and Planning Agencies. *Global Interdependence and American States.* Working paper for the annual CSPA conference, 1989.

Denhardt, K. "The Management of Ideals: A Political Perspective on Ethics." *Public Administration Review,* Mar./Apr. 1989, *49,* 187–192.

Gardner, J. *The Nature of Leadership.* Washington, D.C.: Independent Sector, 1986.

Hartman, N. "Love of the Remote." *Ethics,* 1932, *2,* 311–331.

Jaques, E. *A General Theory of Bureaucracy.* New York: Holstead Press, 1976.

Jaques, E. *Requisite Organization.* Arlington, Va.: Cason Hall, 1989.

Jonas, H. *The Imperative of Responsibility.* Chicago: University of Chicago Press, 1984.

Keohane, R., and Nye, J. S. *Power and Interdependence.* Boston: Little, Brown, 1977.

Kingson, E. R., Hirshorn, B. A., and Corman, J. M. *Ties That Bind.*

The Interdependence of Generations. Washington, D.C.: Gerontological Society of America, 1986.

Leopold, A. *A Sand County Almanac and Sketches Here and There.* New York: Oxford University Press, 1949.

Longman, P. *Born to Pay: The New Politics of Aging in America.* Boston: Houghton Mifflin, 1987.

Luke, J. "Managing Interconnectedness: The Need for Catalytic Leadership." *Futures Research Quarterly,* 1986, *2* (4), 73–83.

Luke, J. "Managing Interconnectedness: The Challenge for Public Administration in the Twenty-First Century." In M. T. Bailey and R. Mayer (eds.), *Public Administration in an Interconnected World.* Westport, Conn.: Greenwood Press, 1991.

Luke, J., and Caiden, G. "Coping with Global Interdependence." In J. L. Perry (ed.), *Handbook of Public Administration.* San Francisco: Jossey-Bass, 1989.

Luke, J., Ventriss, C., Reed, B. J., and Reed, C. M., *Managing Economic Development: A Guide to State and Local Leadership Strategies.* San Francisco: Jossey-Bass, 1988.

Meine, C. "A Review of Potter's *Global Bioethics.*" *Environmental Ethics,* Fall 1989, *11,* 281–295.

Mosher, F. C. "The Changing Responsibilities and Tactics of the Federal Government." *Public Administration Review,* 1980, *40* (6), 546.

Neugarten, B., and Neugarten, D. "Policy Issues in an Aging Society." In M. Storandt and G. R. VandenBos (eds.), *The Adult Years: Continuity and Change.* Washington, D.C.: American Psychological Association, 1989.

Neustadt, R., and May, E. *Thinking in Time: The Uses of History for Decision Makers.* New York: Free Press, 1986.

Partridge, E. *Responsibilities to Future Generations.* Buffalo, N.Y.: Prometheus Books, 1981.

Passmore, J. *Man's Responsibility for Nature.* London: Duckworth, 1974.

Potter, V. R. *Bioethics: Bridge to the Future.* Englewood Cliffs, N.J.: Prentice-Hall, 1971.

Potter, V. R. *Global Bioethics: Building on the Leopold Legacy.* East Lansing: Michigan State University Press, 1988.

Regan, T. "The Nature and Possibility of Environmental Ethic." *Environmental Ethics*, 1981, *3*, 16–31.

Roberts, A. "The Politics of Nuclear Power." *Arena*, 1976, *12* (41), 24–25.

Rohr, J. "Ethics in Public Administration: A State of the Discipline Report." In N. B. Lynn and A. Wildavsky (eds.), *Public Administration: The State of the Discipline*. Chatham, N.J.: Chatham House, 1990.

Rolston, H. *Environmental Ethics*. Philadelphia: Temple University Press, 1988.

Rosenau, J. *The Study of Global Interdependence*. New York: Nichols, 1980.

Routley, R., and Routley, V. "Nuclear Energy and Obligations to the Future." *Inquiry*, 1978, *21*, 133–179.

Ruckleshaus, W. "Toward a Sustainable World." *Scientific American*, Sept. 1989, pp. 166–174.

Scott, A. *The Dynamics of Interdependence*. Chapel Hill: University of North Carolina Press, 1982.

Simon, H. A. *Reason in Human Affairs*. Stanford, Calif.: Stanford University Press, 1983.

Smith, A. *Theory of Moral Sentiments*. Oxford, England: Clarendon Press, 1975.

Speth, J. "Turning Point for the Earth." *G.A.O. Journal*, Summer 1989, pp. 23–29.

State of Oregon. *Possible Impacts on Oregon from Global Warming*. Salem, Oreg.: Department of Energy, 1990.

Stone, C. "Efficiency Versus Social Learning." *Policy Studies Review*, 1985, *4* (4), 484–496.

Stuhr, J. "Bioethical Issues in Oregon Public Policy." In L. McCann (ed.), *Oregon Policy Choices: 1989*. Eugene, Oreg.: Bureau of Governmental Research and Service, 1989.

Tocqueville, A. de. *Democracy in America* (2 vols.). New York: Vintage Books, 1945 (originally published 1835, 1840).

Tong, R. *Ethics in Policy Analysis*. Englewood Cliffs, N.J.: Prentice-Hall, 1986.

Ventriss, C., and Luke, J. "Organizational Learning and Public

Policy: Towards a Substantive Perspective." *American Review of Public Administration*, Dec. 1988, *18* (4), 337–357.
Weinberg, A. M. "Social Institutions and Nuclear Energy." *Science*, July 1972, *177*, 32.

PART THREE

Developing New Strategies

for Promoting

Organizational and Individual Ethics

8   Using High Reliability Management

to Promote Ethical Decision Making

Mary E. Guy

The interface between personal and organizational values is a frontier that has yet to be effectively bridged. High reliability management—a managerial approach that simultaneously emphasizes strong organizational norms, reliance on individual judgment, and personal accountability for the welfare of the whole—provides a perspective from which to approach this frontier. It bridges personal ethics with organizational ethics by encouraging employees to internalize a sense of personal responsibility that motivates them to be sensitive to the ethical implications of both the short-term and long-term effects of their actions.

This reliance on individual responsibility is reminiscent of the rugged individualism that characterized American pioneers. But with the 1990s comes a new twist to American individualism: the organizational context in which individual judgment must be practiced involves decision making amidst a web of complexity. Work environments require interdependent tasks to be performed by a diverse work force functioning in ad hoc teams and matrixes. While managers are the catalysts who set the decisional stage so that employees approach problems with common frames of reference, individuals still make their own decisions.

The American character is epitomized by a constellation of attributes that include a perceived right to be informed of all that is happening, an acceptance of systems that reward individual merit, and an approach to problem solving that is more pragmatic than ideological (Brogan, 1956). Because of this, reliance on individual judgment rather than on externally imposed rules of conduct more effectively yields ethical decisions in the unpredictable situations that arise in the workplace.

However, even in the midst of nurturing reliance on individual judgment, administrators must retain a necessary level of management control. For this reason, the approach requires setting "ethical beacons" to serve as guideposts, lighting the path for people to follow as they encounter problems and seek solutions. To be meaningful for the organization as a whole, as well as for individual employees, ethical beacons must reflect both the predominant values that contribute to achieving the mission of the organization and the highest values that individuals bring with them onto the job.

This chapter treats the interface of individual and organizational values as an ethical frontier. It explores decision-making habits and the trade-offs in values that individuals must make on the job. It then explains how strong organizational norms emphasizing ethics can promote both important organizational and individual values.

The Individual-Organizational Interface
as an Ethical Frontier

Ethics is not a weighty subject restricted to the province of high-minded philosophical debate. Ethics is an everyday application of a standard of relating to others. Yet incorporating ethical sensitivity into daily work life remains a challenge. This was demonstrated in the responses to a recent survey of 441 public administrators (Bowman, 1990). Almost two-thirds of the respondents believed that most organizations have no consistent approach for addressing ethical concerns. Furthermore, only 7 percent believed that most organizations have a problem-solving approach that focuses on encouraging ethical behavior and deterring unethical behavior.

These survey results occurred in spite of glaring media coverage that had exposed the ethical trespasses of the 1980s. By the close of a decade that had witnessed an egregious disregard for ethics at the highest levels of government and on the part of both elected and career officials, the Speaker of the U.S. House of Representatives, Jim Wright, had been forced to step down admist charges of ethics violations; the U.S. Department of Housing and Urban Development scandals had bilked taxpayers out of millions of dollars; Pentagon procurement practices relied on all-too-cozy relationships between procurement officials and vendors; Governor Meacham of Arizona was impeached after exhibiting a strident disregard for the rights of minorities and the rule of law; and estimated costs of the savings and loan bailout approached $500 billion. Even as the telling spotlights dimmed, survey respondents concluded that their own agencies had yet to install meaningful preventive measures to forestall further ethical transgressions.

When organizational norms do not encourage and reward ethics, individuals tend not to be as sensitive to the morality of their actions as they would otherwise be. Evidence suggests that individuals will rise to meet high ethical standards when they believe they will be held personally accountable. For example, individuals who are held responsible for the quality of a decision-making task, either individually or as a group, exert more effort than those who participate anonymously and do not expect to be held accountable (Ben-Yoav and Pruitt, 1984; Price, 1987; Weldon and Gargano, 1985). Hagafors and Brehmer (1983) found that having to justify one's judgments to others leads to higher consistency in the rationale used to explain the judgment. There is even evidence that group decision making, when members are called on to justify their reasoning, results in those with higher levels of moral judgment being able to persuade those who rely on lower levels of moral judgment to rise to the occasion and espouse a more ethical solution (Nichols and Day, 1982).

Ethical Satisficing. When personal or organizational values clash, ethical satisficing results. The end product of ethical satisficing is a compromise that will permit satisfaction of ethical parameters at a minimally acceptable level. In this way the decision maker minimizes some values to maximize others. In its purest sense, ethical decision making is the process of defining a problem, generating alternatives, and choosing among them so that the alternative selected maximizes the most important ethical values while also achieving the intended goal. In satisficing, some values are inevitably compromised for others to be maximized. Although this does not necessarily result in an unethical decision, it produces decisions that are only as good as the circumstances permit.

In the classic essay "The Proverbs of Administration," Herbert Simon ([1946] 1987) argued that unidimensional principles of administration behave like proverbs, with each principle being opposed by a contrary but equally true principle. In fact, ethical values behave similarly to mutually exclusive administrative principles because maximizing one often requires minimizing another. For example, while health and human services agencies may want to emphasize caring and timely service, to do so may require sacrificing accountability and fairness. Or, in terms of personnel actions, an emphasis on objectivity and uniform procedures maximizes accountability at the expense of caring about an individual's unique circumstances.

When called on to make complex ethical decisions on the job, employees are likely to be faced with a no-win situation: two or more values are affected by the decision; a comparison between the values is inevitable, such that a greater return to one can be obtained only at a loss to the other; and anticipated consequences can be predicted in terms of only probabilities rather than certainties. To make matters worse, the power to make the decision will be dispersed between multiple people and departments. The situation is further complicated by the fact that the choice cannot be made directly between values. It must derive from among alternatives that differ in the extent to which each embodies particular values or in the emphasis some values receive in relation to others. The choice of how to distribute an annual bonus to a work team provides such an example. Four possible alternatives are

1.   to each person an equal share
2.   to each person according to individual effort
3.   to each person according to individual need
4.   to each person according to usefulness of his or her contribution.

Adopting one rule of distribution over another results in maximizing different values. The first maximizes accountability, in that it is easy to justify the distribution plan, and assumes parity on the part of everyone in the unit. But it does so at the expense of caring about individual contributions and distinguishing between excellence and mediocrity. The second maximizes caring for each person's intensity of effort and respect for each participant. But it does so at the expense of rewarding excellence, since nonproductive employees may devote hours to a task without making a substantive contribution to it. The third maximizes loyalty to individual employees in an appreciation of their unique circumstances but minimizes fairness to others and pursuit of excellence. It rewards people in proportion to what they need rather than what they contribute to the effort. The fourth maximizes the pursuit of excellence while minimizing a respect for everyone's individual skills and abilities. While each of these alternatives is designed to achieve distributive justice, each results in different forms of distribution and sends different messages about what values are most important and which work characteristics are rewarded.

Having to select one of the four rules illustrates the importance of beacons. Plausible explanations can be made to justify selecting any of the four alternatives. But each selection sends a very different message around the organization in regard to what work characteristics will be rewarded. It is important for beacons to be present in the organization's culture to help define the problem, steer the debate, and guide the selection of alternatives so that the final choice sends a message consistent with expectations for personal performance, the overall mission, and the objectives for achieving it.

Effective beacons become heuristics for employees to use. When presented the opportunity, people will rely on an easy-to-understand decision rule rather than reevaluate a situation and search for nuances not immediately noticeable (Arrow and Raynaud, 1986; Simon, 1976). Heuristics, meaning "rules of thumb," are a convenient and quick means for reducing the number of alternatives that must be evaluated. In fact, as the number of alternatives increases, so does the likelihood that heuristics will be invoked (Payne, Braunstein, and Carroll, 1978; Taylor, 1975).

Ethical satisficing preempts the single-minded pursuit of either deontological or utilitarian ethics by blending the promotion of both means and ends. Constructive satisficing cannot be prescribed in a code of ethics or institutionalized in a policy manual, and its results are only as good as the sensitivities and intentions of those making the decisions. The responsibility for making the "right" decision rests on individual judgment. As Terry Cooper (1986) has convincingly argued, the best safeguard against corruption and subversion of democratic government is a commitment to responsible conduct on the part of those working in the public service. Likewise, Kathryn Denhardt (1988) emphasizes that institutional controls in the form of rules, rigid procedures, and close supervision cannot serve as a substitute for individual judgment. Donald Warwick (1981) warns that the most essential courage in the public service is the courage to decide. In the words of Herbert Simon, reason is instrumental: it cannot tell us where to go; at best it can only tell us how to get there. "It is a gun for hire that can be employed in the service of whatever goals we have, good or bad" (Simon, 1983, pp. 7-8). Therefore, it is incumbent on the organization to emphasize which values are most important and to rely on the individuals in the organization to maximize them without unduly minimizing other positive values.

In summary, choices must be made amidst a complex array of pressures and alternatives, and people must come to the best decision they can, given the constraints of the situation. The generation and selection of alternatives are embedded in a complex of other claims on the attention of those making the decision. Decision makers must balance competing demands from superiors, peers, and subordinates while simultaneously pursuing organizational goals. These circumstances comprise "ethical moderators" because they complicate and temper the quality of ethical decision making. High reliability management is a strategy that gets to the heart of this reality. It is a philosophical framework that emphasizes strong organizational norms, reliance on individual judgment, and personal accountability for the welfare of the whole. Because of this combination of emphases, it has the capacity to instill values that simultaneously promote individual responsibility, efficient production, and a humane work environment into the deep structure of the organization.

High Reliability Management as an Ethical Framework

The interface of individual and organizational ethics represents a frontier where employees' personal values and the organization's values must meld rather than conflict with one another. It is at this frontier that the organization can reward individuals who assert their sense of personal responsibility for seeing that the organization's actions are ethical. In an earlier paper, the term *high reliability management* was coined to refer to a managerial perspective for effectively promoting guiding principles that generate high productivity and consistent ethical actions (Guy, 1990). Its emphasis on ethics is as important as its emphasis on productivity. Since decision making exists in a context of trade-offs, it is imperative that norms guide trade-offs by promoting dominant values. It is the predictability of decision makers' frames of reference that lends high reliability to the actions of an organization.

To achieve high reliability, the organization typically has structural interdependence among its units such that the organization is tightly coupled, redundancy is built into critical aspects of the operational procedures, information channels are open, and feedback is swift. Decision rules are known, and employees adhere to them. Authority is nested throughout the organization so that, even though there is clear centralization of command, there is simultaneous decentralization of decision making down to the lowest possible level. The culture of the organization is strong and promotes adherence to group norms. New members are expected to adopt attitudes that legitimate self-sacrificing behavior and promote a sense of personal responsibility for the welfare of the entire work group. Rather than promoting the value of individual achievement, the organization must reward the value of group achievement in such a way that each individual is rewarded for contributing to the unit's overall success. Workers become heroes when everyone in the unit benefits from their action rather than when the individual succeeds in an effort unrelated to the success of the group as a whole.

Emphasizing values can help managers create norms that provide beacons for guiding workers' actions. This is the argument that Peters and Waterman (1982) made about the characteristics of companies that excel, and it is equally true for public agencies. John DiIulio (1989) points out that well-managed schools, prisons, and armies all have two characteristics in common: the cohesiveness of the personnel and the quality and dynamism of their managers. He has studied successful schools, prisons, and armies and finds a common thread: the managers "stand for something." That is, they symbolize a set of values that promote productivity, and they make decisions that reinforce predominant, positive values.

Unless new employees are effectively socialized to the organization, the increasing diversity of the work force threatens high reliability because employees bring divergent frames of reference to the job. The diversity breaks up the entrenched routines established by long-standing networks. An important reason that "old-boy" and "old-girl" networks remain entrenched in communities and large organizations is that all networks have something in common: they define a common set of characteristics about its members. Members went to the same schools; belong to the same clubs, fraternities, or sororities; live in the same neighborhoods; send their children to the same schools; or vacation in similar places. In sum, their past associations form common perspectives. When backgrounds and private lives differ, then people approach issues from different perspectives.

It is necessary to build a common ground that blends employees' values with the organization's values. Otherwise the search for consensus is beset by a mine field of varing perceptions and perspectives. When employees come to the workplace from diverse backgrounds, repeated training sessions are essential for introducing new employees to the organization and for reminding current employees of the organization's goals, objectives, and values. These sessions orient the learner to what the organization "stands for." Both formal and informal training provides a vehicle for developing a well-defined culture with predominant values. The end result is that values are manifested in the way people interact with one another, how the work gets done, and the way the public perceives the agency.

Developing the frontier between the individual and the organization never ends. New employees arrive on the job with their own system of values and priorities that may or may not coincide with those of the organization. Over time, a sort of melding takes place in which employees adopt those values of the organization that are compatible with their own and vice versa (Guy, 1984; Ott, 1989). While an organization's values will appear to predominate, individuals whittle and shape them in the course of their actions to fit their own needs. Thus, to a great extent, individual and organizational values are parallel and coincident with one another, not superior or subordinate.

Ethical Core. A general consensus has developed around ten core values that serve as the foundation for customary moral codes and are central to relations between people (Barry, 1979; Beauchamp and Bowie, 1979; Josephson, 1988; Solomon and Hanson, 1985). These values have withstood the test of time and provide the moral premise for Plato's sense of the the ultimate Good, Kant's categorical imperative, Rawls's principles of distributive justice, and the Judeo-Christian principles embodied in the Golden Rule. They may be remembered by the acronym CHAPELFIRZ: *c*aring, *h*onesty, *a*ccountability, *p*romise keeping, pursuit of *e*xcellence, *l*oyalty, *f*airness, *i*ntegrity, *r*espect for others, and responsible citizenship. Although the ten core values overlap to some degree, they provide a means for sensitizing employees to the ethical implications of proposed actions.

The ten values in CHAPELFIRZ are in the deep structure of American culture. (*Deep structure* is a term coined by Stanley Deetz and Astrid Kersten [1983] to denote the unexamined, unquestioned values of a culture.) When John Rohr (1989) argues that career civil servants should base their ethical behavior on the regime values of equality, property, and freedom, his argument is premised on the deep structure of American society. Serving as the substrate for regime values is the profound acceptance of integrity and respect for others (to afford everyone the right to own property and remain free and equal) and responsible citizenship (to obey the laws of the land).

Each organization must establish its beacons and teach newcomers the importance of maximizing them when choices are presented. Beacons reflect those values in CHAPELFIRZ that the organization wants to predominate and guide decisions at all levels. For these to be transmitted to employees, clientele, enabling bodies, and any other constituent group, they must be seated in the culture of the organization. They are communicated and reinforced through training and, more pervasively, through the habits, traditions, slogans, actions, and customs of the organization.

This strategy does not suggest that managers should try to construct a rigid set of behavioral guidelines and decision rules that anticipate every eventuality. Not only is this not humanly possible; it is also unnecessary and insulting to the work force. Once employees identify with the agency and what it stands for, managerial efforts are better spent equipping employees with a common set of values and priorities on which they, as competent individuals, are empowered to make their own decisions. However, it is up to managers to send clear messages about what values are most important and what trade-offs among important values are justified. In other words, it is up to managers to foster the deep structure on which the culture of the organization will function.

The entire process is fragile, with one instance of an employee experiencing retribution for engaging in courageous ethical conduct obliterating ten instances of rewards. This is why managers must symbolize important values by their actions. People become convinced of what the most important values are by watching the actions of others. Once convinced, they are equipped to solve problems as they arise, in the context in which they occur, in a solution that promotes the values they have seen rewarded.

Agencies that serve multiple political jurisdictions, such as water boards, personnel offices, mass transit systems, regulatory bodies, and taxing agencies, must develop broad-spectrum beacons that provide guidance in a flexible framework. In addition to the internal demands and expectations that affect all organizations and the constraints spelled out in enabling legislation, they must also be responsive to the pushes and pulls placed on them by the jurisdictions they serve. To this end, the norms they develop must allow them to function with high reliability internally as well as externally as they relate to the multiple, and often conflicting, demands and expectations.

High reliability management, regardless of the setting, emphasizes individual responsibility and delegation of authority to the lowest level possible. Steps toward implementing high reliability management include maximizing values in the consciousness of all employees, creating redundancy so that, as much as possible, all segments of the agency endorse similar values and adopt similar actions when confronted with similar situations, seating the important values in the deep structure of the organization, and empowering and rewarding individuals for practicing principled reasoning.

Case Study

An exploration of the following case shows how ambiguous beacons mislead employees, result in unethical behavior, and harm employees as well as the organization. This situation presents a dilemma frequently encountered by those who work in organizations where funding depends on meeting regulatory standards and data for judging compliance is documented by employees of the organization being evaluated. Such is the case for health care organizations whose livelihood depends on their meeting hundreds of standards that change periodically and for which compliance requires the cooperation of many different people working in different departments.

A nurse and a medical records librarian in the city's public hospital were terminated after admitting to falsifying data in a medical record and concealing records during an accreditation review. The falsification and concealment were discovered during an accreditation site visit that was being performed to determine whether the facility met the standards required of hospitals to make them eligible to receive reimbursement from third-party payers, including insurance companies, Medicaid, and Medicare. This review occurred periodically, and the hospital's financial survival depended on passing. The hospital had barely squeaked through the prior accreditation review and had been placed on probation pending the outcome of this review. All the employees knew that if it did not pass the upcoming review, it would have to close its doors.

When the survey team concluded that a nurse had intentionally falsified a notation in a medical record and the medical records librarian had concealed incomplete records from review, they immediately reported their findings to the hospital's chief executive officer. Fearing that the accreditation was in jeopardy unless he took an immediate corrective action that would send a positive signal to the survey team, the administrator denounced the two employees' actions, fired them, and explained to the surveyors that in no way was such an action ever condoned by the hospital.

The infractions had been discovered by the survey team when two things happened. First, when asked to produce some missing records, a clerical employee reported to the surveyors that the medical records librarian had asked her to remove some patient records from the files prior to the start of the review. Second, during the review, one surveyor had found a discrepancy in a patient's record, making it obvious that a notation had been entered after the fact in an attempt to conceal the fact that an important procedure had been omitted from a patient's treatment. The falsification of the record was in clear violation of acceptable procedures and had been done to make the case appear to be in compliance with accreditation standards.

In retrospect, the following facts were brought to light. Both of these individuals had held key positions at the hospital for a number of years. The nurse was popular among her peers and with the hospital administration and had previously won the Outstanding Employee of the Year Award. To win this award, she had been selected on the recommendation of the medical director, and the final selection had been made by the hospital administrator. The medical records librarian had only recently been promoted to her current position. Her previous position had been in the quality assurance office, which investigated unusual incidents, problems of incomplete patient records, and complaints filed by patients and their families. One of the reasons she had been promoted was that she had demonstrated that she was well aware of regulatory standards and was a strict taskmaster when it came to making sure that medical staff consistently met all required documentation guidelines.

To keep the federal inspectors from breathing down its neck when it had been placed on probation at the prior review, the hospital had set an ambitious goal, saying it would comply with governmental standards by the end of year one and exceed those standards in year two. One week prior to the survey, the hospital administrator had called a special meeting to emphasize how important it was that the hospital pass the review and be fully accredited. The ambitiousness of the goal and the importance of passing the accreditation review led to employees' reasoning that if their overzealous compliance helped the hospital, then the hospital would condone it and even protect them if their actions were revealed. However, their ambitions and hospital loyalty resulted ultimately in their dismissal. Headlines in the city newspaper reported the firings and planted a seed of doubt in the minds of the public about the quality of care that the hospital was providing.

As people throughout the hospital whispered with one another about the dismissals, one of the clerks in the medical records office was overheard to say, "Everybody alters a medical record sooner or later, and anyone who tells you they don't is a liar." Someone else said, "We don't doctor the records as much as other hospitals in this town, and they are always laughing at us for not cheating."

This is an all-too-common case of an organization, in this case a hospital, sending out mixed signals to employees. On one hand, employees knew they were to comply with regulatory standards; on the other, employees who were loyal to the hospital interpreted the eagerness of the hospital to pass accreditation as a message that they would be exonerated for violating standards if it would improve the chance of gaining a positive accreditation decision. The mixed message was intrepreted as a beacon that emphasized loyalty to the organization at the expense of honesty. The nurse and the medical records librarian exchanged honesty for expediency in order to make the hospital look good to outside reviewers. These were decisions that they made independently of anyone else. Judging from their prior work performance, they were valued employees who cared about the organization. They made judgments that in their minds maximized the most important value: loyalty to the hospital.

Had there been clear beacons of honesty, accountability, and pursuit of excellence, these two employees would never have found themselves fired from their jobs. Top hospital management, in their eagerness to pass accreditation, had let it be known that the hospital had to pass the inspection and that it was up to all employees to see that this happened. The beacons were not emphasizing that honesty and the intent of the standards also be maximized, Instead, they emphasized passing the accreditation survey by whatever means necessary and to adhere to the letter, but not necessarily the intent, of the accreditation regulations.

Even at its best, high reliability management will not deter all ethical abuses. But it can prevent those violations that result from misinterpretation and insensitivity to the long-range effects of one's actions. Table 2 and the discussion that follows illustrate two scenarios for the case and show which values are maximized, which are minimized, and which are ignored. The table helps to show how the beacons are different for the real case versus the ideal case. Of the ten values in CHAPELFIRZ, two are maximized in the actual case, and eight are maximized in the ideal situation.

In both the actual case and the ideal case, employees cared about the hospital and were loyal to it. In the actual case the employees exchanged honesty for their loyalty to the hospital. No specific promises had been made to any party, so promise keeping is not relevant in this case. The ideal case comes much closer to the pursuit of excellence in terms of a straightforward compliance with standards than does the situation where compliance is only superficial. Fairness did not serve as a beacon in either the real or the ideal case. The ideal case relied on integrity of employees to truthfully meet standards or admit their failure to comply. In the ideal case employees would have shown more respect for others by not falsi-

Table 2. Analysis of Values Maximized and Minimized.

Core Values	Actual Case	Ideal Case
Caring	Max	Max
Honesty	Min	Max
Accountability	Min	Max
Promise keeping	NA	NA
Pursuit of excellence	Min	Max
Loyalty	Max	Max
Fairness	NA	NA
Integrity	Min	Max
Respect for others	Min	Max
Responsible citizenship	Min	Max

fying records than in the real case, where surveyors were left to discover dishonesty. Whenever public funds are involved, responsible citizenship always enters the picture. Public funds are expended in Medicare and Medicaid programs, and thus employees of hospitals become stewards reponsible for meeting standards established to govern the expenditure of those funds.

This situation was played out in the crucible of organizational traditions, problem-solving style, time-sensitive pressures, and sensitivity to organizational beacons. Every hospital's mission statement boasts that its goal is to provide quality care. But employees will ferret out the meaning of "quality care" by watching for what behaviors are rewarded, ignored, and discouraged. In the ideal situation, hospitals not only want to pass accreditation inspection but also want to meet the intent of the standards. This is a different situation than when administrators want to pass accreditation but care only about meeting the letter of the standard, not the spirit.

The beacons that guide employee performance are quite different in these two instances. In the ideal case, the message is to be in compliance with all standards throughout the year. In the actual case, the message is to appear to be in compliance on the days the accreditation team visits the hospital. Beacons in the first scenario focus on honesty, accountability, pursuit of excellence, and integrity. Beacons in the second focus on loyalty to the hospital.

The differences in the beacons produce different behaviors on the part of personnel. In the first, employees will openly pursue avenues to meet standards. In the second, employees will determine what is necessary to meet the standards while the accreditors are present. Secrecy will prevail because it will be necessary to conceal the truth about actual procedures not in compliance with the standards. Individuals left to make decisions in the ideal scenario will be equipped to develop solutions that they can honestly justify. Individuals left to make decisions in the actual scenario will be forced to whitewash conditions that are out of compliance. The ultimate penalty for operating in the ambiguity of the second scenario is that trust among employees wanes. As soon as employees learn that there is not a one-to-one correspondence between management's actions and words, expediency will prevail, and employees are on their own in terms of determining whether to respond to actions or words.

The contribution of high reliability management is that it provides a framework for focusing on the most important values at all levels of the organization while minimizing the probability of misinterpretation. It clarifies the parameters in which exceptions are justified and sets the limits for what is and is not acceptable behavior. Its greatest strength is that it does so without having to define specific rules to cover specific infractions. When individuals are ultimately responsible for their actions, they must also be empowered to make decisions governing their actions.

Employees come to organizations wth their own value hierarchies, which are basic preferences about the relative importance of respective values. Since values shape the way problems are perceived and framed, they are crucial to the realization that something is a problem to be solved rather than a condition to be accepted. Given the different perspectives that personnel bring to any decision, how is it possible for an employer to inculcate a unique set of important values? The answer lies in using and unambiguously reinforcing clear beacons. Beacons are operationalized in easily understood principles found in organizational slogans, rituals, litanies, and policies that reward important values. The messages in such beacons must strike a balance between the needs of individuals and the needs of the agency. When beacons are absent, the pressures that surround decision makers make it difficult to produce quality decisions that consistently maximize desired values. Rarely will any party to problem solving be able to achieve all that is desired. But it is reasonable to expect a compromise that satisfices, or, in other words, is as good as can be, given the constraints of the situation. In this way, a balance is struck that maximizes the interests of all parties as much as possible in the constraints of acceptable action.

Conclusion

The ethical frontier represented at the interface of individual and organizational values represents a rich context in which ethical decision making must occur. It places an imperative on all employees to be sensitive to the ethical implications of their actions, in both the short term and long term, from a personal and an organizational viewpoint. To operationalize this ethical imperative, management must put its trust in each individual's capacity to seek the best solution to problems, respect employees' abilities to reach a satisfactory compromise when preferences conflict, and empower all individuals to exercise their personal judgment, regardless of their rank in the organization.

Self-awareness and being attentive to one's own motives are essential elements of ethical decision making. The many conflict-of-interest statutes around the country are examples of the attempt to legislate ethical decision making. But it is more effective for individuals to govern themselves and their own behavior than for imprecise laws to govern them. Harsh rules and investigative procedures may cause irreparable damage to agency morale and efficiency and still not instill the quality of decision making necessary to equip staff to independently evaluate conflicts and take appropriate action. In the end, no codes of conduct can foresee all the conflicts people will encounter. It is for this reason that the fundamental values in CHAPELFIRZ are important. Equipping staff with the sensitivity to recognize conflicts and assess them in terms of the values that are involved is the most enduring means for actively promoting ethical decisions and actions.

When an organization is successful at developing an internalized sense of personal responsibility for ethical decision making on the part of its employees, it benefits two ways. It satisfies employees' desire to have control over decisions that affect their work, while it also increases accountability for both individuals' and the organization's actions. High reliability management is created and maintained when the most important values of the organization are known to all and there is no hesitance to make decisions that maximize them. Although this is already the goal of most management teams, it is achieved too rarely. High reliability management relies upon a simultaneous emphasis on cultural norms, individual involvement, communication at all levels, and a strong consensus favoring bounded flexibility. Furthermore, it implies a realistic balance between satisfying the needs of the individual and the needs of the organization.

Directions for Future Research. From an ethics perspective, the goal of high reliability management is to produce a sensitivity to ethical values that manifests itself in ethical actions and high standards of conduct at all levels and positions in the organization. For this to happen, there must be a heightened sense of personal responsibility on the part of employees to be sensitive to the ethical implications of their actions and to engage in principled reasoning. This model invites research at both the individual and the organizational level to clarify the relationship between organizational norms, reliance on individual judgment, and perceived accountability for the welfare of the whole. More specifically, the following research questions offer paths for empirical inquiry:

1. How does an organization define its important values and shape them into beacons?
2. What training methods and communication channels serve as effective means for instilling beacons into decision processes?
3. What styles of orientation training are most effective for implementing this management approach?
4. Which values serve as the clearest beacons?
5. Which core values are most often maximized in an organization or its subunits?
6. How receptive are employees and managers to high reliability management?
7. Based on a longitudinal study, how do beacons change over time, both from the organizational perspective and from the individual perspective?
8. How do diverse work forces compare with homogeneous work forces in regard to the effectiveness of organizational beacons?
9. How are ethics abuses sanctioned in organizations with high reliability management?

These questions reach to the heart of the relationship between organizational behavior and human decision processes. To answer them is to advance the frontier that currently exists at the juncture of individual and organizational ethics.

References

Arrow, K. J., and Raynaud, H. *Social Choice and Multicriterion Decision-Making.* Cambridge, Mass.: MIT Press, 1986.

Barry, V. *Moral Issues in Business.* Belmont, Calif.: Wadsworth, 1979.

Beauchamp, T. L., and Bowie, N. E. (eds.). *Ethical Theory and Business.* Englewood Cliffs, N.J.: Prentice-Hall, 1979.

Ben-Yoav, O., and Pruitt, D. G. "Accountability to Constituents: A Two-Edged Sword." *Organizational Behavior and Human Performance,* 1984, *34,* 283–295.

Bowman, J. S. "Ethics in Government: A National Survey of Public Administrators." *Public Administration Review,* 1990, *50* (3), 345–353.

Brogan, D. W. *The American Character.* New York: Random House, 1956.

Cooper, T. L. *The Responsible Administrator: An Approach to Ethics for the Administrative Role.* (2nd ed.) Millwood, N.Y.: Associated Faculty Press, 1986.

Deetz, S. A., and Kersten, A. "Critical Models of Interpretative Research." In L. L. Putnam and M. E. Pacanowsky (eds.), *Communication and Organization: An Interpretive Approach.* Newbury Park, Calif.: Sage, 1983.

Denhardt, K. G. *The Ethics of Public Service: Resolving Moral Dilemmas in Public Organizations.* Westport, Conn.: Greenwood Press, 1988.

DiIulio, J. J., Jr. "Recovering the Public Management Variable: Lessons from Schools, Prisons, and Armies." *Public Administration Review,* 1989, *49* (2), 127–133.

Guy, M. E. "Passages Through the Organization: Old Dogs and New Tricks." *Group and Organizational Studies,* 1984, *9* (4), 467–479.

Guy, M. E. "High Reliability Management." *Public Productivity and Management Review,* 1990, *13* (4), 301–313.

Hagafors, R., and Brehmer, B. "Does Having to Justify One's Judgments Change the Nature of the Judgment Process?" *Organizational Behavior and Human Performance,* 1983, *31,* 223–232.

Josephson, M. "Teaching Ethical Decision Making and Principled Reasoning." *Ethics,* 1988, *1* (1), 27–33.

Nichols, M. L., and Day, V. E. "A Comparison of Moral Reasoning of Groups and Individuals on the 'Defining Issues Test.'" *Academy of Management Journal,* 1982, *25,* 201–208.

Ott, J. S. *The Organizational Culture Perspective.* Chicago: Dorsey Press, 1989.

Payne, J. W., Braunstein, M. L., and Carroll, J. S. "Exploring Predecisional Behavior: An Alternative Approach to Decision Research." *Organizational Behavior and Human Performance,* 1978, *22,* 17–44.

Peters, T. J., and Waterman, R. H., Jr. *In Search of Excellence.* New York: Harper & Row, 1982.

Price, K. H. "Decision Responsibility, Task Responsibility, Identifiability, and Social Loafing." *Organizational Behavior and Human Decision Processes,* 1987, *40,* 330–345.

Rohr, J. A. *Ethics for Bureaucrats: An Essay on Law and Values.* (2nd ed.) New York: Marcel Dekker, 1989.

Simon, H. A. *Administrative Behavior.* New York: Free Press, 1947.

Simon, H. A. *Reason in Human Affairs.* Stanford, Calif.: Stanford University Press, 1983.

Simon, H. A. "The Proverbs of Administration." *Public Administration Review,* 1946, *6,* 53–67. Reprinted in J. M. Shafritz and A. C. Hyde (eds.), *Classics of Public Administration.* Chicago: Dorsey Press, 1987.

Solomon, R. C., and Hanson, K. *It's Good Business.* New York: Atheneum, 1985.

Taylor, R. N. "Psychological Determinants of Bounded Rationality: Implications for Decision-Making Strategies." *Decision Sciences,* 1975, *6,* 409–427.

Warwick, D. P. "The Ethics of Administrative Discretion." In J. L. Fleishman, L. Liebman, and M. H. Moore (eds.), *Public Duties: The Moral Obligations of Government Officials.* Cambridge, Mass.: Harvard University Press, 1981.

Weldon, E., and Gargano, G. M. "Cognitive Effort in Additive Task Groups: The Effects of Shared Responsibility on the Quality of Multiattribute Judgments." *Organizational Behavior and Human Decision Processes,* 1985, *36,* 348–361.

9   Beyond Conventional
Management Practices:
Shifting Organizational Values

Gerald T. Gabris

If administrative ethics is to have any value for the public sector, it must have a deep and meaningful conceptual foundation. While this cornerstone may exist, it is often ensconced in aphorisms or short statements of principle. Vague generalizations such as that appointed administrators should be politically neutral, administrative professionalism connotes a higher-order public duty, or a professional administrator is one who follows the principles of efficiency are subject to varied interpretation and not exceptionally penetrating (Finer, 1941; Gulick and Urwick, 1945; Thompson, 1985). The central theme of this chapter does not challenge the desirability of administrative ethics but questions whether conventional management practices found in most public organizations make the possibility of a higher administrative ethics, especially in the context of current vernacular, rather meaningless and hypocritical.

Professional public administrators often downplay the fact that numerous public organizations are poorly run, employees stressed out, the level of managerial competence low, the degree of organizational stagnation high, and the cost of employing professional administrators substantial (Thayer, 1987). Even though many public organizations manifest a panoply of internal management problems and inefficiencies, public administrators do not want to take any blame, and few actually pursue aggressive problem-solving changes (Ingraham and Ban, 1984). When innovations are attempted and do not work well, public managers blame the system but rarely themselves. They refuse to admit that they often practice management according to Pogo: "I have seen the enemy, and he is us." Thus, mere advocacy of ethical principles is not enough. Many public managers experience difficulty following the administrative ethics they espouse because real-world constraints make the practice of substantive ethics an elusive, complicated, and in some instances dangerous activity.

This chapter investigates constraints and considers, in an admittedly speculative vein, whether the very way public managers administer organizations makes the concept of administrative ethics oxymoronic. Administrators do have ethics, but the type of ethics they practice is not consonant with what they advocate in a general overt sense. This chapter also considers whether public administrators practice an ethics of relativism. What works at a given time and simultaneously enhances self-survival and interest is ethical or at least not unethical. Acquisition of power is the primary survival strategy, even if this means others may be hurt: on the surface smile and tell people what they want to hear but do not trust anyone too much; if necessary, bend the rules but make sure they apply strictly to everyone else. If the above observations sound harsh, they are intendedly so. How organizations are actually managed is substantially different from what is taught in textbooks. This chapter will describe public management ethics and propose several options for pursuing administrative ethics on a higher plane. Before this is done, it will first consider the theory of the founder of modern administrative ethics, Niccolo Machiavelli.

The Primacy of Machiavellian Ethics

Machiavelli, the fifteenth-century Florentine administrator and author of *The Prince* and *Discourses* (1950), fundamentally challenged the ethical theories of the Greeks. Specifically, Machiavelli denies that human reason leads to high levels of virtue and governmental excellence. Speaking through Socrates in *The Republic*, Plato rejects Thrasymachus's contention that might makes right (Bloom, 1968). Machiavelli argues that Thrasymachus is correct. Indeed, one student of political theory avers that Machiavelli invented the concept of the modern executive and that this is a ferocious, power-driven untamed version (Mansfield, 1989). Harvey Mansfield (1989) asserts that Machiavelli clearly identifies the need for a power-driven executive capable of making quick, decisive, and efficient decisions, even if this means bending the normal rules. Executives are designed to handle crisis situations. The ambivalence of the modern executive concerns how to balance the aggrandizement of power by the executive, which is frequently undemocratic, with democratic values and institutions. The argument is made here that by and large we have not adequately contained the dysfunctional side of the Machiavellian executive. If anything, our public agencies exacerbate the negative effects of a Machiavellian perspective of management, while somewhat ironically posturing support for supposedly high ethical standards.

Machiavelli describes in *The Prince* how Agathocles of Syracuse rose from destitute poverty to become ruler of Syracuse (1950, p. 31). How was this accomplished? Agathocles triumphed through cunning, deceit, manipulation, and, ultimately, the murder of the elected senate. By these actions he did not gain glory or honor but did acquire power. In Machiavelli's worldview, power is the raw material for personal survival. His position attained, Agathocles maintained power and rulership for a lengthy period. What, then, are Machiavelli's rules of the game for the effective ruler-manager?

Machiavelli contends that persons who make professions of goodness will eventually come to grief among the many who do not. Therefore, prudence dictates that successful rulers must learn not to be good (Machiavelli, 1950, p. 56). Another rule is that it is better to be feared than loved, because fear is the more powerful force (Machiavelli, 1950, p. 60). This is especially important given the portrayal of ordinary people as greedy, voluble, insouciant, and disloyal. The effective ruler should appear pleasant and play the role yet under the surface practice ruthless manipulation. Ultimately, the ruler-manager must determine whether the ends justify the means (Machiavelli, 1950, p. 66). If one takes Machiavelli's prescriptions seriously, it is clear that few organizations can generate high trust, high openness, low risk, and high owning. Indeed, engaging in the truth can be dangerous. High ethics may be noble but may also set one up for potential extirpation. Most managers are expedient in the Machiavellian context. Above the waterline, they fixate on social norms and verbally support ethical principles but below the surface practice a more competitive, manipulative, and self-oriented style of management. This gauche rationality makes sense because many managers perceive other managers as behaving the same way (Golembiewski and Kiepper, 1988). It makes strategic sense to be Machiavellian when everyone else plays the same ballgame. This returns to the basic question posed by this chapter. Why do so many managers tolerate Machiavellian ethics, which by its very nature debases the plane of organizational excellence, almost certainly ensures suboptimal decision making, damages communications and interpersonal relations, and makes the organization look less efficient to the outside world?

Conventional Management Conditions and Practices

Hierarchy and Positional Power. Most public organizations place heavy emphasis on hierarchy, positional power, and functional specialization (Parsons, 1947). One office or position exerts imperative control over lower offices in the hierarchy. An assumption underlying the principle of hierarchy is that persons in higher positions are smarter, more rational, and more competent than those working under them. Moreover, persons who possess positional power often feel employees lower in the hierarchy are prone to laziness, ennui, and disinclined toward hard work (Taylor, 1911). To move ahead in many public organizations, subordinate managers are frequently obsequious toward supervisors yet autocratic toward their own subordinates (Presthus, 1978). They do this to please those they serve under while at the same time demonstrating power and control over employees reporting to them. Competitive and aggressive people seek positional power in complex organizations (Persthus, 1978, p. 151). They seek positions over others because supervisory positions serve as instrumental avenues to monetary rewards, control, status, and job security, all contributing to personal survival. Competitiveness and aggressiveness, rather than competence, often determine who secures executive power. Herbert Kaufman (1985, p. 49) suggests individuals with aggressive characteristics and strongly competitive predispositions often achieve disproportionate influence over decision-making roles even though they are not the most intellectually gifted persons working for the organization. Their modus operandi is to overwhelm those around them with energy, aggressive behavior, dramatism, persistence, and coercion.

The way public organizations are structured, upward mobility for most careerists resembles a win-lose proposition. Promotion of one person into a position of power often means someone else loses. Upward mobility pressures engrain Machiavellian behavior in the organizational culture. Employees expect managers to express aggressive, macho, competitive, and tough-minded behaviors. Managers are expected to "tell" other employees what to do and to assume greater job wisdom than those working under them. There are thus strong disincentives against admitting ignorance or any weaknesses in a given situation. Knowing they lack sufficient information, managers will often make unilateral decisions simply to conform to managerial role expectations. This means that many decisions are suboptimal and made in information vacuums. Managers make suboptimal decisions for fear of appearing weak. In short, they perceive a need for justifying their positions. If employees can work without managers, then perhaps managers are not functionally pertinent.

Vertical Differentiation. Another tendency convoluting public organizations and encouraging a Machiavellian ethics relates to vertical differentiation. Organizations can be conceived as layer cakes, with different layers representing distinct subcultures and varying worldviews. Perhaps the best description of this pattern is found in James D. Thompson's seminal work (1967).

Thompson suggests that organizations are simultaneously open and closed systems. At the acme of the organization, which he refers to as the institutional level, executives struggle over interfacing the organization with its environment. Executives are receptive to changes they perceive as enhancing organizational adaptation capacity. However, the success potential of these change mandates is frequently unknown, and for all practical situations they represent a form of organizational experimentation. Open system values prevail at this level. Middle managers are expected to carry out the mandates of senior executives and to motivate rank-and-file employees. They often are expected to secure the necessary resources for accomplishing organizational objectives, are more likely to perceive flaws and contradictions associated with top management policy reforms, and therefore exude a more cynical attitude concerning their beneficial impact.

The final category, rank-and-file workers, who are mainly responsible for producing actual organizational outputs, are more concerned with certainty, stability, routinization of tasks, job security, and maintenance of the status quo. They are primarily "closed-system" oriented. They tend to resist change and disruption and often view top management mandates as kneejerk reactions to environmental stimuli that are best ignored (Gabris and Giles, 1983). By implication, employees at different levels perceive their roles and functions quite differently. Senior executives often become frustrated and disappointed when employees exude indifference toward exciting reforms, technical innovations, and new policies. Employees wonder why senior executives try to fix everything that is not broken. Needless to say, these subcultures rarely agree on the value of change.

The fact that different layers of the organization perceive things so differently further exacerbates diminished trust, lack of openness, high risk, and low owning. Lower-level employees do not find higher-level managers credible but perceive them as manipulative, ambitious, and unwilling to follow through on promises or to model the behavior they expect of others (Kouzes and Posner, 1987, p. 21). These perceptions tend to highlight extremes and while based partly on fact are not usually entirely accurate. But tension between levels can mount. Executives handle this tension by relying on positional power and threatening disincentives for nonconformance. Such action reinforces the stereotype of higher-level supervisors as authoritarians, even though the latter often do not espouse such values. Employees perceive higher-level managers as not really practicing what they preach—and as behaving in contradictory styles (Argyris, 1973).

Intergroup Dynamics. Another common feature of conventional public organizations is competition between functional work units deriving from formal structure. In a municipality this is typically reflected through differentiating the organization into separate fire, police, public works, community development, and administration departments. While most organizations strive for interunit teamwork, group dynamics in functionally designed organizations can lead to several normal and predictable dysfunctions. How functional design may increase group conflict is highlighted below.

First, affiliation with formal work groups heightens a sense of membership pride. Employees tend to view their personal work unit as the most salient and derive status and value as organizational contributors from specific work units. While membership pride may sound quaint, it can precipitate invidious comparisons between groups, which breaks down interunit teamwork (Blake and Mouton, 1984). Second, groups develop stereotypes of each other and usually focus on the negatives. One's personal work group is viewed as morally correct, whereas the comparison group is perceived as cunning, sneaky, and untrustworthy. This can lead to winlose competition between departments. If a fire department purchases a new ladder truck one year, then a police department may not get new squad cars. It becomes difficult in this scenario to nurture trusting and team-oriented approaches to management. Most managers think they can solve these group-related problems through managerial prerogatives such as reorganization, replacement, rotation, and cooperation by edict. While these solutions may provide short-term remedies, they do not resolve underlying group norms and decision premises (Blake and Mouton, 1984, p. 11).

Culture and Socialization. Debra Stewart (1985) argues that behaving according to dominant role expectations does not excuse one from practicing administrative ethics. On the surface this argument seems plausible. Yet, when one considers the conforming forces, role expectations, values, socialization patterns, and groupthink pressures below the waterline, it becomes clear why behaving ethically in conventional organizations is so difficult and perhaps unrealistic.

Upon entering an organization one tacitly accepts the organization's culture. Culture is defined as the dominant norms, values, rewards, and power arrangements that influence behavior in the organization (Burke, 1982). It may not be a written rule that supervisors wear a coat and tie to work, yet failure to do so may lead to ostracism, ridicule, and covert criticism. Athough employees enter public organizations with value predispositions and role expectations, they immediately begin internalizing the cultural values of the organization. Expedience dictates that they practice such behavior if they wish to survive and flourish in their new environment. Once socialized, employees are under tremendous pressure to conform. In extreme situations, this can lead to groupthink, or the tendency to view the work unit as morally correct and not subject to questioning (Janis, 1972). Groupthink may be extreme, but individuals are expected to conform to the dominant culture. Can people make independent moral judgments given these power pressures to conform generally? The answer is both yes and no.

If ethical decisions are generally congruent with dominant organizational norms, there usually is no problem. For instance, Lee Smith may be having an affair with a subordinate, Nancy Rodriguez, which in their department is taboo. In this case, if the affair became publicly known, Lee Smith's supervisor would probably not experience difficulty taking corrective action. This would be the moral thing to do. If the organizational norm condones office trysts as normal, then a supervisor who finds office affairs ethically repugnant may be in a real bind. Here, one set of ethical values is juxtaposed against another. In the real world ethical choices confronting managers are complex and usually ambiguous. Clear solutions are often not present. What happens in these situations?

Tolerance of Suboptimal Conditions. The temptation for most managers is to place personal survival and avoidance of conflict at a higher priority than making tough ethical choices. Suppose a city manager finds his police chief to be a highly incompetent administrator whose authoritarian practices are creating severe motivation, stress, and turnover problems in the police department. One might counsel the city manager to take some form of corrective action against the police chief. However, the police chief may be a veteran of twenty years and also have political support in the community. A challenge to the police chief may lead to a major conflict and a question of whether the police chief or the city manager goes.

It is easier and safer to ignore the police chief and act as if no problem exists—in other words, tolerate a suboptimal condition knowing it is damaging the administrative infrastructure. Internal flaws can be tolerated because tolerating them makes personal survival sense. Since these behaviors may also stem from the culture, challenging them may be castigating deeply rooted behaviors. Pressure to accept suboptimal conditions may be easier and stronger than the desire to make difficult ethical decisions. Some administrators stand for principles and become whistle-blowers. These administrators and employees tend to have short organizational lives. It is easy to say, "Act ethically," but much more difficult to practice ethics. Whether most managers really have the freedom or personal willpower to make independent ethical judgments, given the driving force of cultural conforming pressures and expectations, is open to question.

Defensive Routines. One of the ironies of complex organizations is that most managers act as if everything is harmonious, when just beneath the surface problems simmer and tensions brew. A typical approach to internal problems is to ignore them or at best to treat them with Band-Aid solutions. The tendency to ignore problems and to act as if they did not exist is to engage in "defensive routines," short-term solutions to organizational threats and pain that are not solutions to the underlying causes of problems (Argyris, 1985). Consider the constant complainer or negativist who damages the productivity of staff members but for some reason is the apple of the boss's eye. Ordinary employees will often suffer this employee's ineptitude so as to avoid upsetting the boss with seemingly trivial interpersonal squabbles, even though the individual is a major threat to morale. While such defensive routines avoid short-term conflict, they perpetuate problems. Argyris contends that managers should not allow defensive routines to become embedded in the culture and should engage them when possible.

It is often the case that managers act as though Machiavellian behaviors do not exist and avoid discussing potentially damaging consequences. A successful Machiavellian comes across as sincere, suave, convincing, and warm while simultaneously turning the knife. Because of the prevalence of defensive routines, Machiavellian behaviors, which make ethical principles shallow, are difficult to openly address even though everyone is aware of them. They are undiscussable.

Implications for Machiavellian Ethics

Public managers may espouse high-level administrative ethics but tend to practice behaviors of a different ilk. To survive they often adopt behavioral strategies designed to advance positional power, personal interests, job security, status, and dominance in decision making. Power is the end that justifies the means, and any means, even those that may be ethically slippery, are rational if they further power acquisition. The only Machiavellian proviso is "do not get caught." Public managers utilize Machiavellian behaviors because everyone else is perceived as behaving similarly. To admit ignorance, to admit mistakes, or to appear weak is to exhibit vulnerability. Most managers are unwilling to risk appearing vulnerable. Making unilateral decisions in the absence of good information is viewed as sensible, given the perceived consequences.

The Price of Machiavellian Behaviors: Lowering the Plane. Managers tend toward Machiavellian behaviors partially because of the way organizations are structured. The configuration of hierarchical power, vertical and horizontal competitiveness, subcultural variation, and group dynamics contributes to and reinforces Machiavellian worldviews. Most managers find it too risky to break away from the Machiavellian behavioral loop. It is likely that managers hone their Machiavellian skills to a keener edge rather than rejecting them for more enlightened behavioral repertories. What is the price of this tendency?

Whereas the Greeks advocated the pursuit of excellence through the rule of the wise, Machiavelli argues that excellence is irrelevant. Machiavelli's fundamental goal is ruler-manager survival, and survival does not equate with excellence. Some people smoke cigarettes. Excellent health may warrant smoking abstinence, exercise, and commitment to a new lifestyle. The majority of smokers continue smoking in part because moderate smoking is not immediately life threatening. Indulging one's appetites can be satisfying and expedient even if counterproductive in the long-term prognosis. The same logic applies to organizations. Machiavelli realizes his theory lowers the plane of governmental excellence. No longer are the high virtues of excellence and wisdom pursued, because they are generally irrelevant to maintaining a survival mode.

The English philosopher Thomas Hobbes expands on Machiavelli. Hobbes (1950) contends that self-survival is the only individual natural right. As long as a ruler has sufficient power, he or she can maintain the stability of the state, which in Hobbes's view is the main function of the ruler. Maintenance of order is the end of civil society. The implication of Machiavellian behavior is that values are relative. Moreover, high ethics are meaningless in this type of system other than to serve the function of "controlling" those naive enough to believe in them, for example, those who believe in religion. The state, or for our concern, the organization, becomes an imperfect system that has no need for transcending to a higher level. In this conceptual framework, mediocrity is not only normal but also expected. Machiavellian ethics legitimizes organizational mediocrity and encourages people to find comfortable niches in the system, mainly because any attempt to radically change will threaten personal survival. It is much more prudent to go along, to play the game, and to not rock the boat. Discretion is the greater part of valor. System stability, not excellence, is the central value.

The cost is high. This type of system cannot rise above itself because its very nature stimulates degenerative organizational conditions (Golembiewski, 1977). Degenerative organizations are not likely to produce managers capable of substantively following the principles and ethics they publicly espouse. The organizations they manage appear to contradict the values and principles for which they say they stand. The ethics lacks credibility and meaning and basically serves as empty aphorisms.

Ethical Relativity. The problem with relativistic ethics is that it requires us to tolerate anathematic behaviors. Prior to the Civil War, slave owners had to be tolerated because slavery was an accepted legal and culture practice. Today, anyone openly advocating the reinstitution of slavery would probably be viewed as unethical. Does this mean slavery was less unethical 130 years ago?

Similarly, if ethics are relative, it could be argued that Nazi sympathizers were acting ethically in carrying out their orders. They were simply following the legal prescriptions of the regime. Ethics, then, is basically might makes right. Whatever dominant value system exists at a given time defines the acceptable boundaries of ethical behavior, and those boundaries may expand, contract, and change depending on who has power and what they value. This view rejects universal standards designed to guide and direct good behavior.

Aristotle points out that there is a difference between a good citizen and a good man. The good citizen diligently obeys the laws of the state. The good man obeys higher moral laws and directs his behavior toward the higher law when it conflicts with that of the state. Slave owners and Nazi officials should have realized they were violating higher moral laws, such as the sanctity of human life. An ethical Nazi would have refused to condone the slaughter of the Reich.

Acting ethically in situations where higher ethical principles contradict the dominant social norm is risky and dangerous. Yet this is precisely the condition that separates ethical individuals from Machiavellians. Most people, including this author, cannot make the ethical leap. Ethical persons, especially those who advocate the truth, are frequently ostracized and in extreme cases martyred. Consider the fate of most government whistle-blowers. Being ethical is a lonely, dangerous, and risky venture. This is because ethical behaviors that appeal to higher standards threaten most people, who while espousing the higher values actually operate at a lower plane. This is the case in public organizations. This also raises the final question. Can public managers develop higher and less Machiavellian ethical standards? The answer is yes—but how to get there is complicated.

Developing Higher Administrative Ethical Behaviors

Given how we manage and structure our public organizations, are we likely to break out of the Machiavellian maze? Current management practices and structures make it difficult to dent the Machiavellian armor. Some managers try to break away, but the regression rate is high. At the same time, only fundamental movement away from conventional management practices may enable managers to generate enough force to pursue higher administrative ethics in a critical mass context. While many solutions might be considered, three stand out as most potentially applicable.

The Madisonian Solution. James Madison (1969) astutely illustrates in *Federalist* 10 the unlikely prospect of mitigating the causes of faction by attempting to control individual behavior. The remedy would be worse than the disease. Madison's solution was to control the worst effects of faction by making it virtually impossible for any particular political group to gain hegemony over the governmental decisional apparatus. In *Federalist* 51 Madison asserts, "If men were angels, no government would be necessary" (1969, p. 103). In fact, men are not angels; in framing a government, Madison contends, one problem is controlling the governed, and the second is having the government control itself. Why the fuss?

In our government system, we assume that public officials will behave corruptly in a regularized fashion and further that it is necessary to create safeguards against this periodic weakness. This is accomplished not by stating of what "ethical behavior" consists but by the reverse. In our system, we stipulate characteristics of unethical behavior and make them illegal.

Kathryn Denhardt, in a fine analysis of ethical reforms, points out that most "reform efforts focus on acts involving tangible financial gains for individuals" (1989, p. 7). Her contention is that most ethics laws emphasize controlling illegal behavior (defined mainly as financial misconduct) and stress that failure to conform will lead to severe penalties. Denhardt that concludes this is a very narrow rule-oriented definition of ethics that relies chiefly on coercive remedies.

The problem with the Madisonian solution is that it tacitly condones Machiavellian values. It effectively admonishes unethical behavior and warns against getting caught. If one is caught, a penalty must be paid. This is not an underlying solution or a basis for constructing a higher-order ethical model.

The Code of Ethics Approach. A second approach for advancing a newer and higher plane of administrative ethics encourages administrators to adhere to strict codes of ethics developed by their professional associations (Bowman, 1990). Although this perspective is a step in the correct direction, it is likely to fall substantially short of its objective for several reasons. First, one must assume that individuals are cognizant of and pay attention to the ethical principles of their professional organizations. Some of these associations are so diverse that any ethical principles acceptable to all members would have to be so diluted as to become meaningless. Second, most professionals belong to multiple associations. The question becomes, Whose association norms is one to follow? Which association can claim allegiance over all others? Most professional administrators would face competing ethical codes, presumably diluted, which would end up causing more confusion than resolution of tough ethical questions. Finally, and perhaps most important, most professional organizations have no way of enforcing adherence to ethical codes. Who would determine when someone violated an ethical principle, and even if this could be accomplished (which is doubtful), what penalty could be administered to obtain compliance?

The code approach is also subject to Machiavellian manipulation. Many managers would probably swear allegiance to such a code and give the impression they found it useful to disarm critics and veil Machiavellian skirmishes taking place behind the scenes. Ineluctably, public employees may come to the conclusion that although the meek should in principle inherit the earth, the strong will actually retain control. Hence, the code of ethics approach, while conceptually laudatory, will not provide an enduring and penetrating solution to the real problem, namely, the fundamental alteration of conventional management practices and values.

The Organizational Development Paradigm. To enable managers to create moral codes and subsequently practice them, regenerative organizational conditions must be present. According to Robert T. Golembiewski, there must be high trust, high owning, low risk, and high openness (1977, p. 6). Regenerative characteristics must become part of the end-state vision that managers generally espouse. Yet to favor regenerative characteristics does not necessarily mean they will be pursued. To pursue them in earnest implies the organization must take a "proactive" stance toward organization development (OD). In particular, several basic OD steps should be followed.

The organization should engage in substantial diagnostic analysis of current conditions. This analysis should involve a penetrating analysis of employees at all hierarchical levels and in all functional units. It will show where current state problems and weaknesses exist. Managers, working in concert with OD professionals, should then engage in feedback processes and consider what types of interventions might be feasible for increasing trust, building teamwork between levels of management and between different departments, and mitigating risks for innovative activities. Only fostering a greater sense of trust and teamwork and nurturing greater openness and risk taking make a higher administrative ethics possible. This can be done if organizations are willing to take a hard introspective look at themselves.

Fundamental to OD is the assumption that the human person is the elemental building block of the organization. Human integrity, dignity, worth, and contributions to organizational goals are the guiding principles. OD values assume employees are the most important strategic factors in the organization. All reforms must ultimately hinge on this simple fact.

The types of OD interventions and models that advance the human element have been discussed by numerous authors (Burke, 1982; French and Bell, 1989). Does OD work? According to one major study of both public and private OD applications, the OD success rate in the public sector is in excess of 70 percent (Golembiewski, 1985, p. 81). Through review of hundreds of OD articles, it has been determined that OD has been successful many more times than it has failed. Thus, evidence not to the contrary, OD strategies for transforming the organization's culture and embedding a new and more enlightened set of managerial values represent at least one viable solution to the conventional management practices dilemma. This is because OD generally represents a fundamentally different set of values than those commonly found in most public organizations. As a consequence, it signifies a conceptual break from the status quo and may provide the type of momentum necessary for propelling the organization to a higher conceptual plane. High-involvement emphases that move the organization's culture in a more human and team-oriented direction are all steps toward higher ethical possibilities.

By employing an OD-based management system, the organization provides a solid foundation to build meaningful administrative ethics (Burke, 1987). Managers in such organizations can risk being different, cast aside Machiavellian predispositions, and relate to larger issues that affect the organization and its environment. An OD system may allow some managers to transcend narrow personal interests and concern for survival—perhaps to pursue organizational excellence. Decisions can be based on upward flows of communication and sharper evaluations of consequences. Closer approximation of optimal decision making should be possible. Organizational reforms will be more than cosmetic, and employees may experience ownership and buy into new ideas.

When this chapter was first reviewed, several good questions were raised. A recurring issue pertained to the recommendation that organization development serve as a foundation for establishing a more meaningful administrative ethics. One concern was that OD basically stands for a set of values, not techniques. What does OD have to offer? Where OD stands for a distinct set of values, namely, those that stress the importance of trust, human dignity, and excellence in the organization, these values are a sensible foundation on which to build ethical principles. OD also includes a rather extensive and varied set of techniques, most of which have been field-tested. The same cannot be said of conventional management. A second concern was how we know OD will work. Will it be successful? Based on the best research available, that of Robert T. Golembiewski (1985) public sector OD success rates are about 70 percent. This figure is based on several hundred OD interventions using posttest results and evaluated by an outside panel of judges. If this research is insufficient to demonstrate OD success, then what constitutes acceptable empirical evidence? Further, the challenge can be reversed. What clear and strong evidence exists that conventional management practices are successful? A final concern is that Machiavellian managers may abuse OD values to further enhance self-interest. What is to keep some managers from taking advantage of this possibility? The response is simple. Managers who abuse employee value systems for selfish purposes eventually become exposed. That most devious individuals will take advantage of the belief systems of others is perhaps an unavoidable cost with most things in everyday life. Yet better value systems should make it clearer who is violating major ethical principles.

A brief example of how OD can serve to solidify organizational ethics is illustrated by Golembiewski and Kiepper (1988) in an analysis of OD in Metropolitan Atlanta Rapid Transit Authority (MARTA). Initially, the general manager had promised top-level executives medical insurance coverage for the executives' unmarried domestic partners. When this became a costly and politically sensitive personnel issue, the general manager decided to break the promise. This change in policy had its greatest impact on minority executives who did not fit traditional family role models, and they presumed the policy change was racially motivated. Because the initial agreement to provide the medical insurance had been negotiated through an OD contract, the OD consultant convinced the general manager that he was breaking his word and principle by unilaterally dropping a policy originally agreed to in good faith through bargaining. Thus, in this rather practical and simple example, OD contracting protected specific fringe benefit rights of employees from elimination without justification.

To summarize, this chapter has suggested that public managers are socialized into Machiavellian value systems in their normal work organizations. Machiavellian values stress personal survival mainly through power acquisition, deceit, cunning, and manipulation. Survival rather than excellence is the fundamental emphasis. Machiavellian value systems legitimize the acceptance of suboptimal performance levels if such strategies enhance or protect one's organizational position. These values are exacerbated by the use of numerous conventional management practices in the public sector. Functional organization design, hierarchical authority systems, defensive routines, and socializing forces reinforce and solidify suboptimal conditions. For the typical manager overcoming these public sector organizational obstacles can be a formidable and dangerous endeavor, with immediate consequences of lower trust, higher risk, lower communication, and lower owning. Machiavellian values and conventional management practices precipitate "degenerative" organizational characteristics. Given these predominating organizational forces, it will be nearly impossible to develop credible and penetrating administrative ethics on this shaky and unstable foundation. Public sector managers should contemplate experimentation with something new if deeper and more meaningful administrative ethics is to be achieved. Organization development has been presented in this chapter as one potential alternative because it uses fundamentally different value patterns and legitimizes experimentation with innovative management techniques.

Some may suggest that the above scenario is overly idealistic and utopian. It is intendedly so. As Plato said, excellence is an elusive and abstract concept for which to strive. Ethics involve transcendent principles. They not only provoke people to think "What if?" but also motivate them to try. They represent ideals. By comparing the ideal to the current state, we learn in what direction and how far we have to go. These ideals have meaning only if people think they are potentially possible and not contradicted by everyday reality. Conventional management practices in public organizations simply do not create the type of fertile soil in which to plant higher level ethical principles. The soil in conventional organizations is too leached to provide meaningful nourishment. This is why an OD paradigm may be one alternative on which to build a viable administrative ethics.

References

Argyris, C. "The CEO's Behavior: Key to Organizational Development." *Harvard Business Review,* 1973, *2* (51), 55–65.

Argyris, C. *Strategy, Change, and Defensive Routines.* Boston: Pittman, 1985.

Blake, R. R., and Mouton, J. S. *Solving Costly Organizational Conflicts: Achieving Intergroup Trust, Cooperation, and Teamwork.* San Francisco: Jossey-Bass, 1984.

Bloom, A. (trans.). *The Republic of Plato.* New York: Basic Books, 1968.

Bowman, J. S. "Ethics in Government: A National Survey of Public Administrators." *Public Administration Review,* 1990, *50* (3), 345–353.

Burke, W. *Organization Development: Principles and Practices.* Boston: Little Brown, 1982.

Burke, W. *Organization Development: A Normative View.* Reading, Mass.: Addison-Wesley, 1987.

Denhardt, K. "Ethical Integrity and Organizational Performance—The Impact of Ethics Reforms." Paper presented at the annual southeastern conference of the American Society for Public Administration, Jackson, Mississippi, Oct. 1989.

Finer, H. "Administrative Responsibility in Democratic Government." *Public Administration Review,* 1941, *1,* 335–350.

French, W., and Bell, C. *Organization Development.* Englewood Cliffs, N.J.: Prentice-Hall, 1989.

Gabris, G., and Giles, W. A. "Level of Management, Performance Appraisal, and Productivity Reform in Complex Organizations." *Review of Public Personnel Administration,* 1983, *3,* 45–63.

Golembiewski, R. *Public Administration as a Developing Discipline.* Part 2: *Organization Development as One of a Future Family of Miniparadigms.* New York: Marcel Dekker, 1977.

Golembiewski, R. *Humanizing Public Organizations.* Mt. Airy, Md.: Lomond, 1985.

Golembiewski, R., and Kiepper, A. *High Performance and Human Costs: A Public Section Model of Organization Development.* New York: Praeger, 1988.

Urwick, L. *The Elements of Administration,* New York: Harper, 1944.

Hobbes, T. *Leviathan,* New York: Dutton, 1950.

Ingraham, P., and Ban, C. (eds.). *Legislating Bureaucratic Change.* Albany: State University of New York Press, 1984.

Janis, I. *Victims of Groupthink: A Psychological Study of Foreign Policy Decisions and Fiascos.* Boston: Houghton Mifflin, 1972.

Kaufman, H. *Time, Chance, and Organizations: Natural Selection in a Perilous Environment.* Chatham, N.J.: Chatham House, 1985.

Kouzes, J. M., and Posner, B. Z. *The Leadership Challenge: How to Get Extraordinary Things Done in Organizations.* San Francisco: Jossey-Bass, 1987.

Machiavelli, N. *The Prince and the Discourses*. New York: Random House, 1950.

Madison, J. "Federalist #10." In K. M. Dolbeare (ed.), *Directions in American Political Thought*. New York: Wiley, 1969.

Mansfield, H. *Taming the Prince*. New York: Free Press, 1989.

Parsons, T. (ed. and intro.). *Max Weber: The Theory of Social and Economic Organization*. New York: Free Press, 1947.

Presthus, R. *The Organizational Society*. New York: St. Martin's, 1978.

Stewart, D. "Ethics and the Profession of Public Administration: The Moral Responsibility of Individuals in Public Sector Organizations." *Public Administration Quarterly*, 1985, *8*, 487–496.

Taylor, F. W. *The Principles of Scientific Management*. New York: Norton, 1911.

Thayer, F. "Performance Appraisal and Merit Pay Systems: The Disasters Multiply." *Review of Public Personnel Administration*, 1987, *7*, 36–54.

Thompson, D. F. "The Possibility of Administrative Ethics." *Public Administration Review*, Oct./Dec. 1985, *45* (5), 555–561.

Thompson, J. D. *Organizations in Action*. New York: McGraw-Hill, 1967.

10 New Strategies
for Institutional Controls

Judith A. Truelson

Over the past century, the scope and power of government bureaucracies have increased considerably the world over. Public officials, both elected and appointed, have had to confront two serious problems as a result. One is to interpret the intent of ambiguous and sometimes contradictory laws. The other is to exercise appropriate discretion when faced with conflicts in role, authority, and interests. Both involve difficult ethical dilemmas, never easy to resolve and occasionally unresolvable. Rather than tackle them on a personal basis, most officials have relied on their prevailing organizational cultures to determine what is considered ethical, who is allowed to engage at least formally in ethical deliberations, and what range of options is permitted to public managers who make ethical decisions (Denhardt, 1988, pp. 75–76).

In the United States since the Watergate affair there has been particular concern with how public bureaucracies and managers might better be prevented from misusing their powers and discretion and acting unethically. At the federal level since 1978 the emphasis has been on strengthening external controls to hold executives more accountable for the actions of their organizations and personnel under their control and discretion. The motive behind new laws and organizations has been to shed more light on the gap between government promises and actual performance (Rosen, 1989, p. 131) and on possible institutionalized misconduct and misbehavior deliberately covered up in the federal bureaucracy. The assumption, right or wrong, is that it is more feasible to change the institutional arrangements that govern the conduct of public business than to change the attitudes and behavior of the people who conduct that business. Traditionally, public norms have been sought through formal requirements, standards, and sanctions rather than through exhortation, education, and behavior modification. Thus, many of the new federal controls, such as the inspectors general (IGs), waste and fraud hot lines and whistle-blower protection laws, rely on the willingness of individuals in federal organizations to follow the new channels by personally exposing wrongdoing that they observe and experience according to the new precedents that have been instituted.

One notable exception to the emphasis on external controls has been the provision in the Ethics in Government Act of 1978 of the Office of Government Ethics (OGE), which is responsible for ethics education in federal government agencies. Unfortunately, the ethics education program has yet to attend adequately to defiant organizational cultures that inhibit ethical performance. Further, the statutory focus of OGE has defined ethics too narrowly in terms of conflicts of interest and concentrated too selectively on political appointees. Persistent mass media exposure of ethical violations throughout federal government administration has also drawn attention to the limitations and weaknesses of the new external controls and how little use has in fact been made of new channels and opportunities by federal government officials and the public in general in reporting public misconduct. The hot lines, for instance, have not rung that often, and the congressional inquiry into the *Challenger* disaster showed how strongly entrenched the conforming organizational culture in the National Aeronautics and Space Administration (NASA) and its contractors was, so that even after the event the responsible whistle-blowers remained unprotected from organizational retaliation (U.S. Presidential Commission on the Space Shuttle *Challenger* Accident, 1986).

This chapter discusses the resistance of federal agency cultures to external controls and the need for additional nonfinancial internal controls. It presents techniques whereby an existing coordinating unit such as OGE or a possible new unit such as a federal ombudsman office could train public managers in strategies designed to expand ethical awareness and a heightened sense of individual ethical responsibility. Clearly, such ethical awareness has to become part of the organizational culture through peer pressure, dissent channels, and ethical workshops.

The 1990s present an unprecedented opportunity to overhaul the concept of institutional control of administrative responsibility by switching emphasis from external sanctions (too late to prevent wrongdoing) to internal organizational sensitivity and awareness of possible wrongdoing, somewhat like an antenna forewarning of impending misconduct. Obviously both external and internal institutional controls need to be combined and coordinated in a more systematic fashion, but just as important, internal institutional controls need to be defined in terms more of professional pride than of pure adherence to financial guidelines. Administrative values of guardianship, trust, competence, and discipline need to be integrated, not separated from moral and professional concerns with justice, fairness, honor, and the public interest. Organizational cultures, particularly in the public sector, need to emphasize that both the spirit as well as the intent of the law should be followed, and the public's expectation of public norms should be met as well as the organization's perceptions of its own norms.

Resistance of Agency Cultures to External Controls

Control over agency misconduct has been exerted through monitoring by oversight agents external to agency hierarchical structures but still operating within agencies—through IGs and designated agency ethics officers (DAEOs)—and by oversight agents completely external to the agency—congressional committees, the Merit Systems Protection Board (MSPB), and the Office of the Special Counsel (OSC). The exercise of administrative discretion in relation to these controls depends on public managers' willingness and ability to make independent judgments about ethical issues (Cooper, 1986, pp. 43-55; Waldo, 1980, pp. 103-106; Denhardt, 1988, pp. 112-119). These independent judgments require that officials have the authority to act, the power to control, and the freedom to decide between right and wrong so that they may be held accountable to an outside or external judgment for exercising their discretion (Caiden, 1988, p. 25).

The ethics of structure that asserts that administrators are responsible for only those specific duties for which they are legally liable and the ethics of neutrality that portrays ideal administrators as loyal and reliable instruments of the goals of the organization (Thompson, 1985) are sources of three major difficulties with the use of external institutional controls. Conflicts of objective responsibilities and moral ambivalence in agency cultures are particular reflections of these difficulties, which inhibit the exercise of administrative discretion in the use of these controls. The first difficulty has to do with the unpredictability of the role of politics in the functioning of external controls. Second, there is the danger that institutionalization of external controls may lead to cooptation by the organizational power structure. Third, the reactive nature of statutory external controls limits their effectiveness in agency cultures.

Structure, Neutrality, and Politics. The ethics of structure and neutrality elevate administration over politics by suggesting that it may not be possible to determine who is morally responsible for agency decisions and that administrators are to express only those principles reflected in the orders and policies they are charged with implementing. Administrative concerns can then prevent political influences from exerting external control in agencies. On the one hand, the ethics of structure contends that to praise or blame someone for an outcome, it must be assumed that the person's actions or omissions were a cause of the outcome and that the person did not act in excusable ignorance or under compulsion. In public organizations the problem of identifying the persons who caused outcomes in a decision or policy becomes at least as difficult as the problem of assessing the morality of the decision or policy (Thompson, 1980). On the other hand, the ethics of neutrality portrays the ideal administrator as a completely loyal and reliable instrument of the goals of the organization, never injecting personal, public, or professional values into the process of furthering these goals. This ethics reinforces the great virtue of organization—its capacity to serve any social end—regardless of the ends that individuals in it favor (Thompson, 1985, p. 556).

Many, however, support the view that administrative discretion goes beyond carrying out the intentions of legislators or the superiors in the agency. Administrators can and should take the initiative in proposing policies, mobilizing support for them, and questioning policies that may run counter to the public interest (Rohr, 1989, pp. 37–51; Warwick, 1981, pp. 93–127). From this perspective, the effectiveness of external controls depends on the fusion of politics and administration. There has certainly been much support in the 1980s for the view that they should be fused (Rabin and Bowman, 1984). In the case of the *Challenger* space shuttle, for example, officials in the chains of command who knew about the O-ring fault have been criticized for not challenging organizational policy by invoking external controls to halt the launch (Romzek and Dubnick, 1987).

Conflicts of Objective Responsibility and Cooptation. In environments of systemic corruption, in which the goals of organizational loyalty and survival conflict with notions of public accountability and trust (Caiden and Caiden, 1977), there is the danger that institutionalization of external controls may lead to cooptation by the organizational power structure. For example, critics allege that IG hot-line investigations in the military services may be less than independent; they often lead to cases turned over, with little result, to the services' IGs who are usually in the chain of command involved in the allegations (Truelson, 1985).

Based on hundreds of hearings and federal reports, it has been alleged that federal contracting abuses may be described as systemic, engrained, and immune to outside intervention: "Yet, despite the clear evidence of systemic contracting abuses throughout the federal government, the Office of Management and Budget, which has responsibility for issuing and contracting guidelines, has generally failed to bring about a cleanup by the individual agencies. In hearing after hearing before Congress over the last two decades, representatives of the budget office have regularly testified that, while there are a few contracting abuses, some new procedure or modification of an existing regulation will correct the problems. And then things continue as before, until the next set of hearings at which OMB again announces new procedures that are going to correct the problems once and for all" (Hanrahan, 1983, pp. 38–39). The more prevalent systemic corruption in public agencies is, the more intense the conflicts of loyalty and responsibility associated with use of administrative discretion will be.

Moral Ambivalence and Reactive Controls. Moral ambivalence does not deny that administrators must often use their own
judgment in the formulation of policy, but the use of discretion in
this view can never be the occasion for applying any moral principles other than those implicit in the orders and policies of the
superiors to whom one is responsible in the organization (Thompson, 1985, p. 556). These rules are reflected in the culture of the
organization through the basic assumptions and beliefs that are
shared by organizational members that operate unconsciously and
define in a basic taken-for-granted fashion an organization's view
of itself and its environment (Schein, 1985).

Since statutory external controls are primarily reactive, they
lag behind unethical practices that may be engrained in agency
cultures, codifying only those that prove over time to be the most
damaging (Stone, 1975). Research has indicated, for example, that
a number of retaliatory personnel practices that are not prohibited
by whistle-blower protection provisions—for example, refusal to
give an employee meaningful work or reassignment of a nonsmok-
ing employee into the midst of smokers (Glazer and Glazer, 1989;
Truelson, 1986)—have been invoked against whistle-blowers. Even
if statutory controls could be designed and institutionalized to effectively protect whistle-blowers or prevent conflicts of interest or
to eliminate fraud, waste, and abuse, until these controls are passed
and enforced, agency cultures may continue business as usual, taking advantage of the jurisdictional ambiguities, procedural deficiencies, and lack of sanctioning power that plague external
controls.

The ethics of structure and the ethics of neutrality as reflected
in conflicts of objective responsibility and moral ambivalence create
an image of agency culture that defeats external controls by cutting
off the agency culture and insulating it from political accountability. As a result, external controls on administrative responsibility
may fail to be politically responsive, often appear to coopted by
agency values, and fail to cover the range of improper conducts
exhibited in the agency. Since politics and administration cannot
be neatly separated, Friedrich (1940) has concluded that political
accountability—that is, external controls—is inadequate to ensuring responsible administrative conduct and that internal controls

that emphasize responsiveness to public and professional standards of justice and honor are apt to create a more responsive and creative bureaucracy.

Accountability mechanisms internal to the organization have even been considered parallel to those individual controls described by Friedrich as having power to shape behavior not as a matter of external regulations and procedures manipulated by someone else in the form of commands and directives but as a set of internalized attitudes, values, and beliefs (Goodpaster and Matthews, 1982; Friedrich, 1940).

Institutionalizing the Development of Internal Agency Controls

In undertaking programs designed to expand ethical awareness and individual sense of responsibility in agencies, OGE has an advantage over other established units in that it already has officers in each agency—the DAEOs. It has already set up a training program that has reached over three thousand employees, most at the management level. It has developed a guide, *How to Keep Out of Trouble,* distributed to all new political appointees. It is developing a computerized data base on all department and agency ethics programs (U.S. Congress. House, 1988). Statutory authorization for this expanded charge to the agency would, however, probably depend on whether OGE can more effectively fulfill its already mandated functions, as the 1988 reauthorization hearings have recommended. Congress has granted OGE twenty-three additional authorized employees (which will bring the total number of authorized employees to about fifty-three) who will be involved in improvement of monitoring, management, and oversight of the executive branch ethics programs. Means of improvement include requirement and collection of data on the agency ethics programs and development of formal criteria for determining the cases in which OGE will intervene (U.S. Congress. House, 1988). The absence of a strong monitoring and leadership role by OGE in preventing conflicts of interest or the appearance thereof could raise the question of its potential effectiveness as an ethical awareness and training unit.

The President's Commission on Federal Ethics Reform (PCFER) has recommend_d that Congress appoint an independent ethics official, to be confirmed by both houses, who would head a permanent ethics office that would investigate allegations of misconduct, report findings publicly to the ethics committee of the appropriate house, and recommend appropriate sanctions (U.S. President's Commission on Federal Ethics Law Reform, 1989). Enactment of this recommendation would create an office that could serve at least some of the functions of an independent federal employee ombudsman, including a special responsibility for promoting ethics awareness, documenting ethical standards, and coordinating ethics training programs.

Some of the ombudsmanlike functions that this office could assume include coordination of external bureaucratic accountability mechanisms by referring federal employees to the proper agency official or office to lodge their complaint, mediating timely and voluntary solutions when public employee complaints are lodged with these agencies, counseling federal employees on strategy and possible outcomes for invoking the services of these agencies, and educating federal employees on the services offered by the IG, OSC, and the MSPB. In view of the fragmentation of the ethical system, such an office would offer the advantages of providing a degree of coordination presently lacking while also inquiring into major variations and breakdowns in the system and recommending improved techniques. The major advantage, however, of assigning expanded responsibility for promoting ethical awareness and individual responsibility to a new office rather than to OGE is that it would be a *new* office signaling a new and expanded concern with moral accountability. Probably, more problems will surface or surface earlier if an additional communication channel is added to the system.

Launching an agencywide internal controls program such as described in the next section requires a coordinating unit. While OGE might serve the function of ensuring training consistency and promoting inter- and intraagency communication of ethics issues, there may be advantages in creating a new unit that could also serve some ombudsmanlike functions.

Coordinated Agency Training for Ethical
Awareness and Action

A coordinating unit such as OGE could be given responsibility for preparation of a general ethical awareness training package including but not limited to issues of legal compliance. After initial centralized training of the DAEOs in the implementation of this package, the DAEO in each agency could develop a training team in conjunction with existing agency ethics personnel—the IG, inspectors, auditors, and investigators. Each training team would need to set up and implement a system of ethics briefings. In addition to entrance and exit ethics briefings, annual mandatory ethics briefings might also be instituted. (Lois Gibbs Brown, the Department of Defense IG, recently recommended an annual mandatory ethics briefing for all DOD personnel [U.S. Congress. Senate, 1989, p. 53]). Although all agency personnel should be included in this training, special briefings should continue for presidential appointees and should be developed for senior executives, program managers, and other senior staff. The agency training committees would also need to develop a program for institutionalizing ethical awareness in each agency's culture. This program might include techniques such as peer review, ethical dialogue, dissent channels, and articles in publications widely read by employees.

Ethical Awareness Package. A training package for ethical awareness and individual responsibility might exceed legal compliance requirements in several ways: by stimulating the moral imagination, promoting recognition of ethical issues, developing analytical skills, eliciting a sense of moral responsibility, and fostering ethical action. Training techniques for meeting these standards should emphasize examination of what is meant by ethical and unethical behavior, as reflected in codes of conduct and ethics laws, and use of a systematic method of case analysis for development of analytical skills and promotion of responsible ethical action.

Coupling ethics and legislation might be considered inappropriate, since, once an issue is legislated, individuals can no longer freely apply their values to a given situation but are coerced by the sanction of the state into certain types of conduct. It is possible, however, to view the legislative act as a collective ethical judgment (Cooper, 1986, p. 101). During the post-Watergate era, many efforts have been made to codify that judgment. Despite the fact that these codes deal mostly with issues of conflict of interest, they can provide managers with guidance on broader social values including conflicts of responsibility. For example, the Code of Ethics for Government Service states that any wrongdoing public officials observe in the course of their official duties should be brought to the immediate attention of their superiors, and if they fail to act to the attention of public leaders and the public at large (U.S. Congress, 1958).

The PCFER has recommended that OGE be directed by executive order to consolidate all executive branch standards of conduct regulations into a single set of regulations. It has also been recommended that OGE issue a comprehensive ethics manual (U.S. President's Commission on Federal Ethics Law Reform, 1989). As these recommendations are carried out, however, it is vital that OGE move beyond its present function of training to meet the legal requirements of conflict-of-interest laws. The role that OGE has played in briefing, counseling, and advising political appointees who have before-the-fact questions about how conflict-of-interest regulations will affect them needs to be expanded to other categories of employees—procurement officers, auditors, investigators, managers, analysts, lawyers, and so on.

Inclusion of professional codes of conduct such as the American Society for Public Administration code should be emphasized in the training package as well as legal codes in connection with case studies. Placing professional codes in a given agency context can stimulate discussion of questions such as: Have standards in professions represented in this agency remained constant over time, or have they changed? What are the new issues in these professions today, and how do they apply to this agency and these jobs? For what does this agency stand, and how are these ideas acted out in everyday policies and behavior? To what and whom are the agency's obligations and commitments?

Since the case method provides a flexible instructional method for promoting recognition of ethical issues as well as development of analytical skills, OGE or the designated coordinating unit should develop a set of case materials along with questions and instructions in the training package that reflect a wide range of moral dilemmas, including conflicts of interest, responsibility, authority, and roles. To foster development of analytical skills and a sense of individual moral responsibility, trainers should focus on assembling facts bearing on the problem, clarifying the problem by defining the issues, proposing or evaluating suggested solutions or courses of action, and determining which one seems best in view of the circumstances. The following case illustrates the use of this format.

Case of the Conscientious Tax Examiner. Daniel, area supervisor for tax examiners in a federal agency, faced the ethical dilemma of how to get the agency to refund surplus payments instead of simply retaining them when taxpayers in certain categories failed to subtract already withheld sums in calculating that they owed the treasury.

Daniel's perception of the facts indicated that, although the agency had no legal right to keep these overpayments, it was under no specific mandate to return them and had devised no refund procedure. At first, Daniel chose the alternative of going through channels by writing reports urging superiors to change the rules so people would get their surplus payments refunded. After generating a series of reports without result, Daniel began to feel that the operative value in this case was "finders keepers."

When Daniel's immediate supervisor told him that he was not doing his career any good by pursuing this issue, Daniel reassessed his position. According to the code of ethics of Daniel's professional association, ASPA, there were a number of reasons why he should continue to pursue the issue. For example, the code mandates that members of the society should serve the public with respect, concern, and responsiveness; exercise whatever discretionary authority they have under law to promote the public interest; and eliminate all forms of mismanagement of public funds.

Although it has been argued that no individual is a necessary and sufficient cause of any organizational outcome and that it is therefore impossible to ascribe individual responsibility in organizations, trainers can use this case to promote a sense of individual responsibility. Even if Daniel's agency had not refunded surplus payments for many decades and no one presently in the agency had initiated the practice, an official's moral responsibility should not be assessed solely according to the proportionate share she or he contributes to the outcome. In imputing responsibility, consideration should be given not only to the acts that individuals commit but also the the acts they omit. Even though in Daniel's agency no one initiated the wrongful policy, many officials, including Daniel, could be blamed for failing to try to halt the practice (Thompson, 1980, pp. 559–560).

Questions on this case reflecting this method of analysis might include: If you were Daniel, would you have felt responsible for doing something about the situation? What other courses of action were open to Daniel to solve his dilemma? What did this incident reveal about the overall administrative culture in the agency? If you had been Daniel's supervisor, how would you have dealt with him?

Some discussion issues that could be related to a number of training cases would include the extent of personal responsibility in a bureaucracy, use of peer pressure to change agency environments, the role of codes of conduct and ethics laws, and the merits and pitfalls associated with whistle-blowing. Whistle-blowing presents particular challenges to public managers because it flies in the face of long-established behavioral patterns and organizational culture, not just in the federal bureaucracy but throughout American organizations; telling the truth as perceived by the individual, in contradiction to the organizational version, is viewed as "ratting" or squealing, certainly abnormal behavior that is discouraged and penalized. No wonder many federal officials who have had personal knowledge of fraud, waste, and abuse and have wanted to act responsibly and correctly according to external standards have been reluctant to report wrongdoing (U.S. Merit Systems Protection Board, 1984, p. 34).

Most organizational cultures—public and private—define organizational integrity not as conformity to the legally sanctioned requirements of public rectitude but simply as unquestioning obedience and loyalty to the organization, even where wrongdoing has been institutionalized. Organizational survival and expansion take precedence over truthfulness and honesty, certainly over such administrative values as economy, efficiency, and effectiveness (Scott and Hart, 1979, p. 43; Hummel, 1987; Cooper, 1986, p. 34). Public officials, like all organizational members, are pressured and socialized to be "good team players," that is, to go along with the groupthink that prevails and to remain passive when faced with obvious financial mismanagement, incompetence, extravagance, and corruption. Those who are brave enough to defy peer and organizational pressures are shunned and eventually victimized, forcing them to leave of their own accord, or are simply framed and fired (Glazer and Glazer, 1989).

Since Daniel was as committed to safeguarding the public interest as he was to protecting his career, he chose a dual action strategy. He acted to increase the costs to his agency of unethical behavior while raising the visibility of its decision making. He simultaneously elicited the support of a prominent senator, who raised the issue with the agency head, and leaked to the media facts about the agency policy of keeping tax overpayments without telling the taxpayers involved. It was a symbolic victory for Daniel when the acting commissioner of the agency, who agreed that the policy was wrong, ruled that henceforth overly generous taxpayers would get refunds and that those who had overpaid in the past could apply for refunds.

A training package for promotion of ethical awareness and individual responsibility would be designed to encourage employees to discuss dilemmas that confront them and to give them a framework for thinking about and taking ethical action on these dilemmas. Since this training package would not focus merely on legal compliance, it would place laws and compliance into a larger context of values, standards, goals, and obligations.

Institutionalizing Ethical Awareness and Moral Responsibility into Agency Cultures

Integration of ethical awareness and a sense of moral responsibility into agency culture through such internal controls as development and formal distribution of agency codes of ethics, ethics workshops, and dissent channels would reinforce ethics training. Middle managers could appropriately be targeted as key actors in the development of these internal controls. Cases such as that of the conscientious tax collector could also be used to illustrate this middle management role. If choosing to inform an agency IG of wrongdoing (such as miscollection of funds) is considered legitimate by upper management, middle managers may decide to focus on the use of internal controls to develop a more ethical organizational culture. Without upper management's endorsement, of course, middle managers cannot officially change directions; however, they can create opportunities for ethical revitalization and, if mutually supportive, can somewhat override upper managers' opposition to change. If there is negative organizational feedback, managers can use external controls to increase ethical autonomy and to promote due process in the event of ethical conflict between themselves and their organizations.

Assuming that there is positive organizational feedback (that is, no retaliation against the employee for invoking an external control), supervisors may take action to change the ethical environment in the office through peer pressure. If there is an ethics code in the agency, a copy could be provided to every employee. In any case, informal discussions of ethical issues may be arranged. As reinforcement to initial discussions, ethical dialogue can be institutionalized into regularly offered ethics workshops. To the extent that value consensus can be built through group participation, it is likely to have a greater influence on behavior than values announced by the unilateral fiat of supervisors. Employees can also be encouraged to call attention to possible areas of unethical behavior through such dissent channels as peer review of "differing professional opinions," which was set up in 1980 by the Nuclear Regulatory Commission (NRC). Dissent in the NRC context is defined as the expression of one's best professional judgment even though it may differ from a prevailing staff view, disagree with a management position or policy position, or take issue with proposed or established agency practices (Truelson, 1985, p. 25).

Ethics laws, unlike codes of ethics, provide sanctions for those officials caught stepping beyond legal limits. For example, trainers could focus on the fact that if Daniel had been fired after revealing information about the agency practice of not returning surplus tax payments, under whistle-blower provisions of the Civil Service Reform Act of 1978 (CSRA), he could have requested investigation of his termination as a prohibited personnel practice. CSRA created a separate agency, the Merit Systems Protection Board, which has authority to monitor and sanction violations to the merit system and to the rights of federal employees, particularly whistle-blowers; within MSPB, it also created the OSC, which can investigate the activities of agencies, federal managers, and officials. In Daniel's case the OSC and possibly MSPB could have ordered appropriate corrective action against agency personnel, including demotion or dismissal (U.S. Congress. House, 1979). By providing for review of allegations outside the agency and requiring that an agency respond to any substantial allegation of impropriety or wrongdoing, this portion of the whistle-blower provision is the first step toward an administrative system that does not concentrate power in isolated administrative structures (Vaughn, 1984).

Ethics officers and trainers reinforce training for ethical awareness and individual ethical responsibility by encouraging development of institutionalized internal controls in an agency. These controls complement the internal financial controls that already exist in the agency as well as the external controls such as OSC and MSPB that regulate federal employees.

Conclusion

Development of an ethics awareness program and training in assuming individual responsibility in federal agencies would itself constitute an internal organizational control—promoting self-control, integrity, and organizational conscience while discouraging individual moral ambivalence. It would be disturbing if this program were viewed as a substitute for rather than a supplement to individual conscience, especially since it appears that the existing mechanisms for ensuring ethical actions in organizations are inadequate to the task. The primary criticism for using "organizational conscience" as an ethical reform measure is that it remains organizational, and the focus can never be on what the individual or society would consider to be morally right.

The critical challenge of the 1990s is to develop a balance between individual conscience and organizational conscience, as well as congruence between them, in organizations. Clearly, increased interest in high-level attention to internal financial controls in organizations needs to be paralleled at the moral level. Continued study and research also need to focus on the relationship between internal controls such as dissent channels and employee willingness to take responsibility for combating fraud, waste, and abuse. A replication of the 1980 and 1984 MSPB studies of whistle-blowing in the federal government would provide important data for this research.

Caution should be emphasized, however: despite the need to raise the moral level of individual conscience and organizational conscience through the application of both internal and external controls, the adopted perspective must still be founded on the clear and explicit articulation of democratic values. This process is no longer a matter of determining what already works but of experimenting with innovations that limit the independence and autonomy of public officials without unduly handicapping their freedom of action, that reduce the privatization of government without restricting individual privacy, that minimize the occurrence of public wrongdoing without intensifying bureaupathologies, and that increase the public's confidence in public institutions without criminalizing public affairs (Caiden, 1988, p. 35).

References

Caiden, G. E. "Ensuring the Accountability of Public Officials." In J. G. Jabbra and O. P. Dwivedi (eds.), *Public Service Accountability: A Comparative Perspective.* West Hartford, Conn.: Kumarian Press, 1988.

Caiden, G. E., and Caiden, N. J. "Administrative Corruption." *Public Administration Review,* 1977, *37* (3), 301–309.

Cooper, T. L. *The Responsible Administrator: An Approach to Ethics for the Administrative Role.* (2nd ed.) Millwood, N.Y.: Associated Faculty Press, 1986.

Denhardt, K. G. *The Ethics of Public Service: Resolving Moral*

Dilemmas in Public Organizations. Westport, Conn.: Greenwood Press, 1988.

Finer, H. "Administrative Responsibility in Democratic Government." *Public Administration Review,* 1941, *1,* 335–350.

Friedrich, C. J. "Public Policy and the Nature of Administrative Responsibility." *Public Policy,* 1940, *1,* 3–24.

Glazer, M. P., and Glazer, P. M. *The Whistleblowers: Exposing Corruption in Government and Industry.* New York: Basic Books, 1989.

Goodpaster, K., and Matthews, J. B., Jr. "Can a Corporation Have a Conscience?" *Harvard Business Review,* 1982, *60* (1), 132–141.

Hanrahan, J. *Government by Contract.* New York: Norton, 1983.

Hummel, R. P. *The Bureaucratic Experience.* (3rd ed.) New York: St. Martin's, 1987.

Rabin, J., and Bowman, J. S. (eds.). *Politics and Administration: Woodrow Wilson and American Public Administration.* New York: Marcel Dekker, 1984.

Rohr, J. A. *Ethics for Bureaucrats: An Essay on Law and Values.* (2nd ed.) New York: Marcel Dekker, 1989.

Romzek, B. S., and Dubnick, M. J. "Accountability in the Public Sector: Lessons from the Challenger Tragedy." *Public Administration Review,* 1987, *47* (3), 227–238.

Rosen, B. *Holding Government Bureaucracies Accountable.* (2nd ed.) New York: Praeger, 1989.

Schein, E. H. *Organizational Culture and Leadership: A Dynamic View.* San Francisco: Jossey-Bass, 1985.

Scott, W. G., and Hart, D. K. *Organizational America.* Boston: Houghton Mifflin, 1979.

Stone, C. *Where the Law Ends.* New York: Harper & Row, 1975.

Thompson, D. F. "Moral Responsibility of Public Officials: The Problem of Many Hands." *American Political Science Review,* Dec. 1980, *74* (12), 905–916.

Thompson, D. F. "The Possibility of Administrative Ethics." *Public Administration Review,* Oct./Dec. 1985, *45* (5), 555–561.

Thompson, D. F. *Political Ethics and Public Office.* Cambridge, Mass.: Harvard University Press, 1987.

Truelson, J. A. "Protest Is Not a Four Letter Word." *Bureaucrat,* 1985, *14,* 22–26.

Truelson, J. A. "Blowing the Whistle on Systemic Corruption." Unpublished doctoral dissertation, Department of Public Administration, University of Southern California, 1986.

U.S. Congress. *Codes of Ethics for Government Services: Concurrent Resolution of the United States Congress.* 85th Cong., 2d sess., 1958.

U.S. Congress. House. Committee on Post Office and Civil Service. *Legislative History of the Civil Service Reform Act of 1978.* Vol. 1. Washington, D.C.: U.S. Government Printing Office, 1979.

U.S. Congress. House. Committee on the Judiciary. *Reauthorization for the Office of Government Ethics for Fiscal Years 1989– 94: Hearing . . .* Washington, D.C.: U.S. Government Printing Office, 1988.

U.S. Congress. Senate. Committee on Governmental Affairs. Subcommittee on Oversight of Government Management. *Oversight of Department of Defense Ethics Programs, Hearing . . .* Washington, D.C.: U.S. Government Printing Office, 1989.

U.S. Merit Systems Protection Board. *Blowing the Whistle in the Federal Government.* Washington, D.C.: U.S. Government Printing Office, 1984.

U.S. Presidential Commission on the Space Shuttle *Challenger* Accident. *Report to the President.* Washington, D.C.: U.S. Dept. of Justice, 1986.

U.S. President's Commission on Federal Ethics Law Reform. *To Serve with Honor: Report of the President's Commission on Federal Ethics Law Reform.* Washington, D.C.: U.S. Department of Justice, 1989.

Vaughn, R. G. "Statutory Protection of Whistleblowers in the Federal Executive Branch." *University of Illinois Law Review,* 1984, *97,* 615–667.

Waldo, D. *The Enterprise of Public Administration.* Novato, Calif.: Chandler & Sharp, 1980.

Warwick, D. P. "The Ethics of Administrative Discretion." In J. L. Fleishman, L. Liebman, and M. H. Moore (eds.), *Public Duties: The Moral Obligations of Government Officials.* Cambridge, Mass.: Harvard University Press, 1981.

11 Strengthening Ethical Judgment in Public Administration

Debra W. Stewart
Norman A. Sprinthall

For more than a decade ethics has occupied a prominent place in the popular press as well as in the literature of public administration. The dominant popular view has been a minimalist one, holding that we need to focus on management ethics to curb corruption in public organizations.[1] Reinforcing this view, powerful scholarly arguments claim that unethical behavior can be reduced only by organizational strategies that place individuals in fewer compromising situations (for example, rotation and clear guidelines) and by increasing sanctions at the top of the hierarchy for illegal actions (Doig, 1983). Lodging accountability and punishment at the top of the organization in the office of the CEO and reducing "occasions of sin" for individuals through vulnerability assessment have been cast as the most direct strategies for reducing unethical and illegal behavior (Doig, Phillips, and Manson, 1984).

In contrast to the minimalist view, a more proactive perspective on ethics focuses on individual responsibility and assumes that public administrators are moral agents obliged to render moral judgments. This alternative view acknowledges that coupling executive accountability with structures to curb incentive for fraud and abuse is an effective strategy for deterring illegal behavior in complex organizations. However, emphasis on such strategies is flawed to the extent that it implies relieving individuals throughout the organization from personal accountability. Dennis Thompson puts the case most forcefully as he urges the rejection of both the "ethics of neutrality" and the "ethics of structure" as means of releasing individuals from personal responsibility for their actions. The neutrality ethics asserts that administrators should not follow their own moral principles but should neutrally follow the policies and decisions of the organization. The ethics of structure holds that not administrators but the organization should be held responsible for decisions (Thompson, 1985). Thompson rejects both as a substitute for individual responsibility. Quoting Robert Nozick, he concludes, "Responsibility is not a bucket in which less remains when some is apportioned out" (Nozick, 1974, p. 130).

If centering responsibility on individuals in an organization is a good thing, then ethics education becomes an important part of public administration training. Currently, administrative ethics scholarship, with its insights into the values that should guide moral judgment, seems remote from individuals who are asked to render judgments from deep in the organization. The next frontier in scholarship on administrative ethics must address a strategy for improving the moral reasoning capabilities of these administrators in the trenches.

In ethics education there are issues of substance and issues of process. Issues of substance relate to the values that should guide judgment. John Rohr's work on constitutionally grounded regime values (1978) and Terry Cooper's work on the obligations of citizenship in a democratic political community (1984, p. 143; 1987, p. 323) address these substantive issues. The process issues relate to the skills of moral reasoning. Through the decade of the 1980s scholars called for a teaching of administrative ethics that was aimed at improving moral cognitive capabilities (Fleishman and Payne, 1980; Hejka-Ekins, 1988, p. 886; Dwivedi, 1989, p. 12). While some expressed fear that such an approach could simply teach students to be more sophisticated rationalizers of their behavior (Lilla, 1981), this chapter sides with the view that "the development of ethical decision making skills among administrative students ought to be a significant goal of professional ethics education" (Hejka-Ekins, 1988, p. 886).

Toward this purpose, public administration educators recognize the need for providing ethics training in the curriculum. However, progress is being curbed by the dearth of empirical information on how administrators currently reason about ethical quandaries and by the absence of coherent educational strategies to improve current levels. This is not to gainsay recent strides in teaching ethics. The publication by ASPA of the workbook *Professional Standards and Ethics* (Mertins and Brannigan, 1982), an expanding pool of ethics courses offered around the country (Hejka-Ekins, 1988, p. 886), and the growing interest in the study of ethics in public policy programs (Brown, 1986) demonstrate a high level of activity on the issue. But while there exist a solid theoretical understanding of ethics issues and some general instructional strategies for teaching what is known (case studies, simulations), there is no empirical basis for marrying the two. The next step in public administration ethics research is to improve our understanding of the way managers reason when confronted with a moral quandary and to devise educational strategies for strengthening their moral skill and imagination.

Moral Reasoning: Theory and Research

Toward the goal of strengthening the moral judgment of public administrators, the research discussed in this chapter will enable students and practitioners of public administration to assess their own stages of moral reasoning. That assessment can serve as a departure point for education and training.

The present study is based on Lawrence Kohlberg's finding that moral development occurs in a specific sequence of stages across cultures. Kohlberg studied the system of thinking people utilize in dealing with moral questions and identified six stages of moral growth. Stages range from stage 1, straightforward concern about self, to stage 6, concern with the application of universal moral principles, such as those relating to justice and equality (Kohlberg, 1981). Individuals behave in an increasingly consistent and altruistic manner as they approach higher levels of reasoning. Kohlberg's Standard Moral Interview instrument presents general moral dilemmas and classifies individuals by stage according to arguments they invoke in solving these dilemmas. More recently, James Rest (1979) developed an objective adaptation of the Kohlberg interview. In this application Rest collapsed stages 5 and 6 into a "principled reasoning" stage (stage 5). Rest's paper-and-pencil

Defining Issues Test (DIT) permits wider application of moral development studies.

For the Kohlberg-Rest approach to be adapted meaningfully to the public administration context, three conditions must be met. First, the theory must be generalizable. Next, there must be evidence that the "moral stages" correlate with behavior. Finally, the implied direction of moral development must fit our ideals for the public administrator.

On the first point cognitive developmentalists such as Kohlberg and Rest claim universality for their theory. They distinguish between "surface behavior," which varies across cultures and groups, and "deep structure," which addresses the universal level of social experience. Stages of moral development relate to "deep structure" (Rest, 1982, p. 91). A body of empirical evidence supports this claim of cross-cultural validity. Snarey (1985) has reviewed some forty-five studies and has found striking support for cultural similarity.[2] Also supported were the concept of stages and the relation between stage and behavior as a means of addressing the important questions of adult decision making, ethical principles, and behavior. Such principles and behavior are not innate or inborn, nor are they the result of socialization; rather, they result from a gradual interactive process through the less complex stages toward those of greater universality.

On the second point, there has been substantial research that documents a behavioral relationship between levels of moral reasoning and actions. Blasi (1980) has reviewed some eighty works focused on the question of the relation of behavior to the moral judgment stage. He reported a consistently congruent relationship in 80 percent of those studies. The articles reviewed examined human behavior vis-à-vis important complex tasks such as doctor-patient relationships, counselor and teacher interactions with students, and behaviors by ministers, nurses, school principals, and adults in general.[3] Finally, James Rest (1982) has claimed that there are more studies that support both the construct and the predictive validity of this moral stages scheme than any other competing personality theory.

The final point on theory and research in moral reasoning relates to the compatibility of moral judgment and ethical reasoning in Kohlberg with the ideal of public administration. This chapter began from the assumption that public administrators are moral agents obliged to render ethical judgments. From the classical to the contemporary, political theory has acknowledged that there are stages of moral judgment representing different justice orientations. The Kohlberg stages in fact echo some of the classic dialogue from the *Republic* of Plato. At the lowest stage, Plato found reasoning and judgment to be based on physical or materialistic rationales. One need only recall the Socrates-Thrasymachus discussion of the judgments that "might makes right" (Cornford, 1945, p. 14) and that justice is "unlimited self seeking" (Cornford, 1945, p. 30) to find a parallel. Similarly, there is in the *Republic* a parallel to the next stage of the Kohlberg scheme, where reasoning and judgment are largely based on social conformity, the need to be accepted in the social group. This parallel occurs in Glaucon's discussion with Socrates, where Glaucon argues that justice involves helping one's friends and protecting one's social reputation while studiously obeying customs and rules (Cornford, 1945, p. 43).

In fact, it may even be possible to suggest a parallelism between Kohlberg's highest stage, democratic principled thought (a hybrid of Mill's utilitarianism and Kant's categorical imperative), and the Socratic allegory of the cave (Cornford, 1945, p. 227). In Socrates' representation the trees outside the cave are the ideal of perfect universal justice, on which the sunlight of abstract moral reasoning shines. The imperfect realizations of justice are represented by shadows on the cave wall, the distorted and less just representations of public administration in action. In more contemporary terms, principled reasoning may be compared to the perspective taking involved with John Rawls's (1971) veil of ignorance, in which the decisions concerning the distribution of a society's benefits and burdens are made according to a democratic conception of procedural equality. Another parallel to the Kohlbergian paradigm can be found in the work of Hobhouse (1906), who outlined stages of the democratic process as representing increasingly more comprehensive concepts of sovereignty based on justice.

In brief, an important theoretical element in the Kohlberg scheme is the idea that ethical-moral judgment is neither fixed nor relativistic but rather forms a sequence of stages or levels of ethical models. The higher-order models are more democratic and just in their comprehensiveness and thus are broadly compatible with the ideals of public service.

Applying Ethical Stage Theory to Public Administration

When confronting the issue of whether the scheme of stages has applicability to the tasks of the public administrator, there are two immediate questions: Do the tasks require an ability to understand the practical yet ethical dimensions in decision making, and can we measure empirically such practical yet ethical reasoning in a sequence of stages? To begin to answer these questions, an instrument was developed, patterned after the more general measures of ethical-moral judgment from the original work of Kohlberg and Rest. There was one continuing measurement issue that required attention, the question of context. Does the assessment of judgment change according to content or context? If one asks individuals to reason about general, impersonal, or abstract moral dilemmas, will such reasoning change (become higher or lower) if the dilemma is made directly relevant to a person's professional activities? Some previous research had indicated that the reasoning stage varies by context and that the closer the issue is to a individual's immediate role responsibilities, the greater the dissonance and the more varied the responses. Thus, the following measure was created with specific reference to ethical dilemmas often experienced by public administrators in their professional roles.

The content of the dilemmas for the Stewart-Sprinthall Management Survey (SSMS) was created by Stewart based on her lengthy experience in problem-solving discussions with executives in a public sector executive development program. The three dilemmas in the instrument, then, represent real-world issues that administrators actually experience. They are context specific.

The second part of the instrument is a series of rationales for resolving such dilemmas. The participants choose from among twelve alternatives the reasons that best fit how they would solve the problem at hand. The alternative "reasons" that might be important in solving each dilemma were constructed to parallel different Kohlberg levels or stages. For example, for the first dilemma, concerning promotion, a participant who chooses "Does Bob's sense of fairness require that he resist this patronage intrusion whatever the costs to his future effectiveness?" as an important reason would be selecting an answer that represents the highest stage in the scheme. In contrast, selecting "Doesn't Bob need to consider how to pay for his daughter's college tuition if he is fired?" would be congruent with the lowest levels. (Exhibit 3 displays the Kohlberg stages along with some characteristic reasoning at each level.) The alternative choices on the SSMS were created by Sprinthall on the basis of his extensive background in applying the Kohlberg approach to research and practice. The alternatives were further validated through discussions with professional colleagues and advanced graduate students skilled in comprehending Kohlberg theory.

Exhibit 3. Stages of Moral Reasoning.

Stage 1: Concern for Obedience and Punishment

To avoid punishment one must be obedient; fear of punishment is a major motivator.

Stage 2: Concern for Cooperation and Reciprocity in a Single Instance

Cooperative interactions are entered into because each party has something to gain: "Let's make a deal." It is the exchange that makes it fair. Bargains are struck to achieve self-interest. Materialism predominates.

Stage 3: Concern for Enduring Personal Relationships

Maintaining good relationships over time is valued; approval of others is important. Be kind and considerate and you will get along with others; reciprocal role taking; social conformity is the highest value.

Stage 4: Concern for Law and Duty

Authority maintains morality; everyone in society is obligated and protected by the law; respect for the authority of the law is part of one's obligation to society.

Stage P: Principled Reasoning

This mode of reasoning envisions the mind of a hypothetical rational person: What agreement would a hypothetical group of rational people accept? Impartiality is central. Democratic principles of justice and fairness are the core values.

With this background, the next step was to test the instrument with two samples of graduate students in public administration and to compare the results to the most widely used general measure of moral judgment, the DIT (Rest, 1979). The SSMS was patterned after that measure but with context-specific dilemmas and alternative "answers" relevant to the content. A comparison across the stages for the first sample (N = 34) indicated that the SSMS assessed the differences between principled (stage-5) and nonprincipled reasoning with the same degree of accuracy as assessed through the DIT[4] (see Table 3). The only area of difference was the tendency of public administrators to use stage 4 (concern for law and duty) more frequently on the SSMS than on the DIT. With a second sample (N = 50) the results were similar (see Table 4). The amount of principled versus nonprincipled thought was the same, yet again the selection of stage 4 was more common with the SSMS than with the DIT.

To further assess the similarities or differences between the measures, an intercorrelation matrix (see Table 5) was constructed that showed a moderately positive overall correlation between the SSMS total score and the DIT total score. All three of the SSMS individual stories intercorrelated positively with the three total scores on the survey.

Implications: How Ethical Action Might Be Enhanced

Two important conclusions can be drawn from these preliminary findings on moral reasoning in a public administration context. Each holds possible implications for efforts to enhance the quality of public administrators' moral reasoning.

The "Law and Duty" Emphasis. First, the finding that respondents to public administration dilemmas are pulled toward the "law and duty" response rather than distributing responses more evenly across the nonprincipled reasoning options merits further exploration. To put this finding in the context of moral development theory, we stress that it is through experiences that people develop a more elaborate conception of how to arrange cooperation and positive social relationships (Rest, 1986, p. 9). Moral develop-

Table 3. Comparing Principled Reasoning and Stage IV on DIT and SSMS Tests.

P Scores Compared to Stage 4 Scores* (N = 34)		
	DIT	SSMS
P score	41%	38%
Stage 4	34%	48%
P score range	7–83	17–70

*P scores = scores on principled reasoning; Stage 4 scores = scores on reasoning indicating a "concern for law and duty."

Table 4. Comparing All Stages of Moral Reasoning and the DIT and SSMS Tests.

All stage scores compared (N = 50)		
Stage	DIT	SSMS
1 and 2	5%	5%
3	11%	5%
4	33%	47%
P	41%	39%
Meaningless	7%	3%
P score range	(0–83)	(17–70)

Table 5. Intercorrelation Matrix for DIT and SSMS.

Score	SSMS Story 1	SSMS Story 2	SSMS Story 3	SSMS Total
DIT	.34	.24	.34	.42
SSMS story 1	1.00	.24	.20	.67
SSMS story 2		1.00	.30	.65
SSMS story 3			1.00	.76
SSMS total				1.00

ment is development in the way people adjudicate among competing interests. Along with each conception of social organization goes some sense of what is fair. When an individual has to decide right from wrong in a situation, the sense of fairness in adjudicating comes from the underlying sense of social cooperation. As Rest describes it, "various concepts of social cooperation and their accompanying notions of fairness provide heuristics for solving this problem. . . . If a subject can assimilate a particular social problem to one or another concept of cooperation and its accompanying sense of fairness, then the subject will have a basis for judging what is morally right" (Rest, 1986, p. 11).

What appears to be happening in this sample of MPA graduate students is that respondents are assimilating the administrative dilemmas described to them to a stage-4, or "concern for law and duty," scheme of justice. To put this finding in a public administration ethics context, our respondents are taking John Rohr's "low road" versus the "high road" in administrative ethics. This means addressing ethical issues exclusively in terms of adherence to agency rules (Rohr, 1978, p. 52). What explains this finding?

As noted above, Kohlberg has shown that a shift from stage 3 to stage 4 is usually the result of increased occupational responsibility. It may be that the occupational emphases in the public administration stories actually pull respondents in an upward direction toward the "low road." In the case of public administration, it may also be true that law and regulation provide protection to public administrators in the precarious world of political bargaining in which they work. Finally, it could be that the Wilsonian dichotomy between politics and administration is expressed in the belief system of the respondents who opt for stage-4 reasoning because they see it as the clearest expression of the public service ideal. The "goodness" of the rule of law is part of the culture of most public sector organizations and the in-class socialization in much graduate education in public administration.

If the environment of public administration does favor law and duty, it may provide some protection against the ruthless exploitation for personal gain evident in recent Wall Street and defense-contracting scandals (which reflect stage-2 and stage-3 reasoning). But it may also provide a built-in resistance to learning

principled reasoning. The essence of principled reasoning is defer-
ence to democratic values of justice and fairness. To the extent that
public administrators exhibit principled reasoning, they will utilize
these concepts in their decision-making roles. John Rawls has described an ethics of impartiality, justice, and fairness as the underpinning of democratic societies.[5] Where public administrators
utilize these concepts in decision making, they are moving administration toward a democratic ideal.

But is this ideal appropriate for public administrators, given
the role of administration in modern constitutional democracy?
This question speaks to the tension between official obligations and
ethical duties.

The very use of a moral development model as a tool for
knowing about and informing moral action in the administrative
sphere can be challenged on the grounds that "principled" ethical
reasoning (according to Kohlberg and Rest) exceeds the boundaries
of legitimate authority in public administration. Accordingly, our
finding that these respondents are heavily skewed toward law and
duty could be interpreted positively. Most would agree that morally
autonomous public administrators accountable to no one would be
a threat to democratic government. As noted in the introductory
discussion of individual ethical responsibility for administrators,
this chapter is motivated by a belief in the urgency of their assuming
individual moral responsibility. But what does this mean?

In the context of our study, to argue that administrators have
distinct moral responsibility for their actions is to argue that the
best government is one where public administrators can identify
moral issues and reflect on them at a principled level. To advance
this view is not to take sides in the debate about precisely which
authorities should be invoked to support one's principles. Denhardt
invokes "higher law" (1988, p. 42); Rohr argues for regime values
(1978, p. 4); Burke advances "political deliberations" (1989, pp. 100–
141). Nor is it to enter the dispute about how much "politics"
should constrain judgment in public administration (see Burke,
1989, p. 181). Rather it is a position that allows one to agree with
Denhardt's claim that the ethical administrator has a responsibility
to utilize personal moral assessments (Denhardt, 1988, pp. 109–110).
But it also allows one to accommodate Burke's concern that "a

purely moral approach gives insufficient weight to institutional obligations of public officials" (1989, p. 181), obligations that may justifiably trump claims of a morally inspired politics (1989, p. 181). Burke argues against a "purely moral approach" by proposing a "robust and active sense of administering . . . that means acting on responsibilities to protect the integrity of broader democratic processes and the institutional, and especially the administrative enterprise as a whole" (1989, p. 183). But Burke's argument could be a principled reasoning argument, not a law and duty argument. What is critical to understanding the argument in favor of more principled reasoning in public administration is that the emphasis is on why the manager thinks a decision is right or wrong and what considerations count.

To review the stages of moral development theory, they are interpreted primarily as reflecting one's conception of how social cooperation can be organized. Stage 4, or law and duty, reflects emphasis on "society-wide networks of cooperation based on law and roles within secondary organizations," while principled reasoning suggests "ideal principles for constructing societies" (Rest, 1986, p. 179). In a just and fair society organized on democratic principles, the laws and rules that emerge from democratic government and practice have a kind of moral authority that is recognized in principled reasoning and is distinct from blind allegiance to policies, practices, and rules.

It is the capacity to assimilate the legitimate regime values of fairness and justice while maintaining the autonomy to recognize conditions mandating dissent that marks the morally mature administrator. Hence, the resistance to principled reasoning suggested in our preliminary data is a matter of some concern.

Education for Moral Analysis. Second, to the point of educational implications, it is important to underscore the overall levels of reasoning presented by the sample of graduate students. On both instruments the sample selected principled reasons less than half of the time. These instruments are recognition measures. In other words, the subjects do not have to produce their own reasons, as in an interview protocol, but rather pick out the answers they might use from a prescribed list. Research has shown that such objective recognition measures usually overestimate by one stage the actual level subjects might employ if confronted by a situation requiring their own decision making (Kohlberg, 1984). Thus, the base rates reported in that study, if replicated, may indicate that the actual level of reasoning is well below a principled level. A recognition test allows subjects to put their best feet forward, so to speak. Under actual conditions of resolving value judgment dilemmas in their professional roles, we may find that the conventional levels of reasoning, stages 3 and 4, represent by far the preponderant level of analysis and choice.

Given the low rate at which our sample of respondents selected principled reasoning, the most important implication of these findings may be the question of curriculum revision in graduate education for the public service and enhanced in-service training in ethics. Certainly self-assessment is a part of that process. A variety of measures are available to provide students with information about their values and the ethical dimensions of their personalities (see Payne, 1988, p. 276). The purpose of the SSMS is to go beyond self-assessment to strengthen a student's capacity to identify a moral problem, determine courses of action and consequences, and function at a principled reasoning level.

The normative impetus of this chapter calls for reaching farther than controlling behavior of public administrators to improving the quality of ethical action in public sector organizations. If this direction is correct, there is a need to transcend simply describing the level of moral reasoning of incumbent administrators and current students. Kathryn Denhardt argues that public administrators should be trained like moral philosophers, to recognize, analyze, and discuss ethical dilemmas (1988, pp. 184–185). "Through the educational process, students can learn the basic language of philosophy, as well as the necessary background in the moral foundations of public administration" (Denhardt, 1988, p. 185). While there is always a temptation for the practical and concrete to edge out the abstract and theoretical in the public administration curriculum, in this area effective education may depend on the student's capacity to engage in the philosophical enterprise.

Conclusion

In general there is very little natural growth in the emergence of principled reasoning by adults. However, with systematic discussion and analysis of ethical considerations at the graduate level, there is a noticeable increase in the ability to analyze professional issues at higher levels of complexity (Rest, 1986) and more in accord with democratic principles of justice and fairness as outlined by Rawls (1971). The need to conduct more research that profiles how public administrators currently resolve ethical dilemmas marks an obvious frontier of public administration scholarship. There is, however, an equally compelling need to translate these findings into planned approaches for curriculum revision so as to develop a variety of instructional methods designed to promote the ability to resolve ethical problems at a principled level.

Notes

1. Daniel Callahan defines the minimalist ethics by saying, "One may morally act in any way one chooses so far as one does not do harm to others" (1981, p. 265). In the absence of harm one suspends moral judgment. Popular media (newspapers, television, and magazines) express this minimalist ethics in the preoccupation with malfeasant behavior as that behavior evoking moral condemnation (Carroll, 1987, p. 8). This minimalist focus has recently been reflected in press accounts of foreign bribery scandals, insider-trading convictions, and government contracting scandals. The press reports a public outcry for codes and organizational procedures to protect against these expressions of moral and unethical actions (Bennett, 1988; Read, 1988).
2. Snarey (1985) found that the sequence of stages did not hold for eastern tribal-feudal cultures where magical thinking and other forms of nonrational process were the guiding principles for governance. However, these cultures were the only exception to cross-cultural validity.
3. For example, Blasi (1980) reported that in a study of physicians there was a markedly positive correlation between assessed level

of judgment and democratic interactions with patients. Similarly, the best predictor of school principals' ability to lead through consensus building and collaboration was their level of moral judgment. Furthermore, the ability to resist authoritarian orders was directly related to Kohlberg levels in two studies, one with adults in general and a second with college students. Also, willingness to "blow the whistle" on unethical conduct indicated that the Kohlberg level was the best and only predictor of ethical behavior in such "awkward" circumstances (Braebeck, 1984). A follow-up of 1960s' Berkeley, California, student leaders indicated that only those who had reasoned at the more complex levels on the Kohlberg scheme maintained an action commitment to altruistic social problem solving (Nassi, 1981).

4. The typical graduate student in public administration in the pool from which these samples were taken is early to midcareer, in his or her early thirties, pursuing course work while in service. Except for sex, demographics were not collected on this sample, but there is no reason to suspect the sample deviates from the typical public administration graduate student population.

5. A legitimate question can be raised concerning the implied connection in this analysis between Kohlberg, Rawls, and democratic theory. The argument here is that in the moral development approach the individual operating at the highest stage of moral reasoning takes into account those considerations addressed in John Rawls's conception of a properly structured society. The "justice as fairness" ethic described by Rawls corresponds to the Kohlberg-Rest "principled" reasoning (Kohlberg, 1984, pp. 301–303; Hennessy, 1979, p. 219). A major thrust of Rawls's work since the early 1970s has dealt directly with how "justice as fairness" is designed to provide a framework for understanding the conceptual underpinning of modern constitutional democracies, including the individual's relationship to the democratic order (see Rawls, 1985, 1987; for a critical review of these new developments, see "Symposium on Rawlsian Theory of Justice: Recent Developments," 1989; see also

Cohen, 1989; Arneson, 1989). This view of Rawls is adopted in this chapter.

References

Arneson, R. J. "Introduction." *Ethics,* 1989, *99,* 695-710.

Bennett, A. "Ethics Codes Spread Despite Skepticism." *Wall Street Journal,* July 15, 1988, p. 19.

Blasi, A. "Bridging Moral Cognition and Moral Actions: A Critical Review of the Literature." *Psychological Bulletin,* 1980, *88,* 1-45.

Braebeck, N. "Ethical Characteristics of Whistle Blowers." *Journal of Research in Personality,* 1984, *18,* 41-53.

Brown, P. G. "Ethics and Education for the Public Service in a Liberal State." *Journal of Policy Analysis and Management,* 1986, *6,* 56-68.

Burke, J. P. *Bureaucratic Responsibility.* Baltimore, Md.: Johns Hopkins University Press, 1985.

Burke, J. P. "Reconciling Public Administration and Democracy: The Role of the Responsible Administrator." *Public Administration Review,* Mar./Apr. 1989, *49* (2), 180-185.

Callahan, D. "Minimalist Ethics: On the Pacification of Morality." In A. Caplan and D. Callahan (eds.), *Ethics in Hard Times.* New York: Plenum, 1981.

Carroll, A. B. "In Search of the Moral Manager." *Business Horizons,* Mar./Apr. 1987, 7-15.

Cohen, J. "Democratic Equality." *Ethics,* 1989, *99,* 727-751.

Cooper, T. L. "Citizenship and Professionalism in Public Administration." *Public Administration Review,* 1984, *44,* 143-156.

Cooper, T. L. "Hierarchy, Virtue, and the Practice of Public Administration: A Perspective for Normative Ethics." *Public Administration Review,* 1987, *47,* 320-328.

Cornford, F. M. *The Republic of Plato.* New York: Oxford University Press, 1945.

Denhardt, K. G. *The Ethics of Public Service: Resolving Moral Dilemmas in Public Organizations.* Westport, Conn.: Greenwood Press, 1988.

Doig, J. W. "Placing the Burden Where It Belongs." Paper prepared for panel on anticorruption strategies in public agencies, national conference of the American Society for Public Administration, New York, Apr. 1983.

Doig, J. W., Phillips, D. E., and Manson, T. "Deterring Illegal Behavior by Officials of Complex Organizations." *Criminal Justice Ethics,* 1984, *3* (1), 27-55.

Dwivedi, O. P. "Ethics for Public Sector Administrators." Paper prepared for presentation at conference/workshop on business and public sector ethics, Cambridge, U.K., July 1989.

Fleishman, J. L., and Payne, B. L. *The Teaching of Ethics.* Vol. 8: *Ethical Dilemmas and the Education of Policymakers.* Hastings-on-Hudson, N.Y.: Institute of Society, Ethics and the Life Sciences, Hastings Center, 1980.

Hejka-Ekins, A. "Teaching Ethics in Public Administration." *Public Administration Review,* 1988, *48* (5), 885-891.

Hennessy, T. C. "An Interview with Lawrence Kohlberg." In T. Hennessy (ed.), *Value/Moral Education.* Mahwah, N.J.: Paulist Press, 1979.

Hobhouse, L. T. *Morals in Evolution: A Study in Comparative Ethics.* London: Chapman & Hall, 1906.

Kohlberg, L. *The Philosophy of Moral Development.* San Francisco: Harper & Row, 1981.

Kohlberg, L. *Essays on Moral Development.* Vol. 2. New York: Harper & Row, 1984.

Lee, L., and Snarey, J. "The Relationship Between Ego and Moral Development." In D. Lapsley and C. Power (eds.), *Self, Ego, and Identity.* New York: Springer-Verlag, 1988.

Lilla, M. T. "Ethos, 'Ethics,' and Public Service." *The Public Interest,* Spring 1981, *63,* 3-17.

Mertins, H., and Brannigan, P. J. (eds.). *Professional Standards and Ethics: A Workbook for Public Administration.* Washington, D.C.: American Society for Public Administration, 1982.

Nassi, A. "Survivors of the Sixties: Comparative Psychological and Political Development of Former Berkeley Student Activists." *American Psychologist,* 1981, *36* (7), 753-761.

Nozick, R. *Anarchy, State, and Utopia.* New York: Basic Books, 1974.

Payne, S. "Values and Ethics-Related Measures for Management Education." *Journal of Business Ethics,* 1988, *7,* 273-277.

Rawls, J. *A Theory of Justice.* Cambridge, Mass.: Belknap Press, Harvard University Press, 1971.

Rawls, J. "Justice as Fairness: Political Not Metaphysical." *Philosophy and Public Affairs,* 1985, *14,* 223–251.

Rawls, J. "The Idea of an Overlapping Consensus." *Oxford Journal of Legal Studies,* 1987, 7, 1–25.

Read, E. W. "Contractors' Ethics Plans Get Scrutinized." *Wall Street Journal,* July 21, 1988, p. 4.

Rest, J. *Development in Judging Moral Issues.* Minneapolis, Minn.: University of Minnesota Press, 1979.

Rest, J. *Moral Development: Advances in Research and Theory.* New York: Praeger, 1986.

Rest, J. "Kohlberg Defended." *Personnel and Guidance Journal,* 1982, *60,* 387.

Rohr, J. A. *Ethics for Bureaucrats: An Essay on Law and Values.* New York: Marcel Dekker, 1978.

Snarey, J. "Cross-Cultural Universality of Social-Moral Judgment." *Psychological Bulletin,* 1985, *97,* 202–232.

"Symposium on Rawlsian Theory of Justice: Recent Developments." *Ethics,* July 1989, *99,* 695–944.

Thompson, D. F. "The Possibility of Administrative Ethics." *Public Administration Review,* Oct./Dec. 1985, *45* (5), 555–561.

Walker, L. "Sex Differences in the Development of Moral Reasoning: A Rejoiner to Baumrind." *Child Development,* 1986, *57,* 522–526.

12 Improving Ethical Decision Making
Using the Concept of Justice

Gerald M. Pops

Stephen Bailey, a former dean of Syracuse University's Maxwell School, wrote in 1962 that almost every issue in public administration is charged with an ethical dilemma. Nevertheless, he added, the executive rarely has the time or the patience for constructing balanced ethical judgments: "The ethical dilemmas of policy making in the modern world are complex beyond description. The internal dialogue of the decision maker, on those rare occasions when he has the time for ethical reflections, is fraught with paradox, anomaly, and the imponderable. Not acting in the public interest is far less a question of malevolence than of conceptual inadequacy; far less a question of fact than of meaning. And when a conceptual breakdown occurs, conscience often becomes paralyzed. For the decision maker, the result is hunch—hunch rationalized after the fact into the dignity of thoughtful reflection" (1962, p. 98).

Bailey's reflection may have been on Nicholas Henry's mind more than a decade later when, with John Rawls's conceptualization of justice in mind, he wrote, "What is needed for the public administrator is a simple and operational conceptualization of the public interest that permits him to make a moral choice on the basis of rational thinking" (1975, p. 40).

Rohr (1978) and Terry Cooper (1982) took their turns supplying guidance for the making of ethical administrative decisions. Rohr suggested "regime values," a fairly discrete set of values enunciated by the Supreme Court (property, equality, freedom, and others) that might be internalized and applied by a thoughtful and inquiring administrator. Cooper thought that moral judgment could be drawn from the individual administrator's various roles as

261

citizen, organizational member, and thinking person. Ethical responsibility, he reasoned, flows from linking obligations of public participation, laws and policies, certain prescribed inner qualities (such as accepting ambiguity, cultivating courage, and possessing a sense of fairness), and accepting a legitimate organizational role ("constitutional bureaucracy").

While helpful to administrators in thinking about various aspects of what it means to be ethical, these guidelines are not likely to have satisfied Bailey and Henry, nor have they been widely embraced in the field as comprehensive conceptual frameworks that can be applied by administrators to real situations. Denhardt, on reviewing the history of thought in the field, remained skeptical about giving advice to administrators. She insists on the widest possible range of moral judgment for the administrator: "While it is possible to give the administrator some guidance as to what the appropriate moral principles ought to be, it is not possible to give such specific guidelines or to develop a sophisticated enough process for arriving at moral judgments to assure that the administrator will not have to rely ultimately upon an individual moral judgment" (1988, p. 113).

The thesis of this chapter is that the concept of justice, fitted to the current role and responsibility of public administrators, can be designed to serve as a clear and usable criterion (or, more correctly, as a set of criteria) to the making of a wide range of normative decisions in public organizations. As such, it can serve as the cutting edge in the fashioning of guidelines for public administration ethics.

Grounded in constitutionalism, repeated constantly in the rhetoric of politics and public service, central to social and religious philosophy, and applicable to the quality of both outcomes and process, justice is an idea that ought to be taken seriously by public administrators. The fact that it has not yet been taken seriously is testament not to its critical importance, which is universally acknowledged, but to disagreement concerning its meaning and application in particular situations.

A great deal can be done to define justice in the public administrative context so that it can assist in the making of normative decisions. Its current lack of use, in great measure, is due to its

peculiar history and to the oddly separate paths that public administration and administrative law have traveled, a history recounted
briefly below.

Review of the Literature

Justice in public administration has been defined in general by the
values of democratic political tradition and in an operational sense
by administrative law. The term *administrative justice* has usually
been applied to encompass the rules of procedure prescribed by the
courts and legislatures for administrative adjudicative hearings and
the holdings of courts relative to the powers and discretion of administrative agencies. This tradition differs markedly from the Eu-
ropean tradition, which defines the substantive policy output of
public administration as part of administrative law (Schwartz,
1976).

Most of this law was developed in two waves of public policy
change: congressional standardization of the rules applicable to formal agency adjudications and rule making, enacted in 1946 and
codified in Title V of the United States Code, and the "administrative due process explosion" brought about by the Warren and early
Burger Supreme Courts and the activist Court of Appeals of the
District of Columbia in the 1970s (Shapiro, 1983; Rosenbloom,
1983; Pops, 1990).

The first sea change emerged from an accommodation between the American Bar Association and the Roosevelt administration. The bar had strenuously objected to the randomized experimentation going on in various New Deal programs with respect to
fact-finding, licensing, and regulatory decisions (Landis, 1938). On
the basis of the compromise worked out by the Attorney General's
Committee on Administrative Procedure (1941), the Administrative
Procedure Act of 1946 provided for formal hearing rules, semi-
autonomous hearing officers, and judicial review of formal adjudicative decisions.

The "administrative due process explosion," occurring
roughly during the period from 1960 to 1975, was part of a broad
movement to positively redefine constitutional rights in the context
of the modern administrative state (noted and anticipated by Red-

ford, 1969). The scope and nature of administrative hearings required by law and the range of parties that could initiate and participate in them were greatly expanded. The adjudicative decisions of ordinary administrators (not just formal hearing officers) at all levels of government and in nonregulatory as well as regulatory agencies, previously outside of administrative law and the zone of interest of the courts, suddenly received judicial recognition and scrutiny. Such persons as public school principals, prison wardens, and mental health administrators now were obliged by the courts to (1) determine when hearings *had* to be held as a matter of constitutional right and, when required, (2) determine the procedural elements that had to be provided given the particular circumstances. The courts prescribed more or less informal hearing requirements for many situations for which no hearings previously had been required, such as disciplinary prodecures for public school children. Just in case administrators were slow to get the point, the Supreme Court vastly expanded the potential personal liability of public officials and the governmental unit employing them and opened the door to citizen suits for violation of rights secured by the federal Constitution and laws. In addition, hearing requirements for rulemaking and licensing proceedings were made much more trial-like.

Administrative justice in the broad sense, as a standard of decisions by all public administrators, and not simply as process and scope of discretion elements in a lawyer- and court-dominated subsystem of administrative decision making, began to be systematically thought about in the 1970s. Two of the causes of this new way of thinking about justice both in and by public organizations were the definitive publication of John Rawls's ideas on "justice as fairness" (1971) and the alternative dispute resolution (ADR) movement. Rawls's writing marked the first small shift away from the conventional, judicialized approach to administrative justice toward looking at the justice of public organization decisions in the broad sense. The ADR movement addressed an efficiency concern that slow, expensive trial-type procedures were impeding or preventing the settlement of disputes. Whereas Rawlsian thinking challenged public administrators to think about the criteria for making just administrative decisions, ADR focused on the instruments and procedures that could be used to shortcut judicialized procedures.

The administrative due process explosion, which reached its high point in the early 1970s after the Supreme Court's decision in *Goldberg* v. *Kelly* (1970), stimulated a group of legal scholars to think about reforming the administrative hearing process to produce more just outcomes rather than more legally correct procedures. The seminal thinker in the movement was Henry J. Friendly, a federal appellate judge (1975). Other important figures included law professors Milton Carrow, Paul Verkuil (1978), Jerry Mashaw (1974), and Robert Dixon (1972). Collectively called "mass justice theorists" and structured about Carrow's Center for Administrative Justice in Washington, D.C., the group was concerned with how adjudicative decision systems could be designed so as to be responsive to the needs of fairness in the different agency environments. They were also concerned with the management of huge case volumes, a concern that gave them their name. Among their recommendations were the increased use of rule making, the deformalization of hearing requirements, and the substitution of professional, analytical judgment for generalist judgment obtained through adversarial process. The United States Supreme Court sounded a sympathetic chord when it restricted the scope of formalized hearings in *Mathews* v. *Eldridge* (1976).

Rawls focused on the role of government institutions in the fashioning of social justice. He persuasively argued that justice is the central virtue of institutions ("the political constitution and the principle economic and social arrangements"), which sets the stage for and determines all other values (1971, p. 7). Rejecting utilitarianism, which permits the possibility of imposing sacrifice on some in the interests of advantage to the many, in all its various forms, he employs moral discourse to arrive at a definition of just or fair institutions. The discourse assumes hypothetical persons who lack vested interests that would naturally result from their social positions (they are in the "original position"). Such persons would agree on the following principles of justice in social institutions: "*First,* that each person is to have an equal right to the most extensive total system of equal basic liberties compatible with a similar system of liberty for all, *and Second,* that inequality must be arranged so as to be both of greatest benefit to the least advantaged and attached to offices and positions open to all under conditions of fair equality of opportunity" (Rawls, 1971, p. 302).

Justice as fairness was embraced by public administration scholars soon after the publication of Rawls's book *A Theory of Justice,* and its meanings were projected to the functioning of public organizations under the label "social equity theory" (Frederickson, 1973, 1974). The theory linked Rawls to themes popular in public administration at that time: participation, organizational democracy and the sharing of power, and employee rights. Generally, these themes reflected the antiinstitutional flavor of the era (see also Marini, 1971).

Although social equity theory seemed a promising line of normative theory development, it was overtaken by events of the 1970s and strong criticism of Rawls's formulation of justice from the philosophy community. Disillusionment with the Johnson administration's War on Poverty, the passing of the events of Watergate into history, and the related effects of double-digit inflation, shrinking government revenue resources, and "cutback management" took center ground. Robert Nozick (1974) and others attacked Rawls on theoretical grounds, and public choice theory revitalized the utilitarian theory that Rawls had put on the defensive.

The work of the mass justice theorists, in its concern for cutting through formalization, presaged the ADR movement, which is now very much with us. ADR has emphasized negotiation as a preferred decision mode and has extensively used such third-party mechanisms as mediation and arbitration to resolve community, environmental, and public labor disputes. Such methods are even being experimented with in regulatory rule making (Harter, 1983; Susskind and McMahon, 1985). Employment of these methods has caused some elements of procedure long revered by lawyers and regarded by them as essential to justice—for example, hearings on the record, use of neutral decision makers, and the right to appeal— to be challenged.

Finally, the ethics movement in public administration, of which this chapter is a part, has underscored the need for a normative theory of decison making to guide public administration in a world filled with practical value dilemmas, antagonistic political demands, and the decline of the public service's reputation and morale (National Commission on the Public Service, 1988), but also a world in which the reality of administrative discretion and responsibility continues. Such an environment sets the stage for the introduction of conceptual frameworks such as the one presented in this chapter to guide the decisions of public managers and scholars.

The Idea of Reclaiming Administrative Justice

In the 1930s, administrative justice was an era of growth and activity in public administration. Although based on the British judicial habit of using court-appointed special masters, the models used in American agencies did not utilize judicial institutions. Innovative ideas for gaining social policy goals in the context of specific investigations and disputes were coming from administrative leaders in the Roosevelt administration. This experimentation pursued an approach far different than the conventional approach used in private legal practice to investigate, hear, and resolve disputes. The latter used adversarial process, judicial review, and lawyers and formal procedure.

Reflecting the fact that administrative justice was being forged by public administrators instead of lawyers, the teaching of administrative justice in our institutions of higher education was concentrated in political science and public administration programs. Law students, when they were exposed to administrative law, were taught by political scientists or public administration professors in joint government law classes. Administrative law was not yet considered a part of the regular law school curriculum (Dimock, 1980).

The forces combined in the years just prior to World War II to push administrative justice away from the province of public administration and toward the domination of the legal profession. The first was the organized effort, already recounted, of the American Bar Association to make uniform and judicialize the practice and procedures of administrative justice. The second was the willingness of the intellectual community of public administration (although not practitioners) to let that happen. Leonard White, author of the first public administration textbook in 1926, typified the antilaw bias of the public administration community by arguing that "the study of administration should start from the base of management rather than the foundation of law" (White, 1955, p. xvi).

The compromise effected between the extreme position of the bar calling for judicial review of all administrative decisions (actually incorporated in the Walter-Logan Bill of 1939, which was passed by Congress but vetoed by President Roosevelt) and the New Dealers led to an uneasy peace in the 1940s and 1950s. The case of *Ramspeck* v. *Federal Trial Examiners Conference* (1953), in which the Supreme Court spurned efforts of the bar to insulate hearing officers more completely from agency influence, set the tone. But the 1960s and 1970s were characterized by the increasing judicialization of federal and state hearing officer corps, the huge expansion of administrative hearings held by the courts to be required by the due process clause of the Constitution, expanded judicial review of administrative decisions, and the appearance of lawyers and lawyers' strategies in more of the agencies' decision processes.

Blease Graham (1986) argues that legal methods have proven cumbersome and inappropriate for many of the administrative disputes to which they have been applied. Administrative law judges (AIJ), who have become very specialized in particular areas of the law (for example, black lung disability disputes), tend to lack knowledge of the bases of the laws and policies under which they are operating. Administrative decisions, which must survive exhausting judicialized procedure, often come slowly and are not responsive to policy goals. What is needed is for public administrators, who have the vision of where public policy ought to be headed, to be in control. More of the decisions should take into account political factors, factors that administrative law judges and lawyers seem unable to appreciate.

Rosenbloom (1983) and Cooper (1988), however, take the opposite view. Public administration students, they argue, should study administrative law and internalize the process values of lawyers. This direction is justified by the many bad and arbitrary decisions administrators have made in the past relative to employee and citizen rights and liberties. Constitutional norms and legal profession intervention have worked well to reduce these abuses, they argue.

The irony is that some leaders of the administrative law establishment, including officers of the Administrative Conference of the United States, have expressed concern that the administrative decision process has become overjudicialized. In the view of Loren Smith (1985), past chairman of the conference, the current administrative decision process, heavily invested as it is with judicialized process, does not give the proper weight to political factors and does not serve the mission that the Constitution envisions for the agencies.

Should we teach students conventional administrative law? Or, in the spirit of the criticism of the narrowness of the legal approach to administrative decision making, should we prepare students in other ways? Should we stress the dangers of abusing individual rights and liberties of citizens and employees or the dangers that judicialization holds for effective administrative action? The answer seems to lie in doing both. We should attempt to inculcate in our students the principles of due process and fair treatment. However, we should also begin to study the conditions and contingencies that dictate whether judicialized decision making or some other form of decision making (strategic planning methods, for example) is most appropriate. Certainly there are conditions that favor judicialized process, particularly those in which personal hardships could be visited on individuals (as in disciplinary actions).

In view of the growing recognition in the legal community that judicialized process is overused and because of the growing costs of applying it in administrative settings, this author subscribes to the Graham thesis that public administration should be exploring an enlarged role in defining and controlling agency decision processes. Most conflict situations in public administration that could benefit from the application of justice principles are not sufficiently important to attract judicial protection or the interest of lawyers. If public administrators could learn to internalize principles of justice in all of their decisions, they could justify reclaiming the whole of administrative decision processes, in which lawyers could be used as adjuncts and advisors instead of norm setters and decision makers.

Justice as a Criterion for Ethical Judgments

The thesis of this chapter is that justice is a concept that can fill at least part of the need of public administration for reasonably objective, rational guidelines that can be used to analyze and resolve ethical dilemmas. An ethics of public administration must of necessity deal with the making of decisions in several arenas: policy-making, organizational design and management, program development, professional judgments, and personal behavior. Moreover, because the enterprise of public administration defines, through its practices, what government is for so many of our people, there is a need to ground our ethics in a comprehensive and comprehensible theory of the state. Finally, because we live in a society that pays homage to the Constitution and to democratic process, we need a theory of ethics that reflects these values as well. Can these special needs be met by justice?

According to political scientist Charles Anderson, public policy decisions should be evaluated by using one or more of the core values of American government: justice, authority, and efficiency. "How we perceive a problem depends on how we propose to evaluate it," Anderson begins, and he adds that "[e]ach step in the process of decision making depends on the initial stipulation of values to be served" (1979, p. 712).

Authority, which is legitimated or rightful power, is a prerequisite for regarding a problem or project as appropriately the subject of public action. Likewise, efficiency "is a necessary consideration in any system of policy evaluation," since "it is a legitimate criticism of any [decision] that there are better alternatives for achieving stipulated values" (Anderson, 1979, p. 719). "Efficiency is best regarded as an instrumental value, a tool for comparing policy options in terms of other values, a 'tie-breaker' between policy options that have passed minimum test of acceptability on grounds of authority and justice" (Anderson, 1979, p. 720). Efficiency plays an important role in serving administrative justice. Delivering a public policy implies the obligation to deliver as much of it as is practicable. Also, treating people fairly implies expanding the number of persons that can be served. This definition of social justice by Roscoe Pound is instructive as to the relationship of efficiency to administrative justice: "An adjustment of relations and ordering of conduct as will make the goods of existence . . . go round as far as possible with the least friction and waste" (1959, p. 65).

For justice to be a usable concept, it must be carefully defined so that it is not as broad as "social justice." There is endless quarreling as to the meaning of the broader, distributive aspects of social justice. Rescher (1966), for example, lists nine different distributive standards. Social equity theory, in casting its lot with Rawls's equal liberties and the disadvantaged, ran aground in a sea beset by conflicting conceptualizations of social justice. If we limit justice to the more definitive meaning it has in *administrative* decisions, we can make it more manageable. This can be done by tying it to constitutional norms that circumscribe role and responsibility. The term *administrative justice* will be used to designate this more limited sense of justice.

Administrative justice embraces both authority and efficiency values as important and necessary components in and subordinate to the core concept of justice. Justice is, to quote Rawls, "the first virtue of social institutions, as truth is of systems of thought" (1971, p. 3). Justice is a familiar concept that is a constant in our history and consistent with our constitutional traditions. Indeed, it appears prominently in the very first sentence of the United States Constitution: "WE THE PEOPLE OF THE UNITED STATES, in Order to form a more perfect Union, establish Justice, insure domestic Tranquility, provide for the common defence, promote the general Welfare, do ordain and establish this Constitution for the United States of America."

Our political leaders, both in and out of power, make constant reference to justice, as do our political interest groups and political parties. Every human being knows what it is to experience a "sense of injustice" (Deutsch, 1985). Moreover, and critical to our concern here, each citizen looks to government as the proper agent to right injustice. The core concept of justice is as simple as it is universally appealing: "To each according to their due." The idea draws power from its simplicity.

Public administration, functioning in the framework of the

Constitution and democratic principles, distributes the economic and moral goods of society in accordance with law and policy determined by elected representatives and courts. Sometimes it participates in deciding on what the distribution of economic and moral goods ought to be based (administrative policy-making) and almost always takes the leading role in carrying out the distribution that is decided on (implementation). There are two major instances in which public administration engages in administrative policy-making and in so doing determines the ends of distributive justice: first, when it is directed to do so by its political superiors (express delegation); second, when it possesses and is expected to exercise discretion based on its expertise and special knowledge (knowledge authority). Its managerial discretion gives it the power to make ethical judgments in the area of implementation. When implementing policy, whether that policy originates in the political branches or through its own discretion, public administration is the contact point for the interaction of citizen and government. The citizen's perspective of his government and its justness will be hugely influenced by the manner in which the policy product is delivered.

Public administration, as we are reminded frequently, suffers from a crisis of legitimacy. However wise an administrator or an agency might be, he or she or it should not, in a democracy, substitute judgment for that of popularly elected political leadership. To do so undermines the political accountability necessary for a democracy's viability. If administrators can identify the underlying focuses or vectors of change undertaken by political leadership and ratified by followers, then the legitimacy of all governmental actors is expanded. If the people are to "receive their due," they must receive what their elected representatives and judiciary have intended them to receive as they have expressed it in law. The latter's policy must be given a fair trial; if it works well, credit should be given. If it fails, failure should be noted and properly attributed to those who made the policy. If the administrator's goals intervene between the policymaker and the citizen, political accountability is lost, and democracy is compromised.

Democratic, constitutional governance demands of public administration the latter's voluntary subordination to the guidance of the "political" branches of government. The proper role of the public administrator is one of "constitutional balance wheel" (Rohr, 1986) and "agent" (Kass, 1989).

We can derive from these basic notions of authority—derived from democratic principles and constitutional norms—one of the basic tenets of administrative justice. Simply stated, it is the requirement that the administrator *deliver to the public that which legitimate public policy has promised.*

The one major exception to the demand that public administration play a constitutionally subordinate role to political leadership occurs in the case of the evil regime. The political leadership may generate policies so repugnant to social justice that they must be opposed on the basis of individual conscience, with all the authority and moral force that public office affords. The venality of the Hitler and Idi Amin regimes must be resisted by resignation at least and by active subversion if possible. Witness the brave disobedience by Danish administrators working under Nazi domination during the occupation; they refused to carry out German orders to have all Jewish residents identify themselves and state their property holdings (Frederickson and Hart, 1985). Hopefully, such situations are rare in developed democracies, but administrators were asked during the Nixon presidency to take actions intended to subvert the merit system and to harass citizens identified as political "enemies."

The second tenet of administrative justice is one of procedural justice: *accord to individuals and organizations due process and fair treatment.* The procedural rights due under the constitutions, laws, and policies of the nation, states, municipalities, and public organizations must be given to each and every person. Legality is a necessary but insufficient condition for the realization of justice. Procedural justice goes beyond what the law requires to meet the reasonable expectations that persons hold regarding what it means to be treated fairly. This involves meeting perceptions as well as rights.

Being true to democratic and constitutional precepts in helping to chart and carry out the distribution of economic and moral goods, and treating persons fairly in the process, form the foundation of the moral obligation of public administration to act justly and the basis of its legitimacy. As Freedman put it: "It is surprising that more attention has not been given, in the search for sources of administrative legitimacy, to the quality of administrative justice.

The procedural rules by which an institution reaches substantive decisions inevitably convey a telling indication of the fairness of its methods, the extent of its interest in protecting individual rights, and the depth of its commitment to attaining just results. In many important respects, the desire and the capacity of government to devise fair procedures for the discharge of its decision-making responsibilities are the essence of democratic practice" (1978, p. 11).

The essential outlines of administrative justice may now be stated. A just public administration is one that maximizes the distribution to the people that the lawmakers have promised (a goal function) and accord them due fair treatment in the process of carrying out this distribution (a process function).

It may be objected that the concept of administrative justice may be difficult to apply, that in given cases it means different things to different people, and that in any event politics are likely to intervene. There are two responses to this concern. First, public administration *is* political; it is an integral part of the political process (Appleby, 1952). Disagreement over what once-formulated public policy promises, and to whom, forms much of the stuff of politics. Therefore, it should distress no one to find that decision criteria *must* reflect political concerns and factors. Administrative justice does not seek to create social justice in spite of democratically adopted policy; rather, it incorporates the principles and compromises that are a part of such policy. Second, the fact that there may be disagreement over what justice requires in the individual case should not be allowed to decrease the urgent need to continue to seek it in both its collective and individual senses. There are guidelines in administrative justice that are clear and relatively unambiguous and that make administrative decision making less arbitrary and more predictable. The individual public administrator need not be left in a vacuum to decide for him- or herself moral standards for choice. The criteria set out below help to focus the administrator's attention on the goals of public policy while treating persons and interests fairly in the context of each case.

A Framework for Making Just Administrative Decisions

Criteria for making a just administrative decision have been described elsewhere in detail (Pavlak and Pops, 1989) but are presented here in somewhat simplified form. Basically, the criteria group around two sets of factors, the first having to do with the content of the decisions (the "goal function") and the second involving the methods by which the decisions are reached (the "process function").

The goal function of administrative justice, giving the people what their democratic-constitutional system has ordained, requires that the public administrator (1) keep the purpose of the public policy firmly in mind, (2) be uniform and consistent in making administrative policy, (3) focus on the citizen as the chief object and beneficiary of public action instead of the organization or a particular individual, and (4) deliver as much just decision making as is possible.

Under the heading of purpose, an administrator must be able to *separate the principle embedded in the policy from the rules that are its announced means for implementation and, in the event of conflict, choose the principle over the rule.* A discontinuity between principle and rule may exist for several reasons. Policymakers may have erred in their judgment that selected means would serve adopted goals. Means that subvert or at least do not pursue the policy's stated ends may have been intentionally introduced. Here is where the public administrators' special knowledge, experience, and expertise count heavily. Here their legitimacy is strongest and their confidence in their abilities most solid. Justice requires that administrators press for rules rationally related to the ends sought or use their discretion to reinterpret or ignore the obstructing or unhelpful rules. But then, in the close case, when reasonable people can disagree whether a particular rule is rationally related to a policy end, administrators owe an obligation to pursue the policy and give it a fair chance to succeed.

The formal, Aristotelian principle of justice dictates that like cases must be treated alike (and unlike cases treated unalike in proportion to the quality in which they are different). Equality of treatment is both a goal function and a process function, but the result of equal treatment must, by definition, be a goal of administration in a democratic society.

Those client groups identified by lawmakers as targets of largesse or attention must be served before organizational and personal interests. Mass justice theory contributes the good sense notion that greater efficiency is also a necessary criterion of administrative justice. More justice, in more cases, serves the ends of society.

The process side of administrative justice ordains that people be treated fairly. In general, dealing fairly with people means giving them a meaningful voice in the decision process, ensuring the accuracy of the factual bases of decisions, excluding personal bias of decision makers, being very open about how the decision is to be made, and explaining the reasons for the decision once it is made.

Fair treatment borrows heavily on constitutional concepts of due process as developed by the courts. Due process tends toward the rendering of fair decisions in disputes between individuals, and between individuals and government in which the latter is treated as though it were an individual. According to the Fourteenth Amendment to the Constitution, neither federal or state governments can deprive the citizen of life, liberty, or property without "due process of law." The essential elements of due process are giving of adequate notice, excluding bias, affording the opportunity to be heard, and permitting the right of appeal. Employing the elements of due process should come as no surprise to public administrators. The courts have been forcing agencies to practice an enlarged brand of "due process" for the last thirty years (Rosenbloom, 1983). But distilling the essence of these elements and delivering them in the ways that Redford (1969) advises take some practice and organized thinking. Providing fair procedure does not mean the automatic provision of a court-style hearing. In fact, one of the most disturbing developments in the past generation, in terms of fairness, has been the overuse of judication, legal rules, and lawyers in the administrative process. "Overjudicialization" and "legalization" and their ill effects on program administration have been recognized not only by the legal scholars of the mass justice school but also by leaders of the established practicing bar and bench (Smith, 1985). This recognition has led to increasing use of and experimentation with alternative modes of dispute resolution.

Fairness requires that adjudication and adversarial process be used only under circumstances that promote just results. This means, in the usual case, that judication should be limited to situations where there exist (1) a small number of parties, (2) a focus on a factual issue where contending versions of the facts are being urged, and (3) a standard that can be applied (Horowitz, 1977). Since judication is a costly and time-consuming process, the settlement of disputes by this means under circumstances not amenable to adversary procedures (that is, large number of parties, focus on a policy issue, lack of a clear standard to use for decision) produces inefficiency, inaccuracy, and the injection of idiosyncratic notions of policy. These factors lead to injustice. Agency resources are squandered on the settlement of fewer claims and with poorer results.

The Paradigmatic Value of Justice as a Basis of Ethics

The current search for guidelines for moral behavior and value dilemma resolution underscores the need for a comprehensive and comprehensible set of principles for making normative decisions. Such a quest is imposed on public administration by the fact of its considerable discretionary power and the need to justify the exercise of that power. Public administrators are at the contact point of a vast distribution system that allocates social, economic, and political goods. Their effectiveness should be measured by three values: authority, justice, and efficiency. Justice is the principal value of the three because it is oriented to both achieving constitutional ends and serving democratic and equitable process values. The concept of administrative justice, as articulated in this chapter, subordinates to it both authority and efficiency.

As a foundation for a theory of administrative ethics, administrative justice has many advantages. Its formulation is consistent with our constitutional and legal traditions. It is a concept with universal appeal and the potential for increasing the legitimacy of the public administration enterprise. Its place in the American mainstream suggests that it already is being used by the general public to evaluate the work of public organizations.

Harmon and Mayer (1986) analyze the conditions for the acceptance of a new normative approach or paradigm in public administration. Such a formulation, they say, would have to

1. guide decisions relative to the making of public policy as well as interorganizational and intraorganizational matters (decisions of staffing and resolving personnel disputes, for example) and personal matters
2. take into account those factors that inevitably convert a normative issue into more complex issues involving factual elements and judgments about the relationship of actions to consequences
3. recognize the necessity and inevitability of administrative discretion
4. be consistent—that is, be applied in much the same way by different administrative actors in different decision settings
5. lend legitimacy to the public administration enterprise
6. be understandable and capable of being applied by ordinary administrators in the course of their duties, that is, usable

There are a significant number of other paradigmatic "hopefuls," including efficiency, public interest, and constitutionalism. Each of these has its supporters, and each has certain strengths and failings when measured against the demands set out by Harmon and Mayer.

Efficiency. The efficiency paradigm dominated the field of public administration during roughly the first half of this century. Although its various formulations differ greatly (Waldo, 1948), its essence seems fairly straightforward. It measures the worthiness of administrative decisions by their effect on the ratio of outputs (in terms of organizational objectives) to inputs (budget and political supports). What is wrong with efficiency as a paradigm is familiar to any student of public administration. Means are appraised only in terms of their "payoff" on organizational "product" rather than in terms of their own merits (the "instrumental" view of organizational conduct). Yet, ironically, efficiency is criticized because it may result in a concentration on subgoals or proxies of ends because ends in the public sector are elusive and difficult to measure. Thus, despite the claim that efficiency focuses on output-input ratios, it may in reality divert attention away from the real ends of government activity. Despite these and other criticisms, efficiency is nonetheless an ethical premise—it makes an implicit statement about the proper role and conduct of public administrators and public agencies. The problem is that it is the wrong ethical premise because it assumes away administrative policy discretion.

Public Interest. The chief objections to public interest as a normative basis for ethical decision making lie in its inability to meet Harmon and Mayer's first, fourth, and sixth criteria. It is highly subjective and impossible to clearly articulate and consistently apply in individual cases. Its subjectivity and variability clearly affect its usability.

Constitutionalism. Rohr (1986) tells us that constitutionalism is not so much a normative basis for decision making as an attitude that imparts a perspective. The public administrator who adopts a constitutional approach gains, in Harmon and Mayer's perspective, an appreciation of administrative discretion, consistency in action, and legitimacy. It clearly conveys a sense of role and responsibility to public administration. Perhaps its greatest strength lies in its infusing the actions of public administrators and public agencies with legitimacy. Its use is less successful in gaining a handle on interorganizational or intraorganizational matters, the linkage between normative premise and fact-consequence issues, or the understanding of ordinary administrators (who would have to learn a good deal about the legal-constitutional system). Constitutionalism serves reasonably well as a paradigmatic approach to *policy* ethics but works less well with organizational, professional, and personal ethics. It is clear, however, that any paradigm for normative decision making in public administration in the United States must build in the concept of constitutionalism.

Administrative Justice. Administrative justice works to guide organizational and personal decisions as well as it does to guide policy issues. Since it incorporates a decision methodology in which factual accuracy and clear standards for judgment are essential, it necessarily relates ends back to factual sources and promotes consistency. Its use of an output dimension (that is, the criterion that commands the active pursuit of legitimate public policy goals) brings constitutionalism into its scope and thus allows it to meet the test of legitimacy. Since individual decision makers are expected to identify the purposes of public policy and act to pursue the purpose even to the prejudice of specific rules contrary to such purpose, the concept recognizes the essentiality of discretionary authority in the administrator. Finally, the fact that administrative justice is in important part based on familiar notions of due process and common fairness makes it understandable to many if not most administrators and lends to it additional legitimacy. Therefore, administrative justice may lay claim to meeting each of Harmon and Mayer's six paradigmatic conditions.

Institutionalizing Administrative Justice

Inculcating administrative justice in our public organizations, no matter how forceful the logic of the argument, requires some thinking about strategies and tactics. Such innovations as inspectors general, ombudsmen, and encouraging whistle-blowers are being addressed elsewhere in this volume. These have been tried with varying degrees of success and are no doubt helpful. However, something more fundamental is needed. We can say, somewhat tautologically, that we should structure our organizations and induce an organizational climate and culture in ways conducive to their doing justice. How do we do that?

Public administration academicians may make a contribution by both reexamining their abundant literature so as to extract and organize ideas that can contribute to the doing of administrative justice and looking out beyond their familiar reading lists to incorporate much fertile thought that is invigorating other fields, namely, social psychology, law, conflict management, and labor relations.

Illustrative of the rich literature capable of being reexamined in the new light of administrative justice is Weber's theory of bureaucracy. The basic characteristics of bureaucratic organization he identified—hierarchy, rules, impersonality, and filling positions based on technical competence—have long been attacked in the literature of organizational theory as productive of mischievous consequences and thus dysfunctional to some extent. However, if we begin to accept justice as infusing both organizational ends and means, bureaucracy may take on a somewhat more favorable aura for the student of organization. The characteristics of bureaucracy may actually work in the direction of ensuring justice (as well as promoting injustice). For example, hierarchy can be appreciated from the perspective of the role it plays in guaranteeing an independent review of a decision, one of the procedural criteria of administrative justice, and the record-keeping function actually promotes accuracy in the making of decisions (witness the many cases in which inmates have been kept too long in prison).

Professionalism. Another thing that can be done is to recognize the potential strength of our professional organizations and begin to include justice in our professional rhetoric, goal statements, and professional curricula. A real commitment to justice should strengthen our legitimacy among members of the general public and promote internal cohesion in public agencies. The legal profession has managed to dominate the field of administrative justice with great authority and with perhaps less positive effect than would have been the case had public administration filled a partnership role. Many injustices in administration flow directly from the inappropriate application, *by the legal system,* of legal norms and practices in the decision making of public organizations, as when, due to excessive formality in the processing of claims, a large part of the total volume of claims is neglected.

Conclusion

A research agenda for studying how justice can be used in making ethical decisions in public administration extends to (1) inquiry into the nature of perceived injustices at the hands of public administration by both citizens and public employees; (2) the behaviors, attitudes, and moral qualities of public administrators that are associated with or perceived to be associated with the doing of justice; and (3) the structural arrangements that favor or constrain such administrative behavior, attitudes, and qualities. Some injustices are imposed by administrator wrongdoing or nondoing; others are the result of conditions the administrator has little to do with (lack of adequate program funding, faulty legislative design, and so on). More studies such as that of Bardach and Kagan (1982) are needed to explore the complex relationship that exists between rule enforcement, administrative discretion, and effective compliance. Some injustices are the result of system failure and are not attributable to individual decision makers; others are attributable to personal motives and incentives that shape the roles and drive the behavior and attitude formation of administrative decision makers.

Justice is simply too important to leave to the lawyers. What once was the frontier of public administration—giving the people their due—can yet again become the frontier. Justice is everyone's business. Academic public administration should study the demands and processes of justice as they affect public policy development and implementation and the fair treatment of those subject to the application of administrative power. Public administration in general, both academic and practitioner communities, should move aggressively to reclaim administrative justice as the proper sphere of their endeavor.

References

Anderson, C. W. "The Place of Principles in Policy Analysis." *American Political Science Review*, 1979, *73*, 711–723.

Appleby, P. H. *Morality and Administration in Democratic Government*. Baton Rouge: Louisiana State University Press, 1952.

Attorney General's Committee on Administrative Procedure. *Final Report*. Senate Document no. 8, 88th Cong. 1st Sess., 1941.

Bailey, S. K. "The Public Interest: Some Operational Dilemmas." In C. J. Friedrich (ed.), *NOMOS V: The Public Interest*. New York: Atherton Press, 1962.

Bardach, E., and Kagan, R. A. *Going by the Book: The Problem of Regulatory Unreasonableness*. Philadelphia: Temple University Press, 1982.

Cooper, P. J. *Public Law and Public Administration*. (2nd ed.) Englewood Cliffs, N.J.: Prentice-Hall, 1988.

Cooper, T. L. *The Responsible Administrator: An Approach to*

Ethics for the Administrative Role. Port Washington, N.Y.: Kennikat Press, 1982.

Denhardt, K. G. *The Ethics of Public Service: Resolving Moral Dilemmas in Public Organizations.* Westport, Conn.: Greenwood Press, 1988.

Deutsch, M. *Distributive Justice: A Social-Psychological Perspective.* New Haven, Conn.: Yale University Press, 1985.

Dimock, M. E. *Law and Dynamic Administration.* New York: Praeger, 1980.

Dixon, R. G., Jr. "The Welfare State and Mass Justice: A Warning from the Social Security Disability Program." *Duke Law Journal,* 1972, *1972,* 681-741.

Frederickson, H. G. "Creating Tomorrow's Public Administration." *Public Management,* 1973, *53,* 2-4.

Frederickson, H. G. (ed.). "A Symposium: Social Equity and Public Administration." *Public Administration Review,* 1974, *34,* 1-51.

Frederickson, H. G., and Hart, D. K. "The Public Service and the Patriotism of Benevolence." *Public Administration Review,* Sept./Oct. 1985, *45,* 547-553.

Freedman, J. O. *Crisis and Legitimacy: The Administrative Process and American Government.* Cambridge, Eng.: Cambridge University Press, 1978.

Friendly, H. J. "Some Kind of Hearing." *University of Pennsylvania Law Review,* 1975, *123,* 1267-1317.

Gerth, H. H., and Mills, C. W. (eds.). *From Max Weber: Essays in Sociology.* New York: Oxford University Press, 1946.

Goldberg v. *Kelly,* 397 U.S. 254 (1970).

Graham, C. B., Jr. "Justice and Administration: Rediscovering Neglected Traditions." Paper presented at annual meeting of the American Society for Public Administration, Anaheim, Calif., Apr. 1986.

Harmon, M. M., and Mayer, R. T. *Organization Theory for Public Administration.* Boston: Little, Brown, 1986.

Harter, P. J. "Dispute Resolution and Administrative Law: The History, Needs, and Future of a Complex Relationship." *Villanova Law Review,* 1983, *29,* 1393-1419.

Henry, N. *Public Administration and Public Affairs.* Englewood Cliffs, N.J.: Prentice-Hall, 1975.

Horowitz, D. L. *The Courts and Social Policy*. Washington, D.C.: Brookings Institution, 1977.

Kass, H. D. "Exploring Agency as a Basis for Ethical Theory in American Public Administration." *International Journal of Public Administration*, 1989, *12* (6), 949–969.

Landis, J. M. *The Administrative Process*. New Haven, Conn.: Yale University Press, 1938.

Marini, F. (ed.). *Toward a New Public Administration: The Minnowbrook Perspective*. Scranton, Pa.: Chandler, 1971.

Mashaw, J. L. "The Management Side of Due Process: Some Theoretical and Litigation Notes on the Assurance of Accuracy, Fairness, and Timeliness in the Adjudication of Social Welfare Claims." *Cornell Law Review*, 1974, *59*, 772–824.

Mathews v. *Eldridge*, 424 U.S. 319 (1976).

Merton, R. *Social Theory and Social Structure*. New York: Free Press, 1957.

National Commission on the Public Service. *Leadership for America: Rebuilding the Public Service*. Washington, D. C.: National Commission on the Public Service, 1988.

Nozick, R. *Anarchy, State and Utopia*. New York: Basic Books, 1974.

Pavlak, T. J., and Pops, G. M. "Administrative Ethics as Justice." *International Journal of Public Administration*, 1989, *12* (6), 931–948.

Pops, G. M. "Administrative Law as Public Policy: The First Fifty Years." *Journal of Policy History*, 1990, *2* (1), 98–117.

Pound, R. *Jurisprudence*. St. Paul, Minn.: West, 1959.

Ramspeck v. *Federal Trial Examiners Conference*, 345 U.S. 128 (1953).

Rawls, J. *A Theory of Justice*. Cambridge, Mass.: Belknap Press, Harvard University Press, 1971.

Redford, E. S. *Democracy in the Administrative State*. New York: Oxford University Press, 1969.

Rescher, N. *Distributive Justice: A Constructive Critique of the Utilitarian Theory of Distribution*. Indianapolis, Ind.: Bobbs-Merrill, 1966.

Rohr, J. A. *Ethics for Bureaucrats: An Essay on Law and Values*. New York: Marcel Dekker, 1978.

Rohr, J. A. *To Run a Constitution: The Legitimacy of the Administrative State.* Lawrence: University Press of Kansas, 1986.

Rosenbloom, D. H. *Public Administration and Law: Bench v. Bureau in the United States.* New York: Marcel Dekker, 1983.

Schwartz, B. *Administrative Law.* Boston: Little, Brown, 1976.

Shapiro, M. "Administrative Discretion: The Next Stage." *Yale Law Journal,* 1983, *92,* 1487–1522.

Smith, L. A. "Judicialization: The Twilight of Administrative Law." *Duke Law Journal,* 1985, *1985,* 427–466.

Susskind, L., and McMahon, G. "The Theory and Practice of Negotiated Rulemaking." *Yale Journal on Regulation,* 1985, *3* (1), 133–165.

Verkuil, P. R. "The Emerging Concept of Administrative Procedure." *Columbia Law Review,* 1978, *78,* 258–329.

Waldo, D. *The Administrative State: A Study of the Political Theory of American Public Administration.* New York: Ronald Press, 1948.

Walter-Logan Bill. Senate Bill 915, 76th Cong. 1st Sess., 1939.

White, L. D. *Introduction to the Study of Public Administration.* New York: Macmillan, 1926.

White, L. D. *Introduction to the Study of Public Administration.* (4th ed.) New York: Macmillan, 1955.

13   Legitimizing Administrative Discretion
Through Constitutional Stewardship

Douglas F. Morgan
Henry D. Kass

[W]hen a tradition is in good order it is always partially constituted by an argument about the goods the
pursuit of which gives that tradition its particular
point and purpose.

     So when an institution—a university, say, or a
farm or hospital—is the bearer of a tradition of practice or practices, its common life will be partly, but
in a centrally important way, constituted by a continuous argument as to what a university is and ought
to be or what good farming is or what good medicine
is. Traditions, when vital, embody continuities of
conflict [MacIntyre, 1984, p. 222].

American public administration, like a university, a farm, or
a hospital, is the bearer of a tradition of practices that reflects a
continuous debate about what public administration ought to be.
As with all such debates, these normative visions affect the kind of
ethical obligations public administrators are expected to assume.
Over the past fifteen years of teaching and working with experienced career administrators, we have been struck by their capacity
to entertain seemingly contradictory elements of the public administration tradition and the equally contradictory obligations they
engender. For example, we have seen administrators justify their
actions primarily as neutral agents of efficient and effective policy
implementation. At other times we have seen them invoke a pluralist political model to legitimate their efforts to negotiate compro-

mises and build consensus. On still other occasions we have seen administrators resort to the language of the public interest to justify actions that may seem unpopular to vocal constituencies they serve. As outside observers we have always been curious about two questions: To what extent do practitioners seriously and simultaneously embrace all of these seemingly contradictory threads? To what extent do such threads form some larger pattern in the fabric of American administrative practice? In short, in what sense can it be said that these threads constitute what Alasdair MacIntyre calls a common practice or, instead, reflect merely a pragmatic desire to use whatever justification will work to get the administrator's job done?

To help us explore these questions we assembled a focus group of six experienced senior-level local administrators.[1] They consisted of the chief administrative officers of three city and county jurisdictions and three senior-level department heads. Each has a reputation among professionals in the field for being an outstanding public servant with high ethical standards. Each has had a distinguished career and advanced rapidly at a young age to a position with high levels of discretionary authority. Under the pledge of confidentiality the panel members were each asked to take turns presenting ethical problems they have encountered to the group for discussion and decision. Our assumption was that these discussions would provide us with an opportunity to observe how practitioners viewed the relationship among the constituent elements of their administrative practice.

In the remainder of this chapter we will outline the defining characteristics of the phenomena of ethical practice we have observed in our panel of public administrators. This discussion will surface three dominant "continuities of conflict," to use MacIntyre's phrase, which seems to contend for dominance and, together, constitute the American administrative ethos. As we shall see, neutral technical competence, maintaining balance among competing interest groups, and serving the public interest are all frequently used by our panel of administrators to justify the exercise of administrative discretion. In the second section of the chapter we will argue that reliance on each of these justifications is shaped in large part by three problems confronted by practicing administrators: the complex and uncertain *environment* in which they function, the *ambiguity* of their role in our constitutional system of government, and the *conflicting values* among the constituents they serve. We will conclude by arguing that constitutional stewardship provides us with the best model for understanding the continuities in conflict in American administrative practice. In short, properly understood, the contradictory language of administrative practice mirrors the broader contradictions inherent in successfully perpetuating our regime of ordered liberty.

Dialogical Elements in the American Administrative Ethos

We surfaced three dominant values that provide different standards for guiding the discretionary exercise of authority by our focus group of practitioners. At times they see themselves as keepers of competent government; at times they portray themselves as balancers of competing interest groups. When these fail or appear inappropriate to the task, they invoke the public interest. To borrow a phrase from Bellah and others (1986), our administrators seem to invoke three separate languages of discourse. The first language of efficiency and effectiveness relies heavily on Weber and Wilson's (Shafritz and Hyde, 1987) politics-administration dichotomy and emphasizes the importance of neutral competence. The second language draws on our pluralist political tradition and emphasizes the need to maintain a balance among competing political interests. The third language of the public interest is more difficult to categorize, but it rests on a notion of stewardship that obligates career administrators to protect those deeper communal values at the core of our rule of law system. As we will argue in the final section of this chapter, our use of the term *language* to designate each of the three major elements of the American administrative ethos captures the important role we believe dialogue among these elements must play in helping to maintain the continuities in conflict that are so critical to the health of our democratic polity.

The First Language of American Public Administration: Neutral Competence. Members of our panel frequently invoke the language of efficiency and effectiveness to justify administrative action. In addition, much of what they do and how they do it might easily be interpreted in terms of living in a means-end world in which policy ends are established solely by elected officials, leaving career administrators to tend to matters of efficient and effective administration. For example, all of our administrators are reluctant to assume public leadership roles in divisive policy issues, arguing that such business is the prerogative of elected public officials. They seldom, if ever, are willing to assume at the outset of a problem presented for discussion that it poses a deeply troubling value choice or conflict. Before concluding that this is the case, they raise a host of questions. For example, they want to know what is likely to happen if one waits for this or that piece of potentially relevant information. They want to know how a question might be posed to turn a set of decision-making choices away from conflict-generating values toward a more neutral information-gathering and decision-structuring process.

There are obvious reasons why the language of administrative neutrality has considerable appeal for members of our administrative panel. It enables them to tame what have been characterized as wicked problems (Rittel and Weber, 1973) by banning politics from the administrator's world. By normative fiat the manager becomes a dealer in "tame problems" (Rittel and Weber, 1973), ones that can be defined and resolved by technical expertise and logic. This encourages the administrator to conduct a very limited analysis of the situation, largely to see if the principles of technical rationality can be made to apply in some fashion.

Despite its appeal, our focus group of practitioners ultimately reject two of the key assumptions on which the first language rests: (1) the ability and desirability of banning politics from the administrator's world and (2) the ability to separate means from ends. Our administrators are very much aware that they cannot find a safe haven from interest group pressures that constantly surface in the formulation, execution, or evaluation of public policy. They are so preoccupied with such pressures that they characteristically define a problem and anticipate a course of action based on what the "crazies" will say or do. "Crazies" are defined by members of our focus group as single-issue interests who collectively seek to make every public concern a "wicked problem," that is, a matter of fundamental value conflict (Rittel and Weber, 1973; Zammuto, 1982).

Even if it were possible to ban politics from the administrative arena, our focus group expresses reservations about whether this would be desirable. While the first language may simplify the administrator's world ethically and politically, it does so at the cost of making administrators politically irrelevant. Irrelevance is not something that sits easily with a group so deeply committed to an ethics of serving others.

Wicked problems are not the only nemesis of the first language of American public administration. It is also plagued by the requirement that administrators clearly distinguish means from ends. The model of neutral competence requires that the administrator assiduously avoid any participation in the formulation of the ends of government. This, according to the first language, is an activity reserved to the elected legislative body. However, members of our panel find this separation extremely difficult to maintain in practice, mainly because so many administrative and technical issues have a value and thus a policy content. For example, one of the most difficult ethical cases faced by our panel involved a city manager who realized that the seemingly innocuous process of putting certain technical and administrative issues on the city council agenda could be politically explosive during an election period. The first language gave our manager little guidance and no responsibility to consider the political ramifications of his technical and administrative position. However, he fully realized that the administrative decision to bring certain issues to the council table at election time would have profound political impacts not only on policy but also on the electoral process itself. To make his ultimate decision to withhold the issue until after the election, he was forced to consider the other languages in the ethical dialogue, those of pluralist politics and the public interest.

The Second Language of American Public Administration: Pluralist Politics. Since members of our administrative panel all practice in political systems that are basically pluralist, it is not surprising that we found considerable evidence of this normative model being used to justify actions at two major stages of the administrative process. The first occurs at the problem-setting stage, where members of our panel go about the task of defining the situation for action. The second occurs at the action-taking stage, where panel members seek to justify what should be done.

At the problem-defining stage pluralism provides an ethical basis for the major process used to resolve the interest group conflicts that continually threaten the competent operation of government. This is well illustrated by one of the cases presented for discussion by a member of our panel. In the face of a sex-discrimination charge made by a group of employees against one of his departmental deputies, the administrator established a labyrinthine investigative process that would have met the strictest courtlike presumption of innocence. However, in this case appearances would have been deceiving. When called on to explain why such strict prophylactic processes had been used, the administrator emphasized the importance of accommodating a variety of competing interests that included the consequences on future relationships with the employee union, the desire to protect competent managers, the needs of the accused, and the impact of the process on the overall morale and capacity of the organization.

Members of our administrative panel not only rely on the pluralist ethic to shape *how* they approach the policy process; more importantly, they also use the language of interest group accommodation to justify policy outcomes. In a case presented for discussion, one of our participants succeeded in persuading a member of his elected board to refrain from pushing more restrictive reading access standards on the local public library because of the conflict this would foster at the board level. Even though the protection of fundamental First Amendment issues was at stake for the administrator, he relied instead on the value of avoiding interest conflict at the elected board level in persuading the official to refrain from pushing for the adoption of more restrictive standards.

These cases are typical of how the pluralist ethic affects both the process and substance of ethical decision making by members of our panel. The ethic encourages administrators to perform two roles critical to the successful functioning of the political process. At times they are required to be "balancers of interests" and at other times to be "facilitators of consensus." These injunctions obviously put administrators at odds with the more traditional bureaucratic principles inherent in the classical model, which emphasize the mobilization of rational analysis by career administrators over the mobilization of the political power of interest groups. Under the pluralist model at best the technical competence emphasized by the first language becomes a mere tool for shaping the outcome of the interplay among competing interest groups rather than a mode of calculating the most rational alternatives to politically determined ends. Politically, analysis may be valued more for its ability to mobilize power than for its power to reveal truth.

The pluralist model encourages participants to become experts at calculating their own interests and making those interests known to the power holders in the political system. This fosters a partial approach to the public interest rather than the more comprehensive approach sought by those with technical competence and trained in analysis (Lindblom, 1987). The partial approach is defended for two reasons. First, it is much simpler for each participant to calculate his own preferences than for each to try to calculate the preferences of all. The danger of omitting important values is much greater when participants neglect the values in their immediate care in favor of what seems to them a broader view. How can anyone know what is being neglected if everyone speaks for someone else and no one for himself? How can we expect participants to act "to protect the interests of others (which they believe they should take into account but which are not theirs) as well as those who have these interests" (Wildavsky, 1984, p. 166)? A second defense of pluralism is that it is "more efficient for resolving conflicts, a process that lies at the heart of democratic politics. Because the approach is partial, it does not require its practitioners to discover all or most possible conflicts and to work out answers to problems that may never materialize" (Wildavsky, 1984, p. 167).

When a reliance on pluralism or efficiency fails to provide members of our administrative panel with sufficient justification for action, they tend to fall back on an abstraction called "the public interest." In almost all cases this abstraction is not reducible to a mere sum of the partial interests they are seeking to accommodate.

The Third Language of Public Administrative Practice: The Public Interest. The public interest or the common good serves as the ultimate justification for our panel's exercise of administrative discretion. We have observed members of the panel using the public interest to justify action that some would regard as contrary to the strict letter of the law. It has been invoked to justify action involving conflict among a variety of equally choiceworthy goods or to justify choosing the least objectionable among undesirable alternatives. When pressed to define with some specificity what they mean by the public interest, they have little difficulty in doing so. In almost all cases, the public interest is identified with a set of procedural or substantive values that the practitioners believe the community is bound to uphold even when majority sentiment may be against them. Career administrators see themselves as guardians of this historical reservoir of communal self-identity. For example, preserving a treasured natural water supply against short-term commercial interests or standing against local racial prejudice at the risk of being fired were both offered as examples of where the public interest was sufficiently strong to take action at the expense of one's career.

The third language provides a way for our panel of administrators to overcome some severe limitations pluralism places on them. It is, first of all, a way to recognize collective interests over the partial interest of groups in the community. It is also a way for administrators to protect the rights and interests of individuals who are entirely unknown to them as people or may be unrepresented as concrete interest groups. These "abstract others" are usually known by collective nouns such as the poor, the elderly, youth, taxpayers, and, most of all, the public.

Our administrators also have what could be called a sense of intergenerational obligation. As the name suggests, this obligation requires the administrator to become an agent of future generations, to transmit to posterity the most cherished values of the past without allowing that past to become a dead and lifeless hand holding the future hostage. Finally, our focus group is extremely protective of those values whose realization forms the basis of the legitimate authority exercised by the state and its agents, including such rights as free speech, undue invasions of privacy, and respect for various kinds of ethnic, religious, and gender diversity.

The Conditions of Administrative Practice

One of the central questions that prompted our focus group study was how to understand the interactive relationship among the three major elements we have identified in the American administrative ethos. To what extent, if any, do these dialogue threads reflect the larger whole of a healthy professional practice engaged in debate over what Alasdair MacIntyre calls continuities in conflict? An answer is suggested by the conditional and contingent nature of the three languages we have outlined. No member of our focus group is willing to embrace one language to the exclusion of the other. Panel members are seldom if ever willing to assume *at the outset* of a problem presented for discussion that it can be successfully resolved by invoking one language in preference to another. Before settling on a language appropriate to the occasion, panel members raise a host of questions that assume their administrative environment is murky, their role as administrators is ambiguous, and ethical labels are problematical in the public policy process. These contingencies constitute the conditions of administrative practice, thus shaping the terms on which administrators will invoke the various languages in the American administrative ethos. An examination of these conditions will suggest a larger framework for understanding the interplay of the three dialogical threads of the administrative ethos.

Members of our panel continually cite three characteristics of the administrative environment as the basis for their reluctance to give presumptive weight to one language over another. The environment is filled with *complexity;* conditions are in flux, which creates much *uncertainty;* finally, there is considerable potential for *conflict,* which, if not kept in manageable bounds, will prevent managers from getting their jobs done.

Given a complex, uncertain, and conflict-filled environment, our focus group tends to see the decision-making process as a winnowing-down activity that reduces ambiguity sufficiently to define what some have called "the situation for action" (Schon, 1983). The primary problem posed for administrators by this environment is to get "their arms around" the problem or issue so that they can begin to address it. This is not to suggest that administrators draw some kind of clear distinction between facts and values, between means and ends, with administrators in the fact and means business and elected politicians in the values and ends business. No such distinction is made. Rather, the complexity, uncertainty, and potential conflict in their environment mean that administrators do not have enough confidence in the initial stages of a problem to approach it with one language to the exclusion of others.

In addition to being profoundly influenced by the complex and uncertain environment of administrative action, members of our panel see their own role as filled with ambiguity. On the one hand, they regard their primary responsibility as being the efficient and effective delivery of services to the citizenry. On the other hand, their commitment to efficient and effective administration does not embrace the two traditional shibboleths of public administration: the injunction for administrators to be primarily the guardians of "rational" policy development and administration and the injunction to maintain a separation between policy development and execution. Members of our focus group draw no clear distinctions between good administration and good government. Simply put, they are committed to competent government, which means for them at least three things. First, they expect activities in their charge to run smoothly, meaning both cost-efficient administration of the public's business and effective accomplishment of goals. Second, they expect things to be run fairly. Fairness means treating employees and citizens with respect, abiding by the letter of the law, providing the full measure of due process, and being honest. Finally, the panel's commitment to competent government is so broad that there is a tendency for it to embrace the whole of the public interest.

A third characteristic of administrative practice is reflected in the reluctance of our focus group to place an ethical label on an issue. One often hears the comment, "I don't see an ethical problem yet." One participant observed, "Ethics is what you have left after you've tried everything else." Another commented that ethics always involves that "feeling in the pit of your stomach that you always try to avoid." This desire to avoid ethical issues may seem somewhat ironic given the strong commitment by members of our panel to bear the ethical burden of preserving and protecting the public interest. However, the reluctance to engage the ethical dimensions of an issue seems to be grounded in two concerns: the tendency to identify ethical labels with conflict and the fear of having ethical issues become a weapon.

Members of our panel are anxious to avoid conflict, not so

much because they by nature are communitarian souls who shun the pursuit of self-intereȘt but because they spend most of their working hours immersed in various kinds of conflict. As a consequence they are not anxious to contribute more conflict to an already conflict-laden job. Panel members tend to see ethical labels as conflict producers rather than conflict reducers. This is because positions that are cast in terms of differing interests seem for them more capable of compromise than positions cast as differences in values.

Equally important is the desire on the part of panel members to avoid having ethical labels used as weapons in an ever-escalating public debate in which various self-righteous standards are erected as a litmus test of one's intentions and good works. They point out that many a reputation has been ruined and career destroyed by careless ethical charges that, once made, can never be fully or adequately refuted. This is especially the case for public administrators, who have a special moral and legal obligation to protect both the privacy of their employees and the citizens at large.

In summary, our discussions of ethical case problems with a panel of career administrators have surfaced three major conditions of administrative practice that greatly influence how and when administrators will invoke the various languages that are part of the American administrative ethos.

1. Public managers view their environment as filled with uncertainty, complexity, and conflict. Consequently, they see themselves as involved in an ambiguity-reduction decision-making process in which ethical considerations are kept out of public dialogue whenever they are likely to escalate conflict, increase administrative complexity, or introduce additional measures of uncertainty.

2. Career administrators see their role in normative terms with two responsibilities. The first is to promote competent government, and the second is to serve as stewards of the public interest. This role becomes ambiguous when career administrators have to take a position opposed by their elected political superiors.

3. Ethical principles are viewed as a mixed blessing because of their potential for escalating conflict and being used as weapons by others. These characteristics of American administrative practice suggest a framework for ordering the relationship among the three dialogical elements of the American administrative ethos.

Constitutional Stewardship: Ordering the Relationship Among the Three Dialogical Elements of the American Administrative Ethos

The three conditions of American administrative practice we have identified cannot be fully understood or appreciated apart from the structure of constitutional authority peculiar to our system of government. For example, the complexity of the environment in which career administrators operate is largely a product of a deliberately contrived system of separation of powers, checks and balances, and division of authority. These arrangements not only create greater environmental complexity but also contribute significantly to the role ambiguity faced by career administrators operating in a tripartite system of government that seemingly makes career administrators entirely subordinate to the will of the sovereign. But who is the sovereign in our constitutional democracy? The most recently expressed will of the elected representatives? The elected chief executives and their appointees? The decisions of our courts? The constitutional system under whose authority all of these collective wills act? And what is the administrator to do when these wills are contradictory or, more characteristically, silent about how career administrators should exercise their discretionary authority? Such questions remind us that the conditions and languages of administrative practice cannot be understood apart from the problematical character of our constitutional scheme of ordered liberty.

We will show in this section how both the conditions and languages of administrative practice reflect deeply rooted strains in our constitutional system of government. We will argue that the maintenance of a healthy balance among these strains constitutes a career administrator's highest ethical duty, what we have labeled *constitutional stewardship*. The justification for performing this role builds on the recent work of several scholars who assume that career administrators participate in ruling and that such participation creates an ethical obligation to our constitutional system of government as a whole (Rohr, 1978, 1986; Wamsley and others,

1987; Rosenbloom and Caroll, 1989). We go beyond their argument in two ways, first by outlining the major constituent elements of this ethical obligation and second by showing the relationship between these elements and the dominant languages of administrative practice.

Constitutional stewardship requires that career administrators commit themselves to a deeply problematical task. This is not only because our constitutional structure and the values it is designed to protect are in conflict but also because the steward operates in two deeply held traditions that pull in opposing directions. On the one hand, the first language of our administrative ethos seeks to constrain the application of administrative expertise to technical and instrumental questions. On the other hand, the pluralist ethos emphasizes the accommodation of concrete and short-term interests. The stewardship model seeks to reconcile this tension by arguing that both traditions are part of the substantive ends sought by our constitutional order.

The first language of neutral competence recognizes that competent government is as necessary to preserving a regime of ordered liberty as is protection against abuse of authority by the King Georges of the world. As another George recognized in seeking to obtain food and supplies for his troops wintered at Valley Forge, efficient and effective execution of policy directives is critical for the success of our democratic order. There is little debate that competent government was a major objective of those who framed our constitutional system. There is only debate over whether the administrator's role in promoting this competence ought to be intrepreted narrowly to include only technical expertise or more broadly to include the practical wisdom acquired in the daily administration of the affairs of government (Morgan, 1990).

As with the ethos of neutral competence, the pluralist tradition honors a major constitutional objective: to promote individual liberty without allowing it to be endangered by too much power at the center or too little power at the edges where the majority can tyrannize the minority. The accommodation of conflicting interests by career administrators is not only prudent; our liberal democratic order makes such accommodation a matter of constitutional duty.

Taken together, the first and second languages of administrative practice help to establish the normative terms for properly exercising one's role as a constitutional steward. By seeing these traditions as in rather than outside our constitutional heritage, the administrator is challenged to balance three dialogical elements of the American administrative ethos when confronted with a decision. The first language of technical expertise must be conjoined with a consideration of the actual interests likely to be impacted by administrative decisions. The stewardship model insists that the public interest is ultimately served when both elements of our administrative ethos enter into a dialogue with the constitutional processes and principles that are at the very foundations of the republic. The result is a three-way constitutional dialogue that reflects the problematical character of our democratic order—an order committed to competent democratic government where the majority rules but not at the expense of minority rights. In short, constitutional stewardship gives the career administrator the role and ethical duty of using the ordering and commanding language of the Constitution to redress potential deficiencies and excesses of either pluralism or technical rationality. By the same token, this language can be used by constitutional stewards to judge between competing ethical obligations these languages may place on them.

As work with our focus group makes clear, in actual practice the constitutional stewardship model initially requires that career administrators give presumptive weight to the momentum of pluralist politics and instrumental technical rationality. This presumption ends, however, when pluralism or reliance on technical rationality challenges or fails to protect or further our constitutional system and its constitutive values. At this point, those who seek to change, reinterpret, or momentarily suspend the constitutional system must bear the burden of showing that their views have constitutional validity. This means that any revision in the constitutional system must be justified ultimately on the basis of a communitarian and intergenerational rather than a particularistic and transitory interest.

What we have said so far about the substantive nature of ethical obligations as a constitutional steward has some obvious implications for the *form* of ethical dialogue. Ethical reasoning under the stewardship model conforms to a method described by

Jonsen and Toulmin (1988) in their discussion of the history of casuistry. It is a process that gives presumptive weight to an initial set of principles or values. These principles act as warrants to assist in the resolution of the case at hand. The weight given to a particular principle "depends on the similarities between the present case and the precedents; and its soundness can be challenged in situations regarded as exceptional" (Jonsen and Toulmin, 1988, p. 35). As Jonsen and Toulmin observe, it is a method widely used in clinical practices in such divergent fields as law, medicine, and public administration. Edward Levi, in his *Introduction to Legal Reasoning* (1949), documents how this process is characteristically applied by judges confronted with the challenge of deciding on the applicability of common law principles.

The process of ethical reasoning associated with constitutional stewardship gives a superior position not only to constitutional principles but also to the dialogue from which these principles emerge. As with all ethical reasoning based on the dialogical process, general warrants are not given the status of unassailable ethical universals. Constitutional principles and interpretations can be challenged ethically by actors in an administrative situation, providing (1) they are willing to assume the burden of overcoming the presumptive weight attached to such principles and (2) they ground their challenge on constitutional considerations.

In some ways the process of ethical reasoning characteristic of constitutional stewardship resembles the practical reasoning associated with pluralist politics. In both models considerable importance is placed on a careful consideration of the special circumstances in a case and the consequences the decision has for concrete interests. However, the difference between the two is critical. By according a special status to constitutional principles and processes, the stewardship model enables us to distinguish the pragmatic calculation encouraged by the pluralist tradition from the type of principled accommodation and change characteristic of constitutional stewardship. This difference enables us to distinguish clever administrative decision making from the exercise of sound moral judgment. We would argue that the application of the reasoning process associated with our stewardship model exemplifies as well as embodies the Aristotelian concept of phronesis.

We believe the stewardship model provides the best explanation for understanding the actions of members of our administrative panel as they seek justification for resolving particularly troublesome ethical problems. First, it helps to clarify the confused decisional environment in which they see themselves operating. Second, it explains and justifies the administrator's unwillingness to apply ethical labels to troublesome and conflictual issues in a casual manner. Finally, it legitimates the exercise of administrative discretion by nonelected officials.

Constitutional stewardship helps to reduce the ambiguity of the public administrator's operating environment by ordering the three moralities that compete for the administrator's allegiance. The stewardship model accomplishes this by making our constitutional heritage the penultimate authority over the dual claims of technical rationality and pluralist politics. Pluralism is inclined to fall prey to its worse excess—the pursuit of narrowly conceived self-interest—unless it is tempered by the larger set of constitutional values in which pluralism must operate. By the same token, the values of efficiency and economy associated with technical rationality can never be successful ethical ends in themselves. These values only become ethical insofar as they serve ethical ends. By subordinating technical rationality to the service of legitimate constitutive values, one avoids confusing techniques of practice with the ethical purposes they are designed to serve.

Constitutional stewardship both explains and justifies our panel's reluctance to place ethical labels on issues unless there have been a full examination of the situation for action and an exploration of the consequences of various courses of action. Conflict in the administrative arena frequently reflects thinly veiled and strongly felt social conflicts over such fundamental issues as abortion, race, property rights, religion, free speech, and so on. Consequently, the administrator, as an unelected constitutional steward, wishes to see such conflicts raised only when she or he is on firm ethical, political, and administrative ground. Moreover, there is additional evidence that our administrative panel's caution is related to a desire to discourage the casual use of constitutional issues to pursue the narrow ends of pluralist, single-issue politics.

Finally, constitutional stewardship helps our administrators deal with one of the most troublesome issues they face: conflicts with elected officials over ethical problems. Once administrators take an oath to uphold the constitutional system, they face the same stewardship responsibilities as elected officials. As our judicial heritage demonstrates, popular election is not the only basis for acquiring the obligation to exercise the responsibilities of constitutional stewardship. As some have argued, the institutional position of the administrator can from time to time place him or her in a better position than most elected officials to protect cherished constitutional institutions and values (Morgan, 1990; Rohr, 1986). Therefore, it is understandable why an administrator on some occasions may as a matter of duty oppose the will of an elected official.

However, such audacity can be the Achilles' heel of constitutional stewardship. Few would disagree that to have a constitutional system one must have an administrative ethics that endorses the superiority of constitutional values. However, it is also reasonable to argue that two hundred years of constitutional debate have shown that the Constitution and its institutions possess more than their share of ambiguity. Therefore, is it not dangerous to place the interpretation of constitutional principles in the hands of unelected officials who will often be called on to judge not only their own actions but those of elected officials as well? What will protect the republic from possible self-serving, arbitrary, and capricious administrative actions undertaken in the name of an ethical obligation to uphold the Constitution?

There are three possible answers. The first lies in the constitutional steward's ethical obligation to maintain an open dialogue in the furtherance of constitutional values and processes. An open and seriously attended dialogue acts as a constant ethical and political check on possible arbitrary action by the administrator. This may, in fact, explain why our administrators are so careful to let dialogue run its course before they exercise their ethical obligations.

The second check against self-serving use of the stewardship ethics lies in the administrators' strong commitment to both the reality and the appearance of integrity. Members of our administrative panel are preoccupied with the appearance of integrity as a necessary and at times sufficient condition for administrative legitimacy. As one panel member observed, the only thing career administrators may have at the end of their careers as a testimony to their public accomplishments is the ethical integrity they have left behind. Such a deep-seated concern for public appearances provides a strong check against self-indulgent use of one's role as a constitutional steward.

A final barrier against abuse is the built-in internal check that results from the tensions inherent in the commitment of our focus group to competent democratic government. As we have noted, members of our panel tend to define competence broadly to include three sometimes contradictory languages of American administrative practice. Dialogue among these languages helps to maintain the "continuities of conflict" that we believe are vital to preventing abuses of the exercise of American administrative discretion and maintaining the health of the democratic polity it is designed to serve.

Conclusions and Directions for Future Research

Our research indicates that public administrators assume an obligation to balance three ethical claims. The first is the claim of neutral competence, which commits them to effective and efficient administration of policy directives established by the electoral process. The second claim of pluralism commits career administrators to the accommodation of competing interests to establish a working consensus without which no diverse political system can long survive. Finally, our panel is committed to the promotion of the larger public interest, which goes beyond the need for technical competence and interest group accommodation.

When pressed to define what is meant by the public interest, members of our panel are able to articulate a complex ordering of moral claims that we believe is best captured by the language of constitutional stewardship. This language subsumes both the first language of neutral competence and the second language of pluralism, but it does so in a manner that accurately reflects the problematical nature of our democratic enterprise.

The focus group technique used in our research has proved quite promising in adding greater depth to some of the existing literature dealing with the ethical conduct of public administrators.

For example, the technique provides us with an opportunity to forge linkages between two kinds of research on administrative ethics that have previously not had much interaction: the literature that deals with the ethical role of the public administrator in our constitutional system (Rohr, 1986) and survey research that examines the ethical attitudes and values of the American public administrator (Bowman, 1990).

Two specific questions that point a direction for future research are raised by our focus group study. To what extent are our findings consistent with the views of elected officials, professional technical employees, and lower-level managers not represented on our panel? To what extent do views of ethical obligation vary with organizational levels and amounts or kinds of discretionary authority? Such questions need to be addressed to determine the extent to which the constitutional stewardship role outlined here can be successfully employed as an empirical, explanatory, and normative model for the exercise of discretionary American administrative authority.

Note

1.   The data obtained are part of a larger ongoing research project that seeks to examine the way in which the administrative, legal, and political climate in which local government administrators operate affects their sense of ethical obligation, decision making, and action. The research employs a small number of respondents whose views and experiences are examined in depth. The object is to capture the complex, subtle interaction of values that constitute the respondents' structure of ethical meaning. This approach is similar to that used by Bellah and others (1986) and, more specifically, Lane (1962).

The in-depth interweaving technique used for this study is patterned after the "focal group research model" (Merton, Fiske, and Kendall, 1956; Lane, 1962; Krueger, 1988; Morgan, 1988), which was selected for three reasons. First, it discourages the investigators from imposing their own cognitive structure on the respondents in the form of detailed questionnaires. Second, it permits the researchers to focus on ethical dilemmas actually faced by the participants rather than those "imported" by scholars in the form of "canned" cases. Third, by focusing the research on *dialogue,* the authors were able to observe *patterns* of meaning that normally are inaccessible through other techniques.

The focal group consists of six executive-level public administrators chosen for their reputation as highly effective government officials. The group meets monthly for three to four hours, usually preceded by dinner. So far (as of August 1990) over twenty-seven hours of dialogue have been recorded. The group's discussions are focused by using cases drawn from the participants' own experience as "stimulus materials." A simple case discussion format is used, and comments are recorded on audiotape and with process notes. The notes and tapes are later cross-referenced during content analysis. Emphasis is on a free-flowing give-and-take among the panel members over the case materials with minimum intervention by the researchers.

References

Aristotle. *The Nichomachean Ethics.* In R. McKeon (ed.), *Introduction to Aristotle.* New York: Random House, 1947.

Bellah, R., and others. *Habits of the Heart: Individualism and Commitment in American Life.* New York: Harper & Row, 1986.

Bowman, J. S. "Ethics in Government: A National Survey of Public Administrators." *Public Administration Review,* May–June 1990, *50,* 345–353.

Jonsen, A. R., and Toulmin, S. *The Abuse of Casuistry: A History of Moral Reasoning.* Berkeley: University of California Press, 1988.

Kass, H. D., and Catron, B. (eds.). *Images and Identities in Public Administration.* Newbury Park, Calif.: Sage, 1990.

Krueger, R. A. *Focus Groups: A Practical Guide for Applied Research.* Newbury Park, Calif.: Sage, 1988.

Lane, R. E. *Political Life: Why People Get Involved in Politics.* Glencoe, Ill.: Free Press, 1959.

Levi, E. *An Introduction to Legal Reasoning.* Chicago: University of Chicago Press, 1949.

Lindblom, C. "The Science of Muddling Through." In J. M. Shafritz and A. C. Hyde (eds.), *Classics of Public Administration* (2nd ed.). Chicago: Dorsey Press, 1987.

MacIntyre, A. *After Virtue.* (2nd ed.) Notre Dame, Ind.: University of Notre Dame Press, 1984.

Merton, R. K., Fiske, M., and Kendall, P. *The Focused Interview.* New York: Free Press, 1956.

Morgan, D. F. "Administrative Phronesis: Discretion and the Problems of Administrative Legitimacy in our Constitutional System." In H. D. Kass and B. Catron (eds.), *Images and Identities in Public Administration.* Newbury Park, Calif.: Sage, 1990.

Morgan, D. L. *Focus Groups as Qualitative Research.* Newbury Park, Calif.: Sage, 1988.

Rittel, H.W.J., and Weber, M. "Dilemmas in a General Theory of Planning." *Policy Sciences,* 1973, *4,* 151–169.

Rohr, J. A. *Ethics for Bureaucrats: An Essay on Law and Values.* New York: Marcel Dekker, 1978.

Rohr, J. A. *To Run a Constitution: The Legitimacy of the Administrative State.* Lawrence: University Press of Kansas, 1986.

Rosenbloom, D. H., and Caroll, J. D. *Toward Constitutional Competence: A Casebook for Public Administration.* Englewood Cliffs, N.J.: Prentice-Hall, 1989.

Schon, D. *The Reflective Practitioner: How Professionals Think in Action.* New York: Basic Books, 1983.

Shafritz, J. M., and Hyde, A. C. (eds.). *Classics of Public Administration.* (2nd ed.) Chicago: Dorsey Press, 1987.

Stivers, C. "The Shape of the Stone: A Feminist Reflection on Practical Wisdom in Public Administration." Paper presented at the Public Administration Theory Network Workshop, American Society for Public Administration annual conference, Los Angeles, Calif., Apr. 1990.

Vickers, G. *The Art of Judgment: A Study of Policy Making.* London: Harper & Row, 1983.

Wamsley, G., and others. "The Public Administrator and the Governance Process: Refocusing the American Dialogue." In R. C.

Chandler (ed.), *A Centennial History of the American Administrative State.* New York: Free Press, 1987.

Wiek, K. *The Social Psychology of Organizing.* (2nd ed.) Reading, Mass.: Addison-Wesley, 1979.

Wildavsky, A. *The Politics of the Budgetary Process.* (4th ed.) Boston: Little, Brown, 1984.

Zammuto, R. F. *Assessing Organizational Effectiveness.* New York: New York University Press, 1982.

Name Index

Subject Index

International Personnel Management Association (IPMA), 17, 29
Interstate Commerce Commission (ICC), 13
Interviews of public managers, 40–41, 56–58
Introduction to Legal Reasoning (Levi), 300
Iran-Contra affair, 94–95

J

Judgment, 68, 190; ethics as practice of, 79–85; justice as criterion for, 270–274; strengthening, 243–258
Justice: administrative, 263–281; and ethical decision making, 261–282; literature on, 263–267; mass justice theory, 265, 276; in moral foundation of public administration, 106–109; paradigmatic value of, 277–280; procedural, 273–274; Rawls's theory of, 106, 144, 257–258, 264, 265–266

K

Kadi justice, 78
Kohlberg's scale of moral maturity, 47–49, 53
Kohlberg's stages of moral reasoning, 245–248, 249, 257

L

Law and duty: emphasizing to enhance ethical action, 250–254; in stages of moral reasoning, 249
Law and legal issues, 39, 52–56, 59
Leadership, 158–178
Learning, public, 125–126
Liberalism, 116–119, 131
Literature: on justice, 263–267; on public administration ethics, 37–40, 100–102
Logical positivism, 72–73
Lying (Bok), 103

M

Machiavellian ethics, 4, 205–222; and defensive routines, 213–214; and ethical codes, 217; and hierarchy and positional power, 208–209; price of, 214–215; primacy of, 206–208, 221–222; and vertical differentiation, 209–210
Macroethics, 36
Management: case study of mixed signals from, 195–200; high reliability, 4, 191–202; role in ethics, 176–177; scientific, 12–13; style of, 38, 46–47. *See also* Public managers
Man's Responsibility for Nature (Passmore), 170
Mass justice theory, 265, 276
Mathews v. *Eldridge*, 265
Maturity, ethical, 47–49, 53
Maxwell School of Citizenship and Public Affairs, 13, 18
Medicaid, 195, 199
Medicare, 195, 199
Merit Systems Protection Board (MSPB), 227, 232, 236, 239, 240
Methodology: of bureaucratic ethos, 13–14; of democratic ethos, 17; for interviewing public managers, 40–41, 56–58
Metropolitan Atlanta Rapid Transit Authority (MARTA), 221
Microethics, 36
Minimalist ethics, 243, 256
Modernist theory, 140–144, 148–149
Moral ambivalence, 230–231
Moral analysis, education for, 254–255
Moral dualism, 114–131
Moral foundations of public administration, 91–111; barriers to consensus on, 93–99; benevolence, 104–106, 108, 109; emerging consensus on, 99–109; honor, 95, 102–104, 108, 109, 111; justice, 106–109
Moral maturity, 47–49, 53
Moral reasoning, 67–68, 243–258;

Today's public managers face complex ethical dilemmas, often having to weigh personal and professional values against current public opinion and the law. In a climate of increasing concern over ethical conduct in governmental institutions—heightened by a decade of well-publicized cases of both willful and negligent abuses of public trust—administrators confront new challenges in the practice of public service. In this book, editor James S. Bowman brings together the contributions of cutting-edge research to create the first comprehensive reference on the theory and practice of ethics in public administration. Through in-depth interviews with public executives, focus group data, philosophical inquiry, and case studies, leading experts in the field develop an overview of the prevailing ethical environment in the public sector, provide fresh approaches to thinking about government ethics, and offer new strategies for improving ethical decision making.

In part one the authors analyze the political and cultural climate in which public